WCF 4.5 Multi-Layer Services Development with Entity Framework

Third Edition

Build SOA applications on Microsoft platforms with this hands-on guide

Mike Liu

PUBLISHING

BIRMINGHAM - MUMBAI

WCF 4.5 Multi-Layer Services Development with Entity Framework

Third Edition

First published: December 2008
Second Edition: June 2010
Third Edition: December 2012

Production Reference: 1101212

Published by Packt Publishing Ltd.
Livery Place
35 Livery Street
Birmingham B3 2PB, UK.

ISBN 978-1-84968-766-9

www.packtpub.com

Cover Image by Artie Ng (artherng@yahoo.com.au)

Credits

Author

Mike Liu

Reviewers

Chad Gordon Carter

Jason De Oliveira

Andrew Rea

Jeff Sanders

Edward Spencer

Acquisition Editor

Andrew Duckworth

Lead Technical Editor

Azharuddin Sheikh

Technical Editor

Prasad Dalvi

Project Coordinator

Yashodhan Dere

Proofreader

Aaron Nash

Indexer

Tejal Soni

Graphics

Aditi Gajjar

Production Coordinator

Manu Joseph

Cover Work

Manu Joseph

About the Author

Mike Liu studied Mathematics and Software Engineering at Nanjing University and Brandeis University, graduating with a Bachelor's degree and a Master's degree respectively. He is a **Sun Certified Java Programmer** (**SCJP**), Microsoft Certified Solution Developer for Visual Studio 6.0, and Microsoft Certified Solution Developer for .NET. He has been working as a Software Engineer/Architect on various platforms (DOS, Unix, and Windows), using C/C++, Java, VB/VB.NET, and C#.

Mike started using C# for production development back in the year 2001 when C# was still in beta stage and he is now working as a Senior Software Engineer for an investment management firm in Boston Mass.

Mike had his first book *MITT: Multi-user Integrated Table-processing Tool Under Unix* published in 1993, and second book *Advanced C# Programming* published in 2003. The previous two versions of this book — *WCF Multi-tier Services Development with LINQ* and *WCF 4.0 Multi-tier Services Development with LINQ to Entities* — were published in 2008 and 2010.

Many thanks to the editors and technical reviewers at Packt Publishing. Without their help, this book wouldn't be of such high quality. And thanks to my wife Julia Guo, and to my two sons, Kevin and James Liu, for their consideration and sacrifices while I was working on this book.

About the Reviewers

Chad Gordon Carter is a completely self-taught web developer. He has been developing applications since 1998, using classic ASP. Currently, Chad is developing in ASP.Net 4.0 Framework and using common tools such as Telerik and DevExpress.

Chad is currently working professionally for a financial investment company in Buckhead, Georgia. Additionally, Chad owns a web development company and co-owns a flight school in Ball Ground, Geogia.

> I would like to thank my wife and son who have relentlessly put up with my all night geek sessions.

Jason De Oliveira works as CTO for Cellenza (http://www.cellenza.com), an IT consulting company specialized in Microsoft technologies and Agile methodology, in Paris (France). He is an experienced Manager and Senior Solutions Architect, with high skills in Software Architecture and Enterprise Architecture.

Jason works for big companies and helps them to realize complex and challenging software projects. He frequently collaborates with Microsoft and you can find him quite often at the **Microsoft Technology Center** (**MTC**) in Paris.

He loves sharing his knowledge and experience via his blog, by speaking at conferences, by writing technical books, by writing articles in the technical press, by giving software courses as MCT, and by coaching co-workers in his company.

Microsoft has awarded him since 2011 with the **Microsoft® Most Valuable Professional** (**MVP C#**) Award for his numerous contributions to the Microsoft community. Microsoft seeks to recognize the best and brightest from technology communities around the world with the MVP Award. These exceptional and highly respected individuals come from more than 90 countries, serving their local online and offline communities and having an impact worldwide. Jason is very proud to be one of them.

Please feel free to contact him via his blog, if you need any technical assistance or want to exchange on technical subjects (`http://www.jasondeoliveira.com`).

Jason has worked on the following books:

- *.NET 4.5 Expert Programming Cookbook* (English)
- *Visual Studio 2012 - Développez pour le web* (French)

> I would like to thank my lovely wife Orianne and my beautiful daughter Julia for supporting me in my work and for accepting long days and short nights during the week and sometimes even during the week-end. My life would not be the same without them!

Andrew Rea has been working in Software Development for over eight years. Primarily working with web technologies on the .NET Platform, Andrew has worked on several high traffic websites, for well known brands in the United Kingdom. Early in Andrew's career, he worked with VB6 and Classic ASP, moving into the .NET 1.X framework and continuing through to the latest versions using C#. Andrew is also an avid Python, Node.js, and C/C++ developer. Currently Andrew is employed as the Lead Technical Architect for a global brand in the Accommodations and Destinations sector of the travel industry.

Jeff Sanders is a published author, technical editor, and accomplished technologist. He is currently employed with Symbolic Systems in the capacity of a Portfolio Director and Sr. Solutions Architect.

Jeff has years of professional experience in the fields of IT and strategic business consulting, leading both sales and delivery efforts. He regularly contributes to certification and product roadmap development with Microsoft, and speaks publicly on Microsoft enterprise technologies. With his roots in Software Development, Jeff's areas of expertise include collaboration and content management solutions, operational intelligence, digital marketing, enterprise project management, distributed component-based application architectures, object-oriented analysis and design, and enterprise integration patterns and designs.

Jeff is also the CTO of DynamicShift, a client-focused organization specializing in Microsoft technologies, specifically Office365/BPOS, SharePoint Server, StreamInsight, Windows Azure, AppFabric, Business Activity Monitoring, BizTalk Server, and .NET. He is a Microsoft Certified Trainer, and leads DynamicShift in both training and consulting efforts.

He enjoys non-work-related travel, spending time with his wife and daughter, and wishes he had more time for both.

He may be reached at `jeff.sanders@dynamicshift.com`.

Edward Spencer is an experienced .NET developer having worked at a number of software houses in the UK. He has worked on large systems for household names, encompassing a wide range of technologies. He has been developing applications with .NET since 2005. His main areas of interest and focus are web-based applications.

www.PacktPub.com

Support files, eBooks, discount offers and more

You might want to visit www.PacktPub.com for support files and downloads related to your book.

Did you know that Packt offers eBook versions of every book published, with PDF and ePub files available? You can upgrade to the eBook version at www.PacktPub.com and as a print book customer, you are entitled to a discount on the eBook copy. Get in touch with us at service@packtpub.com for more details.

At www.PacktPub.com, you can also read a collection of free technical articles, sign up for a range of free newsletters and receive exclusive discounts and offers on Packt books and eBooks.

http://PacktLib.PacktPub.com

Do you need instant solutions to your IT questions? PacktLib is Packt's online digital book library. Here, you can access, read and search across Packt's entire library of books.

Why Subscribe?

- Fully searchable across every book published by Packt
- Copy and paste, print and bookmark content
- On demand and accessible via web browser

Free Access for Packt account holders

If you have an account with Packt at www.PacktPub.com, you can use this to access PacktLib today and view nine entirely free books. Simply use your login credentials for immediate access.

Instant Updates on New Packt Books

Get notified! Find out when new books are published by following @PacktEnterprise on Twitter, or the *Packt Enterprise* Facebook page.

Table of Contents

Preface

WCF is Microsoft's recommended model for building services and Entity Framework is Microsoft's preferred ORM for accessing underlying data storages. Learning WCF and Entity Framework has become essential and critical for every software developer to survive in this SOA world.

This book is a step-by-step tutorial to guide you through learning WCF, Entity Framework, LINQ, and LINQ to Entities. You will be guided to create five WCF and Entity Framework solutions, of which three are multi-layered real-world WCF service solutions, so you will not only be reading, but also be coding through the book, to gain practical experience of WCF and Entity Framework. Various test clients will be associated with each solution and all solutions can be built and run independently of other solutions. Clear instructions and relevant screenshots will make sure you won't get lost in the world of WCF and Entity Framework. Configuration files, host applications, test clients, and WCF services for each solution will also be available to download for you to examine, modify, and debug from the outside in.

This book focuses on the essentials of using WCF and Entity Framework, rather than providing a reference to every single possibility. It leaves the reference material online where it belongs, and concentrates instead on practical examples, code, and advice.

What this book covers

Chapter 1, Web Services and Windows Communication Foundation, covers basic concepts of web services and WCF.

Chapter 2, Implementing a Basic HelloWorld WCF Service, discusses how a simple `HelloWorld` WCF service is implemented, hosted, and consumed.

Chapter 3, Hosting and Debugging the HelloWorld WCF Service, discusses various hosting and debugging techniques of WCF services.

Chapter 4, Implementing a WCF Service in the Real World, explains how to create a layered WCF service with an interface layer and a business logic layer.

Chapter 5, Adding Database Support and Exception Handling, explains how to add a data access layer and fault message handling to the previously created WCF service.

Chapter 6, LINQ: Language Integrated Query, discusses LINQ-related language features such as anonymous types, extension methods, and lambda expressions.

Chapter 7, LINQ to Entities: Basic Concepts and Features, covers the basic concepts and features of LINQ to Entities such as LINQ to Entities designer, querying and updating tables, deferred execution, and lazy/eager loading.

Chapter 8, LINQ to Entities: Advanced Concepts and Features, covers advanced concepts and features of LINQ to Entities such as stored procedure, inheritance, concurrency control, and transaction support.

Chapter 9, Applying LINQ to Entities to a WCF Service, discusses how to recreate the data access layer of a WCF service with LINQ to Entities.

Chapter 10, Distributed Transaction Support of WCF, explains how to add distributed transaction support to a WCF service.

Chapter 11, WCF Security, covers basic security features and settings of WCF, and hosts a WCF service with Basic Authentication, SSL, and Windows Authentication.

Chapter 12, Extending WCF Services, explains various extension points of WCF services and extends a WCF service with custom behaviors.

What you need for this book

You need the following software:

- Microsoft .NET Framework 4.5
- Microsoft Visual Studio 2012 Ultimate, Premium, or Professional
- Microsoft SQL Server 2012, 2008, 2005, or Express
- Internet Information Server 7.0, 7.5, or 8.0
- Windows 7 or Windows 8

Who this book is for

This book is for C#, VB.NET, and C++ developers who are eager to get started with WCF and Entity Framework, and want a book that is practical and rich with examples from the very beginning.

Developers and architects evaluating SOA implementation technologies for their company will find this book particularly useful because it gets you started with Microsoft's tools for SOA and shows you how to customize our examples for your prototypes.

This book presumes basic knowledge of C# or C++. Previous experience with Visual Studio will be helpful but is not required, as detailed instructions are given throughout the book.

Conventions

In this book, you will find a number of styles of text that distinguish between different kinds of information. Here are some examples of these styles, and an explanation of their meaning.

Code words in text are shown as follows: "For a Microsoft ASMX web service, you can see the WSDL by adding ?WSDL at the end of the web service URL, say http://localhost/MyService/MyService.asmx?WSDL."

A block of code is set as follows:

```
namespace MyWCF.EasyNorthwind.MessageContracts
{
  /// <summary>
  /// Service Contract Class - GetProductResponse
  /// </summary>
  [System.ServiceModel.MessageContract(IsWrapped = false)]
  public partial class GetProductResponse
  {
    private MyWCF.EasyNorthwind.DataContracts.Product product;
    [System.ServiceModel.MessageBodyMember(Name = "Product")]
    public MyWCF.EasyNorthwind.DataContracts.Product Product
    {
      get { return product; }
      set { product = value; }
    }
  }
}
```

Any command-line input or output is written as follows:

```
"C:\Program Files\Microsoft SDKs\Windows\v8.0A\bin\NETFX 4.0 Tools\
SvcUtil.exe" http://localhost:1054/HostDevServer/HelloWorldService.
svc?wsdl/out:HelloWorldServiceRef.cs /config:app.config
```

New terms and **important words** are shown in bold. Words that you see on the screen, in menus or dialog boxes for example, appear in the text like this: "If the **Open Project** dialog box pops up, click on **Cancel** to close it."

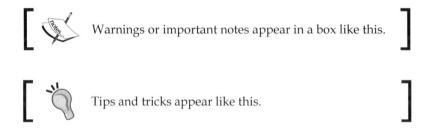

> Warnings or important notes appear in a box like this.

> Tips and tricks appear like this.

Reader feedback

Feedback from our readers is always welcome. Let us know what you think about this book—what you liked or may have disliked. Reader feedback is important for us to develop titles that you really get the most out of.

To send us general feedback, simply send an e-mail to feedback@packtpub.com, and mention the book title via the subject of your message.

If there is a book that you need and would like to see us publish, please send us a note in the **SUGGEST A TITLE** form on www.packtpub.com or e-mail suggest@packtpub.com.

If there is a topic that you have expertise in and you are interested in either writing or contributing to a book, see our author guide on www.packtpub.com/authors.

Customer support

Now that you are the proud owner of a Packt book, we have a number of things to help you to get the most from your purchase.

Downloading the example code

You can download the example code files for all Packt books you have purchased from your account at `http://www.PacktPub.com`. If you purchased this book elsewhere, you can visit `http://www.PacktPub.com/support` and register to have the files e-mailed directly to you.

Errata

Although we have taken every care to ensure the accuracy of our content, mistakes do happen. If you find a mistake in one of our books—maybe a mistake in the text or the code—we would be grateful if you would report this to us. By doing so, you can save other readers from frustration and help us improve subsequent versions of this book. If you find any errata, please report them by visiting `http://www.packtpub.com/support`, selecting your book, clicking on the **errata submission form** link, and entering the details of your errata. Once your errata are verified, your submission will be accepted and the errata will be uploaded on our website, or added to any list of existing errata, under the Errata section of that title. Any existing errata can be viewed by selecting your title from `http://www.packtpub.com/support`.

Piracy

Piracy of copyright material on the Internet is an ongoing problem across all media. At Packt, we take the protection of our copyright and licenses very seriously. If you come across any illegal copies of our works, in any form, on the Internet, please provide us with the location address or website name immediately so that we can pursue a remedy.

Please contact us at `copyright@packtpub.com` with a link to the suspected pirated material.

We appreciate your help in protecting our authors, and our ability to bring you valuable content.

Questions

You can contact us at `questions@packtpub.com` if you are having a problem with any aspect of the book, and we will do our best to address it.

1
Web Services and Windows Communication Foundation

A web service is a software system designed to support interoperable machine-to-machine interaction over a network. Web services have been around for a while, but it is the **service-oriented architecture (SOA)** that makes web services much more popular today. Now with **Windows Communication Foundation (WCF)**, a new era has begun for developing services, including web services, on the Microsoft platform.

In this chapter, we will learn concepts and definitions related to SOA, web services, and WCF. We will discuss each of the following in detail:

- What is SOA?
- Web service and its relation to SOA
- Standards and specifications for web services
- What is WCF?
- Use of WCF for SOA
- WCF architecture
- Basic WCF concepts
- WCF production and development environments

What is SOA?

SOA is the acronym for **service-oriented architecture**. SOA is an architectural design pattern by which several guiding principles determine the nature of the design. Basically, SOA states that every component of a system should be a service, and the system should be composed of several loosely-coupled services. A service here means a unit of a program that serves a business process. Loosely-coupled here means that these services should be independent of each other so that changing one of them should not affect any other services.

SOA is neither a specific technology nor a specific language. It is just a blueprint or a system design approach. It is an architectural model that aims to enhance the efficiency, agility, and productivity of an enterprise system. The key concepts of SOA are services, high interoperability, and loose coupling.

Web services

There are many approaches to realizing SOA, but the most popular and practical one is using web services.

What is a web service?

As mentioned in the beginning of this chapter, a web service is a software system designed to support interoperable machine-to-machine interaction over a network. A web service is typically hosted on a remote machine (provider) and called by a client application (consumer) over a network. After the provider of a web service publishes the service, the client can discover it and invoke it. The communications between a web service and a client application to be used can be done by sending XML messages. A web service is hosted within a web server and HTTP is used as the transport protocol between the server and the client applications. The following diagram shows the interaction of web services:

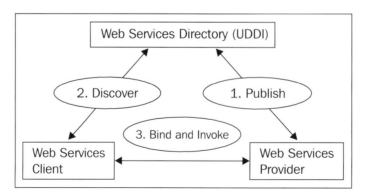

The reason it is called a web service is that it is designed to be hosted in a web server such as Microsoft Internet Information Server, and called over the Internet, typically through the HTTP or HTTPS protocols. This is to ensure that a web service can be called by any application, using any programming language, and under any operating system, as long as there is an active Internet connection, and of course, an open HTTP/HTTPS port, which is `true` for almost every computer on the Internet.

Web services were invented to solve the interoperability problem between various applications. In the early 90s, along with the LAN/WAN/Internet development, it became a big problem to integrate different applications. An application might have been developed using C++ or Java, and run on a Unix box, a Windows PC, or even a mainframe computer. There was no consistent way that was standardized across the industry for one application to communicate with other applications. It was the development of XML that made it possible to share data between the applications across hardware boundaries and networks or even over the Internet.

For example, a Windows application might need to display the price of a particular stock. With a web service, this application can make a request to a URL and/or pass an XML string such as the following:

```
<QuoteRequest><GetPrice Symble='XYZ'/> </QuoteRequest>
```

The requested URL is actually the Internet address of a web service, which upon receiving the preceding quote request, gives a response as follows:

```
<QuoteResponse><QuotePrice Symble='XYZ'>51.22</QuotePrice>
</QuoteResponse/>
```

The Windows application then uses an XML parser to interpret the response package and display the price on the screen.

Each web service has a unique URL and contains various methods. When calling a web service, you have to specify which method you want to call, and then you need to pass the required parameters to the web service method. Each web service method will also give a response package to provide the execution results to the caller.

Not only can new applications, such as web services, be developed, but also the legacy applications can be wrapped up and exposed as web services. So, an IBM mainframe accounting system might be able to provide external customers with a link to check the balance of an account.

WSDL

In order for a web service to be invoked by other applications, the invoking system must know how to call the method in the web service. WSDL is a language that provides the ability for a web service to be able to give a description of the methods available through the web service.

WSDL stands for **Web Services Description Language**. It is an XML format that defines and describes the functionalities of the web service, including the method names, parameter names and types, and returning datatypes of the web service.

For a Microsoft ASMX web service, you can see the WSDL by adding `?WSDL` at the end of the web service URL, say `http://localhost/MyService/MyService.asmx?WSDL`.

Web service proxy

A client application calls a web service through a proxy. A web service proxy is a subclass between a web service and a client. It is normally autogenerated, according to the WSDL of the web service, by a tool such as Visual Studio IDE. It can be re-used by any client application. The proxy contains the stub methods mimicking all the methods of the web service so that a client application can call each method of the web service through these stub methods. It also contains other necessary information required by the client to call the web service such as custom exceptions, custom data and class types, and so on.

The address of the web service can be embedded within the proxy class, or it can be placed inside a configuration file. A proxy class of a web service can be created for a specific language. For example, there could be a proxy class for the Java clients, a proxy class for the C# clients, and yet another proxy class for the COBOL clients. A proxy class can also be generated in a commonly understood way such as in XML format. Different clients written in different languages can re-use this same common proxy class to communicate with the web service.

To call a web service from a client application, the proper proxy class first has to be added to the client project. Then, with an optional configuration file, the address of the web service can be defined. Within the client application, a web service object can be instantiated and its methods can be called just as for any other normal method.

SOAP

There are many standards for web services—SOAP is one of them. **SOAP** was originally an acronym for **Simple Object Access Protocol** and was designed by Microsoft. As this protocol became popular with the spread of web services and its original meaning was misleading, the original acronym was dropped with version 1.2 of the standard. It is now merely a protocol, maintained by W3C.

Now, SOAP is a protocol for exchanging the XML-based messages over computer networks. It is widely used by web services and has become its de facto protocol. With SOAP, the client application can send a request in XML format to a server application, and then the server application will send back a response in XML format. The transport for SOAP is normally HTTP/HTTPS, and the wide acceptance of HTTP is one of the reasons why SOAP is also widely accepted today.

Web services: standards and specifications

Because SOA is an architectural style, and web service is now the de facto standard for building SOA applications, we need to know what standards and specifications are available for web services.

As discussed in previous sections, there are many standards and specifications for web services. Some have been well developed and widely accepted, some are being developed, and others are just at the proposal stage. These specifications are in varying degrees of maturity, and are maintained or supported by various standards and entities. Specifications may complement, overlap, and compete with each other. As most of these standards' committees and specifications are for future web services, not all of them are implemented in current web service frameworks.

The web service standards and specifications are occasionally referred to as **WS-***, although there is neither a single managed set of specifications that this consistently refers to nor a recognized owning body across all of them. The reference term WS-* is more of a general nod to the fact that many specifications are named with **WS-** as their prefix.

Besides XML, SOAP, and WSDL, here is a brief list of some other important standards and specifications for web services.

WS-I Profiles

The **Web Services Interoperability Organization (WS-I)** is an industry consortium chartered to promote interoperability across the stack of web services specifications. It publishes web service profiles, sample applications, and test tools to help determine profile conformance. One of the popular profiles it has published is the WS-I Basic Profile. WS-I is governed by a Board of Directors, and Microsoft is one of the board members. The web address for the WS-I Organization is `http://www. ws-i.org`.

WS-Addressing

WS-Addressing is a mechanism that allows web services to communicate addressing information. With traditional web services, addressing information is carried by the transport layer, and the web service message itself knows nothing about its destination. With this new standard, addressing information will be included in the XML message itself. A SOAP header can be added to the message for this purpose. The network-level transport is now responsible only for delivering that message to a dispatcher that is capable of reading the metadata.

WS-Security

WS-Security describes how to handle security issues within the SOAP messages. It attaches the signature and encryption information as well as the security tokens to the SOAP messages. In addition to the traditional HTTP/HTTPS authentications, it incorporates extra security features in the header of the SOAP message, working in the application layer. Also, it ensures the end-to-end security.

There are several specifications associated with WS-Security, such as WS-SecureConversation, WS-Federation, WS-Authorization, WS-Policy, WS-Trust, and WS-Privacy.

WS-ReliableMessaging

WS-ReliableMessaging describes a protocol that allows SOAP messages to be delivered reliably between the distributed applications.

The WS-ReliableMessaging model enforces reliability between the message source and destination. If a message cannot be delivered to the destination, the model must raise an exception or indicate to the source that the message can't be delivered.

WS-Coordination and WS-Transaction

WS-Coordination describes an extensible framework for providing protocols that coordinate the actions of distributed applications. The framework enables the existing transaction processing, workflow, and other systems for coordination, to hide their proprietary protocols, and to operate in a heterogeneous environment. Additionally, this specification provides a definition for the structure of the context and the requirements for propagating context between the cooperating services.

WS-Transaction describes coordination types that are used with the extensible coordination framework described in the WS-Coordination specification. It defines two coordination types—**Atomic Transaction (AT)** for individual operations and **Business Activity (BA)** for long-running transactions.

WS-AtomicTransaction provides the definition of the atomic transaction coordination type that is used with the extensible coordination framework described in the WS-Coordination specification. This protocol can be used to build the applications that require consistent agreement on the outcome of short-lived distributed activities that have all-or-nothing semantics.

WS-BusinessActivity provides the definition of the business activity coordination type that is used with the extensible coordination framework described in the WS-Coordination specification. This protocol can be used to build the applications that require consistent agreement on the outcome of long-running distributed activities.

Windows Communication Foundation (WCF)

WCF is the latest technology from Microsoft for building services, including web services. In this section, we will learn what WCF is and what it is composed of. We will also learn various .NET runtimes, .NET frameworks, Visual Studio versions, the relationships between them, and what is needed to develop or deploy WCF services. You will see some code snippets that will help you to further understand the WCF concepts although they are not in a completed WCF project. Once we have grasped the basic concepts of WCF, we will develop a complete WCF service and create a client application to consume it, in the next chapter.

What is WCF?

WCF is the acronym for **Windows Communication Foundation**. It is Microsoft's unified programming model for building the service-oriented applications. It enables developers to build the secure, reliable, and transacted solutions that integrate across platforms and are interoperated with the existing investments. WCF is built on the Microsoft .NET Framework and simplifies the development of the connected systems. It unifies a broad array of the distributed systems capabilities in a composable, extensible architecture that supports multiple transports, messaging patterns, encodings, network topologies, and hosting models. It is the next generation version of several existing products—**ASP.NET's web methods (ASMX)** and **Microsoft Web Services Enhancements (WSE)** for Microsoft .NET, .NET Remoting, Enterprise Services, and System.Messaging.

The purpose of WCF is to provide a single programming model, which can be used to create services on the .NET platform, for organizations.

Why is WCF used for SOA?

As we have seen in the previous section, WCF is an umbrella technology that covers ASMX web services, .NET Remoting, WSE, Enterprise Service, and System Messaging. It is designed to offer a manageable approach to distributed computing, broad interoperability, and direct support for service orientation. WCF supports many styles of distributed application development by providing a layered architecture. At its base, the WCF channel architecture provides asynchronous, untyped message-passing primitives. Built on top of this base are protocol facilities for secure, reliable, and transacted data exchange, and a broad choice of transport and encoding options.

Let us take an example that shows why WCF is a good approach for SOA. Suppose a company is designing a service to get loan information. This service could be used by the internal call center application, an Internet web application, and a third-party Java J2EE application such as a banking system. For interactions with the call center client application, performance is important. For communication with the J2EE-based application, however, interoperability becomes the highest goal. The security requirements are also quite different between the local Windows-based application and the J2EE-based application running on another operating system. Even transactional requirements might vary with only the internal application being allowed to make the transactional requests.

With these complex requirements, it is not easy to build the desired service with any single existing technology. For example, the ASMX technology may serve well for the interoperability, but its performance may not be ideal. .NET Remoting is a good choice from the performance perspective, but it is not good at interoperability. Enterprise Services could be used for managing the object lifetimes and defining the distributed transactions, but Enterprise Services supports only a limited set of communication options.

Now with WCF, it is much easier to implement this service. As WCF has unified a broad array of distributed systems capabilities, the get loan service can be built with WCF for all of its application-to-application communication. The following list shows how WCF addresses each of these requirements:

- Since WCF can communicate by using web service standards, interoperability with other platforms that also support SOAP, such as the leading J2EE-based application servers, is straightforward.

- You can also configure and extend WCF to communicate with web services using messages not based on SOAP, for example, simple XML formats such as RSS.

- Performance is of paramount concern for most businesses. WCF was developed with the goal of being one of the fastest-distributed application platforms developed by Microsoft.

- To allow for optimal performance when both parties in a communication are built on WCF, the wire encoding used in this case is an optimized binary version of an XML Information Set. Using this option makes sense for communication with the call center client application because it is also built on WCF and performance is an important concern.

- Managing object lifetimes, defining distributed transactions, and other aspects of Enterprise Services are now provided by WCF. They are available to any WCF-based application, which means that the get loan service can use them with any of the other applications that it communicates with.

- Because it supports a large set of the WS-* specifications, WCF helps to provide reliability, security, and transactions, when communicating with any platform that supports these specifications.

- The WCF option for queued messaging, built on Message Queuing, allows applications to use persistent queuing without using another set of application programming interfaces.

The result of this unification is greater functionality and significantly reduced complexity.

WCF architecture

The following diagram illustrates the principal layers of the WCF architecture. This diagram is taken from the Microsoft website (`http://msdn.microsoft.com/en-us/library/ms733128.aspx`):

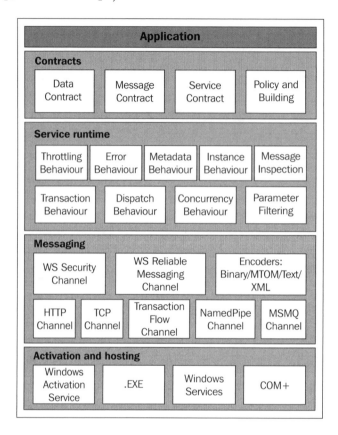

- The Contracts layer defines various aspects of the message system. For example, the Data Contract describes every parameter that makes up every message that a service can create or consume. The Service runtime layer contains the behaviors that occur only during the actual operation of the service, that is, the runtime behaviors of the service. The Messaging layer is composed of channels. A **channel** is a component that processes a message in some way, for example, in authenticating a message.

- In its final form, a service is a program. Like other programs, a service must be run in an executable format. This is known as the **hosting application**.

In the next section, we will learn these concepts in detail.

Basic WCF concepts – WCF ABCs

There are many terms and concepts surrounding WCF such as address, binding, contract, endpoint, behavior, hosting, and channels. Understanding these terms is very helpful when using WCF.

Address

The WCF address is a specific location for a service. It is the specific place to which a message will be sent. All WCF services are deployed at a specific address, listening at that address for incoming requests.

A **WCF address** is normally specified as a URL, with the first part specifying the transport mechanism, and the hierarchical parts specifying the unique location of the service. For example, `http://www.myweb.com/myWCFServices/SampleService` is an address for a WCF service. This WCF service uses HTTP as its transport protocol, and it is located on the server `www.myweb.com`, with a unique service path of `myWCFServices/SampleService`. The following diagram illustrates the three parts of a WCF service address:

Binding

Bindings are used for specifying the transport, encoding, and protocol details required for clients and services to communicate with each other. Bindings are what WCF uses to generate the underlying wire representation of the endpoint (an endpoint is a place where clients can communicate with a WCF service; more details will follow). So, most of the details of the binding must be agreed upon by the parties that are communicating. The easiest way to achieve this is by having clients of a service to use the same binding that the service uses.

A binding is made up of a collection of binding elements. Each element describes some aspects of how the service communicates with clients. A binding must include at least one transport binding element, at least one message encoding binding element (which can be provided by the transport binding element by default), and any number of other protocol binding elements. The process that builds a runtime out of this description, allows each binding element to contribute code to that runtime.

WCF provides bindings that contain common selections of binding elements. These can either be used with their default settings or the default values can be modified according to the user requirements. These system-provided bindings have properties that allow direct control over the binding elements and their settings.

The following are some examples of the system-provided bindings:

- `BasicHttpBinding`
- `WSHttpBinding`
- `WSDualHttpBinding`
- `WS2007HttpBinding`
- `WSFederationHttpBinding`
- `WS2007FederationHttpBinding`
- `NetTcpBinding`
- `NetNamedPipeBinding`
- `NetMsmqBinding`
- `NetPeerTcpBinding`
- `WebHttpBinding`
- `MsmqIntegrationBinding`

Each one of these built-in bindings has predefined required elements for a common task, and is ready to be used in your project. For instance, `BasicHttpBinding` uses HTTP as the transport for sending the SOAP 1.1 messages, and it has attributes and elements such as `receiveTimeout`, `sendTimeout`, `maxMessageSize`, and `maxBufferSize`. You can use the default settings of its attributes and elements, or overwrite them as needed.

Contract

A **WCF contract** is a set of specifications that defines the interfaces of a WCF service. A WCF service communicates with other applications according to its contracts. There are several types of WCF contracts such as service contract, operation contract, data contract, message contract, and fault contract.

Service contract

A **service contract** is the interface of the WCF service. Basically, it tells others what the service can do. It may include the service-level settings such as the name of the service, the namespace of the service, and the corresponding callback contracts of the service. Inside the interface, it can define a bunch of methods or service operations for specific tasks. A WCF service has to contain at least one service contract to service requests.

Operation contract

An **operation contract** is defined within a service contract. It defines the parameters and return type of an operation. An operation can take data of a primitive (native) datatype such as an integer as a parameter, or it can take a message, which should be defined as a message contract type. Just as a service contract is an interface, an operation contract is a definition of an operation. It has to be implemented in order for the service to function as a WCF service. An operation contract also defines the operation-level settings such as the transaction flow of the operation, the directions of the operation (one-way request/reply or duplex callbacks), and the fault contract of the operation.

The following is an example of an operation contract:

```
[FaultContract(typeof(ProductFault))]
GetProductResponse GetProduct(GetProductRequest request);
```

In this example, the operation contract's name is `GetProduct` and it takes one input parameter, which is of the type `GetProductRequest` (a message contract) and has one return value, which is of the type `GetProductResponse` (another message contract). It may return a fault message, which is of the type `ProductFault` (a fault contract), to the client applications. We will cover message contract and fault contract in the following sections.

Message contract

If an operation contract needs to pass a message as a parameter or return a message, the type of these messages will be defined as message contracts. A message contract defines the elements of the message as well as any message-related settings such as the level of message security, and also whether an element should go to the header or to the body.

The following is a message contract example:

```
namespace MyWCF.EasyNorthwind.MessageContracts
{
  /// <summary>
  /// Service Contract Class - GetProductResponse
  /// </summary>
  [System.ServiceModel.MessageContract(IsWrapped = false)]
  public partial class GetProductResponse
  {
    private MyWCF.EasyNorthwind.DataContracts.Product product;
    [System.ServiceModel.MessageBodyMember(Name = "Product")]
    public MyWCF.EasyNorthwind.DataContracts.Product Product
    {
      get { return product; }
      set { product = value; }
    }
  }
}
```

In this example, the message contract's name is `GetProductResponse` and this message contract has one member, which is of the type `Product`.

Data contract

Data contracts are datatypes of the WCF service. All datatypes used by the WCF service must be described in metadata to enable other applications to interoperate with the service. A data contract can be used by an operation contract as a parameter or return type, or it can be used by a message contract to define elements. If a WCF service uses only primitive (native) datatypes, it is not necessary to define any data contract.

The following is an example of data contract:

```
namespace MyWCF.EasyNorthwind.DataContracts
{
  /// <summary>
  /// Data Contract Class - Product
  /// </summary>
  [System.Runtime.Serialization.DataContract(
```

```
  Namespace =
  "http://MyCompany.com/ProductService/EasyWCF/2008/05",
   Name = "Product")]
  public partial class Product
  {
    private int productID;
    private string productName;
    [System.Runtime.Serialization.DataMember(
    Name= "ProductID")]
    public int ProductID
    {
      get { return productID; }
      set { productID = value; }
    }
    [System.Runtime.Serialization.DataMember(
Name = "ProductName")]
    public string ProductName
    {
      get { return productName; }
      set { productName = value; }
    }
  }
}
```

In this example, the namespace of the data contract is `http://MyCompany.com/ProductService/EasyWCF/2008/05`, the name of the data contract is `Product`, and this data contract has two members (`ProductID` and `ProductName`).

Fault contract

In any WCF service operation contract, if an error is returned to the caller, the caller should be warned of that error. These error types are defined as fault contracts. An operation can have zero or more fault contracts associated with it.

The following is a fault contract example:

```
namespace MyWCF.EasyNorthwind.FaultContracts
{
  /// <summary>
  /// Data Contract Class - ProductFault
  /// </summary>
  [System.Runtime.Serialization.DataContract(
  Namespace =
  "http://MyCompany.com/ProductService/EasyWCF/2008/05",
  Name = "ProductFault")]
  public partial class ProductFault
```

```
  {
    private string faultMessage;
    [System.Runtime.Serialization.DataMember(
    Name = "FaultMessage")]
    public string FaultMessage
    {
      get { return faultMessage; }
      set { faultMessage = value; }
    }
  }
}
```

In this example, the namespace of the fault contract is `http://MyCompany.com/ProductService/EasyWCF/2008/05`, the name of the fault contract is `ProductFault`, and the fault contract has only one member (`FaultMessage`).

Endpoint

Messages are sent between endpoints. **Endpoints** are places where messages are sent or received (or both), and they define all of the information required for the message exchange. A service exposes one or more application endpoints (as well as zero or more infrastructure endpoints). A service can expose this information as the metadata that clients process to generate the appropriate WCF clients and communication stacks. When needed, the client generates an endpoint that is compatible with one of the service's endpoints.

A WCF service endpoint has an address, a binding, and a service contract (sometimes referred as **WCF ABCs**).

The endpoint's address is a network address where the endpoint resides. It describes, in a standard-based way, where messages should be sent. Each endpoint normally has one unique address, but sometimes two or more endpoints can share the same address.

The endpoint's binding specifies how the endpoint communicates with the world, including things such as transport protocol (TCP, HTTP), encoding (text, binary), and security requirements (SSL, SOAP message security).

The endpoint's contract specifies what the endpoint communicates, and is essentially a collection of messages organized in the operations that have basic **Message Exchange Patterns** (**MEPs**) such as one-way, duplex, or request/reply.

The following diagram shows the components of a WCF service endpoint:

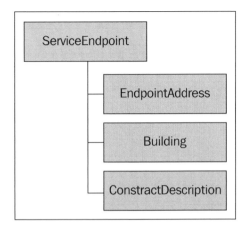

Behavior

A **WCF behavior** is a type of settings to extend the functionality of the original type. There are many types of behaviors in WCF such as service behavior, binding behavior, contract behavior, security behavior, and channel behavior. For example, a new service behavior can be defined to specify the transaction timeout of the service, the maximum concurrent instances of the service, and whether the service publishes metadata or not. Behaviors are configured in the WCF service configuration file. We will configure several specific behaviors in the next chapters.

Hosting

A WCF service is a component that can be called by other applications. It must be hosted in an environment in order to be discovered and used by others. The WCF host is an application that controls the lifetime of the service. With .NET 3.0 and beyond, there are several ways to host the service.

Self hosting

A WCF service can be self-hosted, which means that the service runs as a standalone application and controls its own lifetime. This is the most flexible and easiest way of hosting a WCF service, but its availability and features are limited.

Windows services hosting

A WCF service can also be hosted as a Windows service. A **Windows service** is a process managed by the operating system and it is automatically started when Windows is started (if it is configured to do so). However, it lacks some critical features (such as versioning) for WCF services.

IIS or Windows Activation Services hosting

A better way to host a WCF service is to use IIS. This is the traditional way of hosting a web service. IIS, by its nature, has many useful features such as process recycling, idle shutdown, process health monitoring, message-based activation, high availability, easy manageability, versioning, and deployment scenarios. All of these features are required for the enterprise-level WCF services.

Starting from IIS 7.0, **Windows Activation Services (WAS)** is the process activation mechanism for hosting WCF services. WAS retains the familiar IIS 6.0 process model application pools and message-based process activation and hosting features (such as rapid failure protection, health monitoring, and recycling), but it removes the dependency on HTTP from the activation architecture. IIS 7.0 and above use WAS to accomplish the message-based activation over HTTP. Additional WCF components also plug into WAS to provide message-based activation over the other protocols that WCF supports, such as TCP, MSMQ, and named pipes. This allows applications that use the non-HTTP communication protocols to use the IIS features such as process recycling, rapid fail protection, and the common configuration systems that were only previously available to the HTTP-based applications.

Channels

As we have seen in the previous sections, a WCF service has to be hosted in an application on the server side. On the client side, the client applications have to specify the bindings to connect to the WCF services. The binding elements are interfaces and they have to be implemented in the concrete classes. The concrete implementation of a binding element is called a **channel**. The binding represents the configuration and the channel is the implementation associated with that configuration. Therefore, there is a channel associated with each binding element. Channels stack on top of one another to create the concrete implementation of the binding—the channel stack.

The **WCF channel stack** is a layered communication stack with one or more channels that process messages. At the bottom of the stack, there is a transport channel that is responsible for adapting the channel stack to the underlying transport (for example, TCP, HTTP, SMTP, and other types of transport). Channels provide a low-level programming model for sending and receiving messages. This programming model relies on several interfaces and other types collectively known as the **WCF channel model**. The following diagram shows a simple channel stack:

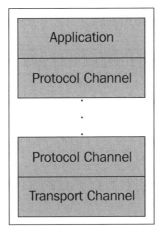

Metadata

The **metadata** of a service describes the characteristics of the service that an external entity needs to understand in order to communicate with the service. Metadata can be consumed by the ServiceModel Metadata Utility Tool (Svcutil.exe) to generate a WCF client proxy and the accompanying configuration that a client application can use to interact with the service.

The metadata exposed by the service includes XML schema documents, which define the data contract of the service, and WSDL documents, which describe the methods of the service.

Though WCF services always have metadata, it is possible to hide the metadata from outsiders. If you do so, you have to pass the metadata to the client side by other means. This practice is not common, but it gives your services an extra layer of security. When enabled through the configuration settings through metadata behavior, metadata for the service can be retrieved by inspecting the service and its endpoints. The following configuration setting in a WCF service configuration file will enable metadata publishing for HTTP transport protocol:

```
<serviceMetadata httpGetEnabled="true" />
```

WCF production and development environments

WCF was first introduced in Microsoft's .NET **Common Language Runtime (CLR)** version 2.0. The corresponding framework at that time was .NET 3.0. To develop and run the WCF services, Microsoft .NET Framework 3.0 or above is required.

Visual Studio is Microsoft's IDE for developing the WCF service applications. Visual Studio 2008 and above support WCF service application development.

The following table shows all of the different versions of the .NET runtimes, .NET Frameworks, and Visual Studios, along with their relationships:

CLR	.NET Framework	Components						Visual Studio
CLR 4.0	.NET 4.5	Metro	HTML5		Portable Class Libraries			2012
	.NET 4.0	Parallel Computing	Dynamic		Covariance and Contravariance			2010 or above
CLR 2.0	.NET 3.5 SP1	ASP.NET MVC	Entity Framework	LINQ to Entities	Cloud Computing			2008 or above
	.NET 3.5	LINQ						2008 or above
		LINQ to SQL	LINQ to XML	LINQ to Objects	ASP .NET AJAX	REST	RSS	
	.NET 3.0	WCF	WPF	WF	CardSpace			
	.NET 2.0	Winforms	ASP.NET		ADO.NET			2005 or above
CLR 1.0	.NET 1.1	Winforms	ASP.NET		ADO.NET			2003
	.NET 1.0							2002

Summary

In this chapter, we have learned and clarified many concepts related to SOA, web services, and WCF. Now, we know that SOA is an architectural design and WCF is Microsoft's unified programming model for building the service-oriented applications.

In the next chapter, we will develop our first WCF service with Visual Studio 2012, so you can have a better understanding of WCF.

2
Implementing a Basic HelloWorld WCF Service

In the previous chapter, we learned several WCF concepts and looked at a few code snippets.

In this chapter, we will implement a basic WCF service from scratch. We will build a `HelloWorld` WCF service by carrying out the following steps:

- Creating the solution and project
- Creating the WCF service contract interface
- Implementing the WCF service
- Hosting the WCF service in IIS Express
- Creating a client application to consume this WCF service

Creating the HelloWorld solution and project

Before we can build the WCF service, we need to create a solution for our service project. We also need a directory in which we will save all the files. Throughout this book, we will save our project source codes in the `C:\SOAWithWCFandLINQ\Projects` directory. We will have a subfolder for each solution we create and under this solution folder, we will have one subfolder for each project.

For this `HelloWorld` solution, the final directory structure is shown in the following screenshot:

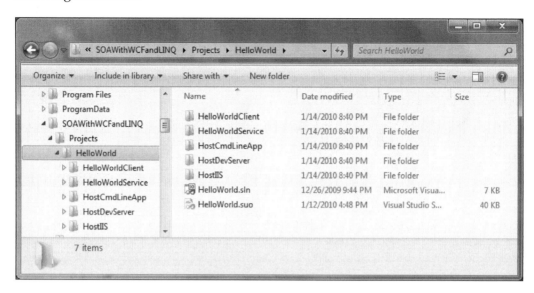

 You don't need to manually create these directories with Windows Explorer; Visual Studio will create them automatically when you create the solutions and projects.

Now follow these steps to create our first solution and the `HelloWorld` project:

1. Start Visual Studio 2012 (you can use Visual Studio Ultimate, Premium, or Professional throughout this book). If the **Open Project** dialog box pops up, click on **Cancel** to close it.

2. Go to menu **File | New | Project**. The **New Project** dialog window will appear:

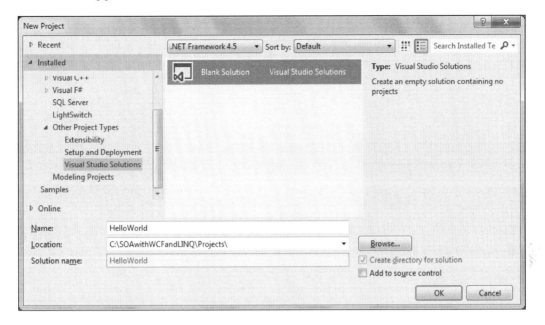

3. From the left-hand side of the window, expand **Installed | Other Project Types** and then select **Visual Studio Solutions** as the template. From the middle section of the window, select **Blank Solution**.

4. At the bottom of the window, type HelloWorld in the **Name** field and enter C:\SOAWithWCFandLINQ\Projects\ in the **Location** field. Note that you should not enter HelloWorld within the location, because Visual Studio will automatically create a folder for a new solution.

5. Click on the **OK** button to close this window and your screen should look like the following screenshot with an empty solution:

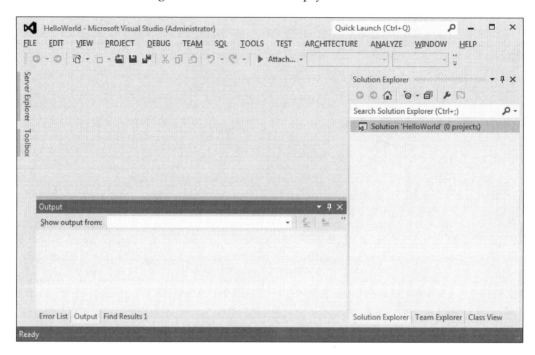

6. Depending on your settings, the layout may be different. But you should still have an empty solution in your **Solution Explorer**. If you don't see **Solution Explorer**, navigate to the menu **View | Solution Explorer** or press *Ctrl + Alt + L* to bring it up.

7. In **Solution Explorer**, right-click on the solution and select **Add | New Project...** from the context menu. You can also go to the menu **File | Add | New Project...** to get the same result. The following screenshot shows the context menu for adding a new project:

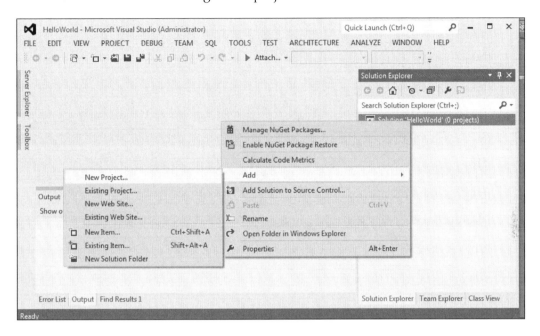

8. The **New Project** window should now appear on your screen. In the left-hand side of this window, select **Installed | Visual C#** as the template, and in the middle section of the window, select **Class Library**.

9. At the bottom of the window, type `HelloWorldService` in the **Name** field. Enter `C:\SOAWithWCFandLINQ\Projects\HelloWorld` in the **Location** field. Again, don't add `HelloWorldService` to the location, as Visual Studio will create a subfolder for this new project (Visual Studio will use the solution folder as the default base folder for all the new projects added to the solution).

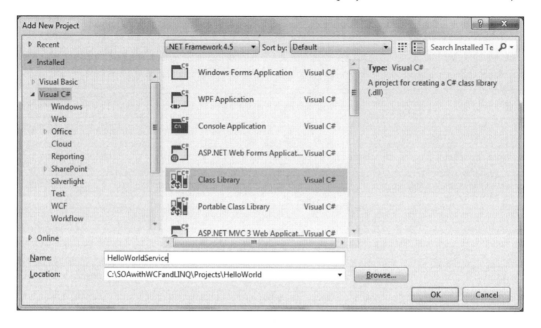

You may have noticed that there is already a template for **WCF Service Application** in Visual Studio 2012. For this very first example, we will not use this template. Instead, we will create everything by ourselves to understand the purpose of each template. This is an excellent way for you to understand and master this new technology. In the next chapter, we will use this template to create the project, so we don't need to manually type a lot of code.

10. Now you can click on the **OK** button to close this window.

Once you click on the **OK** button, Visual Studio will create several files for you. The first file is the project file. This is an XML file under the project directory and it is called `HelloWorldService.csproj`.

Visual Studio also creates an empty class file called `Class1.cs`. Later we will change this default name to a more meaningful one and change its namespace to our own.

Three directories are created automatically under the project folder—one to hold the binary files, another to hold the object files, and a third one for the properties files of the project.

The window on your screen should now look like the following screenshot:

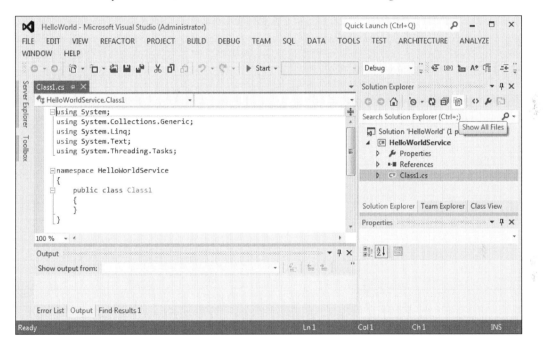

We have now created a new solution and project. Next, we will develop and build this service. But before we go any further, we need to do two things to this project:

1. Click on the **Show All Files** button on the **Solution Explorer** toolbar, as shown in the preceding screenshot. Clicking on this button will show all files and directories in your hard disk under the project folder—even those items that are not included in the project. Make sure that you don't have the solution item selected. Otherwise, you cannot see the **Show All Files** button.

2. Change the default namespace of the project. From **Solution Explorer**, right-click on the **HelloWorldService** project and select **Properties** from the context menu or go to menu item **Project | HelloWorldService Properties...**. You will see a dialog window for project properties. Under the **Application** tab, enter MyWCFServices in the **Default namespace** field.

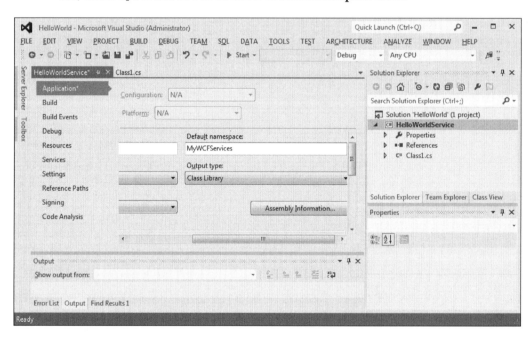

Lastly, in order to develop a WCF service, we need to add a reference to the System. ServiceModel assembly. Perform the following steps:

3. In the **Solution Explorer** window, right-click on the **HelloWorldService** project and select **Add Reference...** from the context menu. You can also go to the menu item **Project | Add Reference...** to do this. The **Reference Manager** dialog window will appear on your screen.

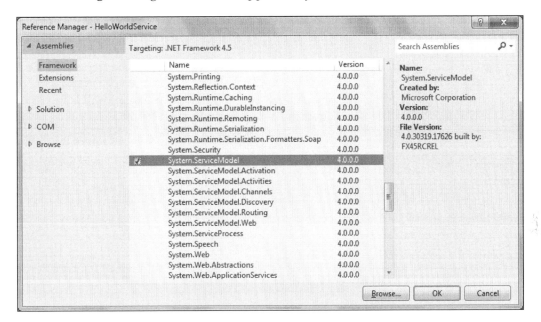

4. Check **System.ServiceModel** from the **Framework** tab under **Assemblies** and click on **OK**.

Now in **Solution Explorer**, if you expand the references of the **HelloWorldService** project, you will see that **System.ServiceModel** has been added under **References**. Also, note that **System.Xml.Linq** is added by default. We will use this later when we query a database.

Creating the HelloWorldService service contract interface

In the previous section, we created the solution and the project for the `HelloWorld` WCF service. From this section onwards, we will start building the `HelloWorld` WCF service. First, we need to create the service contract interface. For that, perform the following steps:

1. In **Solution Explorer**, right-click on the **HelloWorldService** project and select **Add | New Item...** from the context menu. The **Add New Item - HelloWorldService** dialog window shown in the following screenshot will appear on your screen:

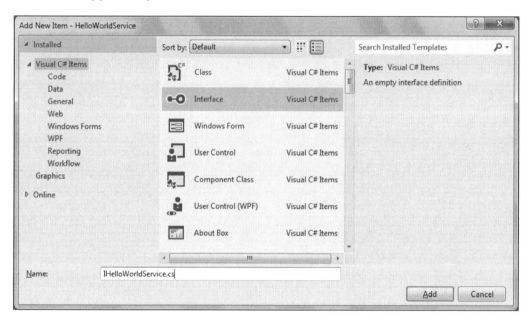

2. On the left-hand side of the window, select **Installed | Visual C# Items** as the template, and from the middle section of the window, select **Interface**.

3. At the bottom of the window, change **Name** from `Interface1.cs` to `IHelloWorldService.cs`.

4. Click on the **Add** button.

Now an empty service interface file has been added to the project, which we are going to use as the service interface.

Follow these steps to customize it:

1. Add a `using` statement:

    ```
    using System.ServiceModel;
    ```

2. Add a `ServiceContract` attribute to the interface. This will designate the interface as a WCF service contract interface.

    ```
    [ServiceContract]
    ```

3. Add a `GetMessage` method to the interface. This method will take a string as the input and return another string as the result. It also has an attribute called `OperationContract`:

    ```
    [OperationContract]
    string GetMessage(string name);
    ```

4. Change the interface to public.

The final content of the file, `IHelloWorldService.cs`, should look as follows:

```
using System;
using System.Collections.Generic;
using System.Linq;
using System.Text;
using System.Threading.Tasks;
using System.ServiceModel;

namespace MyWCFServices
{
    [ServiceContract]
    public interface IHelloWorldService
    {
        [OperationContract]
        string GetMessage(string name);
    }
}
```

Implementing the HelloWorldService service contract

Now that we have defined a service contract interface, we need to implement it. For this purpose, we will re-use the empty class file that Visual Studio created for us earlier, and modify this to make it the implementation class of our service.

Before we modify this file, we need to rename it. In the **Solution Explorer** window, right-click on the **Class1.cs** file, select **Rename** from the context menu, and rename it as HelloWorldService.cs.

 Visual Studio is smart enough to change all the related files that are references to use this new name. You can also select the file and change its name from the **Properties** window.

Next, perform the following steps to customize this class file:

1. Open the HelloWorldService.cs file.

2. Change its namespace from HelloWorldService to MyWCFServices. This is because this file was added before we changed the default namespace of the project.

3. Change its name from Class1 to HelloWorldService, if this is not done for you.

4. Make it implement IHelloWorldService implicitly.

   ```
   public class HelloWorldService: IHelloWorldService
   ```

5. Add a GetMessage method to the class. This is an ordinary C# method that returns a string. You can also right-click on the interface link and select **Implement Interface** to add the skeleton of this method.

   ```
   public string GetMessage(string name)
   {
       return "Hello world from " + name + "!";
   }
   ```

The final content of the HelloWorldService.cs file should look like the following:

```
using System;
using System.Collections.Generic;
using System.Linq;
using System.Text;
using System.Threading.Tasks;
```

```
namespace MyWCFServices
{
    public class HelloWorldService: IHelloWorldService
    {
        public string GetMessage(string name)
        {
            return "Hello world from " + name + "!";
        }
    }
}
```

Now build the project. If there is no build error, it means that you have successfully created your first WCF service. If you see a compilation error, such as `'ServiceModel' does not exist in the namespace 'System'`, this is because you didn't add the `System.ServiceModel` namespace reference correctly. Revisit the previous section to add this reference, and you are all set.

Next, we will host this WCF service in an environment and create a client application to consume it.

Hosting the WCF service in IIS Express

`HelloWorldService` is a class library. It has to be hosted in an environment so that client applications may access it. In this section, we will learn how to host it, using IIS Express. Later in the next chapter, we will discuss more hosting options for a WCF service.

Creating the host application

There are several built-in host applications for WCF services within Visual Studio 2012. However, in this section, we will manually create the host application so that you can have a better understanding of what a hosting application is really like under the hood. In subsequent chapters, we will learn and use the built-in hosting application.

To host the library by using IIS Express, we need to add a new website to the solution. Follow these steps to create this website:

1. In **Solution Explorer**, right-click on the **Solution** file and select **Add | New Web Site...** from the context menu (**Show Solution** must always be enabled in **Options | Projects** and **Solutions** in order to see the solution file). The **Add New Web Site** dialog window should pop up.

2. Select **Visual C# | ASP.NET Empty Web Site** as the template and leave the **Web location** field set as **File System**. Change the website name from `WebSite1` to `C:\SOAWithWCFandLINQ\Projects\HelloWorld\HostDevServer` and click on **OK**.

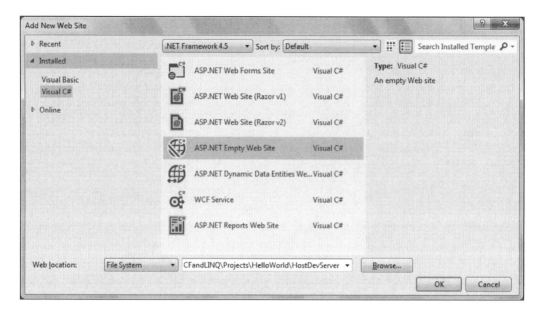

3. Now in **Solution Explorer**, you have one more item (**HostDevServer**) within the solution. It will look like the following:

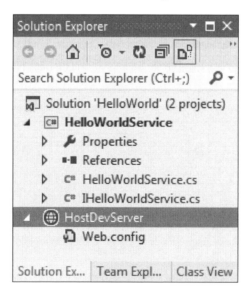

4. Next, we need to set the website as the startup project. In **Solution Explorer**, right-click on the website **HostDevServer** and select **Set as StartUp Project** from the context menu (or you can first select the website from **Solution Explorer** and then select the menu item **Website | Set as StartUp Project**). The **HostDevServer** website should be highlighted in **Solution Explorer**, indicating that it is now the startup project.

5. Because we will host HelloWorldService from this website, we need to add a HelloWorldService reference to the website. In **Solution Explorer**, right-click on the **HostDevServer** website and select **Add Reference...** from the context menu. The **Reference Manager** dialog box should appear, as shown in the following screenshot:

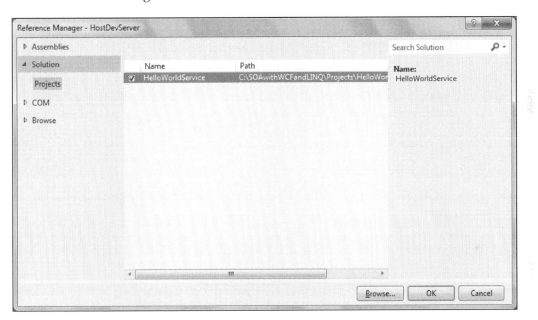

6. In the **Reference Manager** dialog box, click on the **Solutions** tab and then click on **Projects**. Check the **HelloWorldService** project and then click on **OK**. You will see that a new directory (bin) has been created under the HostDevServer website and two files from the HelloWorldService project have been copied to this new directory. Later on, when this website is accessed, the web server (IIS Express) will look for executable code in this bin directory.

Testing the host application

Now we can run the website inside IIS Express. If you start the `HostDevServer` website by pressing *Ctrl + F5* or by selecting **Debug | Start Without Debugging...** in the menu, you will see an empty website in your browser with an error.

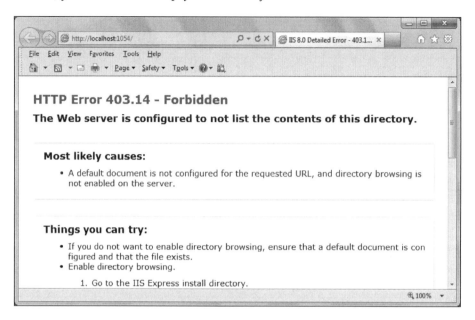

If you press *F5* (or select **Debug | Start Debugging** from the menu), you may see a dialog saying **Debugging Not Enabled** (as shown in the following screenshot). Choose the option **Run without debugging (equivalent to Ctrl + F5)** and click on the **OK** button to continue. We will explore the debugging options of a WCF service later. Until then we will continue to use *Ctrl + F5* to start the website without debugging.

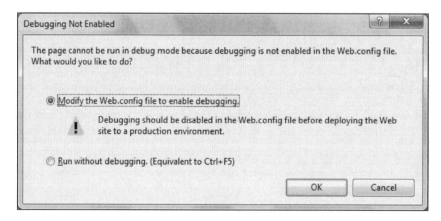

IIS Express

At this point, you should have the `HostDevServer` site up and running. This site actually runs inside IIS Express. IIS Express is a lightweight, self-contained version of IIS optimized for developers. This web server is intended to be used by developers only and has functionality similar to that of the **Internet Information Services (IIS)** server. It also has some limitations, for example, it only supports the HTTP and HTTPS protocols.

When a new website is created within Visual Studio, IIS Express will automatically assign a port for it. You can find your website's port in the **Properties** window of your website, as shown in the following screenshot:

IIS Express is normally started from within Visual Studio when you need to debug or unit test a web project. If you really need to start it from outside of Visual Studio, you can use a command-line statement in the following format:

```
C:\Program Files\IIS Express\iisexpress /path:c:\myapp\ /port:1054 /
clr:v4.0
```

For our website, the statement should be as follows:

```
"C:\Program Files\IIS Express\iisexpress" /path:C:\SOAwithWCFandLINQ\
Projects\HelloWorld\HostDevServer /port:1054 /clr:v4.0
```

 `IISexpress.exe` is located under your program files directory. In x64 system, it should be under your program files (x86) directory.

Modifying the web.config file

Although we can start the website now, it is only an empty site. Currently, it does not host our `HelloWorldService`. This is because we haven't specified which service this website should host or an entry point for this website.

To specify which service our website will host, we can add a `.svc` file to the website. From .NET 4.0, we can also use the file-less (svc-less) activation service to accomplish this. In this section, we will take the file-less approach to specify the service.

Now, let's modify the `web.config` file of the website to host our `HelloWorldService` WCF service. Open the `web.config` file of the website and change it to the following:

```xml
<?xml version="1.0"?>
<!--
  For more information on how to configure your ASP.NET application,
please visit
  http://go.microsoft.com/fwlink/?LinkId=169433
  -->
<configuration>
  <system.web>
    <compilation debug="true" targetFramework="4.5"/>
    <httpRuntime targetFramework="4.5"/>
  </system.web>

  <system.serviceModel>
    <serviceHostingEnvironment >
      <serviceActivations>
        <add factory="System.ServiceModel.
        Activation.ServiceHostFactory"
         relativeAddress="./HostDevServer/HelloWorldService.svc"
         service="MyWCFServices.HelloWorldService"/>
      </serviceActivations>
    </serviceHostingEnvironment>
    <behaviors>
      <serviceBehaviors>
        <behavior>
          <serviceMetadata httpGetEnabled="true"/>
        </behavior>
      </serviceBehaviors>
    </behaviors>
  </system.serviceModel>

</configuration>
```

Note that the `system.serviceModel` node is the only code that we have added to the `config` file.

The `httpGetEnabled` behavior is essential because we want other applications to be able to locate the metadata of this service via HTTP. Without the metadata, the client applications can't generate the proxy and thus won't be able to use the service.

The following is a brief explanation of the other elements in this configuration file:

- `Configuration` is the root node of the file.
- `system.serviceModel` is the top node for all the WCF service-specific settings.
- `serviceHostingEnvironment` is used to specify the hosting environment.
- The `serviceActivations` node is where you specify the service name and its relative address. This configuration element allows you to define the virtual service activation settings that map to your WCF service types. This makes it possible to activate services hosted in WAS/IIS without a `.svc` file.
- Within the `serviceBehaviors` node, you can define specific behaviors for a service. In our example, we have specified one behavior, which enables the service metadata exchange for the service.

Starting the host application

Now, if you start the website by pressing *Ctrl + F5* (don't use *F5* or the menu option **Debug | Start Debugging** until we discuss these later), you will still see the same empty website with the same error. However, at this time we have a service hosted within this website, so just append `HostDevServer/HelloWorldService.svc` after the address (it should look like `http://localhost:1054/`). Then you will get the description of this service, that is, how to get the `wsdl` file of this service and how to create a client to consume this service. You should see a page similar to the one shown in the following screenshot:

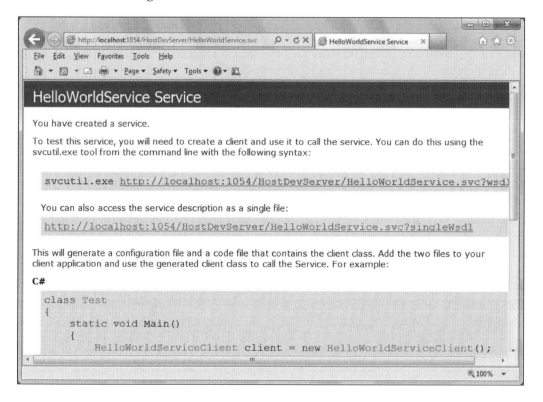

Now, click on the WSDL link on this page and you will get the WSDL XML file for this service. The `wsdl` file gives all of the contract information for this service. In the next section, we will use this `wsdl` file to generate a proxy for our client application.

Creating a client to consume the WCF service

Now that we have successfully created and hosted a WCF service, we need a client to consume the service. We will create a C# client application to consume HelloWorldService.

In this section, we will create a Windows console application to call the WCF service.

Creating the client application project

First, we need to create a console application project and add it to the solution. Follow these steps to create the console application:

1. In **Solution Explorer**, right-click on the solution **HelloWorld** and select **Add | New Project...** from the context menu. The **Add New Project** dialog window should appear, as shown in the following screenshot:

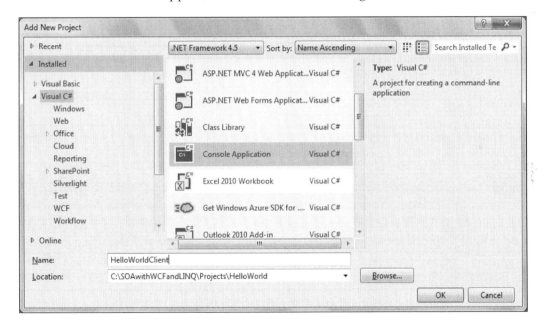

2. Select **Visual C# | Console Application** as the template, change the project name from the defaulted value of ConsoleApplication1 to HelloWorldClient, and leave the **Location** field as **C:\ SOAWithWCFandLINQ\Projects\HelloWorld**. Click on the **OK** button. The new client project has now been created and added to the solution.

Generating the proxy and configuration files

In order to consume a non-RESTful WCF service, a client application must first obtain or generate a proxy class.

We also need a configuration file to specify things such as the binding of the service, the address of the service, and the contract.

To generate these two files, we can use the svcutil.exe tool from the command line. You can follow these steps to generate the two files:

1. Start the service by pressing *Ctrl + F5* or by selecting the menu option **Debug | Start Without Debugging** (at this point your startup project should still be HostDevServer; if not, you need to set this to be the startup project).

2. After the service has been started, open a command-line window, change the directory to your client application folder, and then run the command-line svcutil.exe tool with the following syntax (SvcUtil.exe may be in a different directory in your machine and you need to substitute 1054 with your service hosting port):

    ```
    "C:\Program Files\Microsoft SDKs\Windows\v8.0A\bin\NETFX
    4.0 Tools\SvcUtil.exe" http://localhost:1054/HostDevServer/
    HelloWorldService.svc?wsdl/out:HelloWorldServiceRef.cs /
    config:app.config
    ```

You will see an output similar to that shown in the following screenshot:

Here two files have been generated—one for the proxy (HelloWorldServiceRef.cs) and the other for the configuration (app.config).

If you open the proxy file, you will see that the interface of the service (IHelloWorldService) is mimicked inside the proxy class and a client class (HelloWorldServiceClient) is created for implementing this interface. Inside this client class, the implementation of the service operation (GetMessage) is only a wrapper that delegates the call to the actual service implementation of the operation.

Inside the configuration file, you will see the definitions of HelloWorldService such as the endpoint address, binding, timeout settings, and security behaviors of the service.

> You can also create a proxy dynamically at runtime, or call the service through a Channel Factory instead of a proxy. Beware if you go with the Channel Factory approach, you may have to share your interface DLL with the clients.

Customizing the client application

Before we can run the client application, we still have some more work to do. Follow these steps to finish the customization:

1. Reload the app.config file. When you switch to Visual Studio, 2012, you will be asked to reload the app.config file since it has been changed. Click on **Yes** to reload it.

2. Add the proxy file to the project. In **Solution Explorer**, first select the **HelloWorldClient** project and click on **Show All Files** to show all the files. Now under the HelloWorldClient folder, you will see the proxy file (HelloWorldServiceRef.cs). However, this file is not yet included in the project. Right-click on it and select **Include In Project** to include it in the client project. You can also use the menu **Project | Add Existing Item...** (or the context menu **Add | Existing Item...**) to add it to the project.

3. Add a reference to the System.ServiceModel namespace. Just as we did for the HelloWorldService project, we also need to add a reference to the WCF .NET System.ServiceModel assembly. From **Solution Explorer**, just right-click on the **HelloWorldClient** project, select **Add Reference...,** and check **Assemblies\Framework\System.ServiceModel**. Then, click on the **OK** button to add the reference to the project.

4. Modify program.cs to call the service. In program.cs, add the following line to initialize the service client object:

```
HelloWorldServiceClient client = new HelloWorldServiceClient();
```

Using the default constructor on `HelloWorldServiceClient` means that the client runtime will look for the default client endpoint in the `app.config` file, which is present due to the use of `SvcUtil`.

Then we can call its method just as we would do for any other object:

```
Console.WriteLine(client.GetMessage("Mike Liu"));
```

Pass your name as the parameter to the `GetMessage` method so that it prints out a message for you.

Running the client application

We are now ready to run this client program.

First, make sure the service host application `HostDevServer` has been started. If you have stopped it previously, start it now (you need to set `HostDevServer` as the startup project and press *Ctrl + F5* to start it in non-debugging mode, or you can just right-click on the project **HostDevServer** and select **View in Browser (Internet Explorer)** from the context menu).

Then, from **Solution Explorer**, right-click on the project **HelloWorldClient**, select **Set as StartUp Project**, and then press *Ctrl + F5* to run it.

You will see output as shown in the following screenshot:

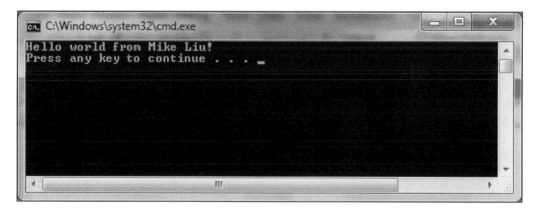

Setting the service application to AutoStart

Because we know we have to start the service host application before we run the client program, we can make some changes to the solution to automate this task, that is, to automatically start the service immediately before we run the client program.

To do this, in **Solution Explorer**, right-click on **Solution**, select **Properties** from the context menu, and you will see the **Solution 'HelloWorld' Property Pages** dialog box:

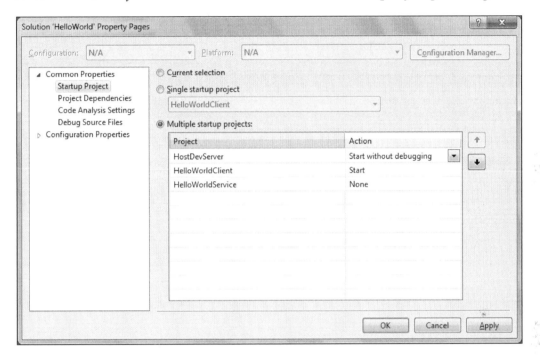

On this page, first select the **Multiple startup projects** option. Then change the action of **HostDevServer** to **Start without debugging**. Change **HelloWorldClient** to the same action.

 HostDevServer must be above **HelloWorldClient**. If it is not, use the arrows to move it to the top.

To test it, first stop the service and then press *Ctrl + F5*. You will notice that HostDevServer is started first, and then the client program runs without errors.

Note that this will only work inside Visual Studio IDE. If you start the client program from Windows Explorer (`C:\SOAWithWCFandLINQ\Projects\HelloWorld\HelloWorldClient\bin\Debug\HelloWorldClient.exe`) without first starting the service, the service won't get started automatically and you will get an error message saying **There was no endpoint listening at http://localhost:1054/HostDevServer/HelloWorldService.svc**.

Summary

In this chapter, we implemented a basic WCF service, hosted it within IIS Express, and created a command-line program to reference and consume this basic WCF service. At this point, you should have a thorough understanding as to what a WCF service is, under the hood. You will benefit from this when you develop WCF services, using Visual Studio WCF templates or automation guidance packages.

In the next chapter, we will explore more hosting options and discuss how to debug a WCF service.

3

Hosting and Debugging the HelloWorld WCF Service

In the previous chapter, we built a basic HelloWorld WCF service and hosted it within IIS Express. In this chapter, we will explore more hosting options for WCF services and learn how to debug WCF services.

In this chapter we will discuss:

- Hosting a WCF service in ASP.NET Development Server
- Hosting a WCF service in a console application
- Hosting a WCF service in a Windows Service application
- Hosting a WCF service in IIS using the HTTP protocol
- Hosting a WCF service in IIS using the TCP protocol
- Testing a WCF service
- Debugging a WCF service from a client application
- Directly debugging a WCF service
- Attaching to a running WCF service process

Hosting the HelloWorld WCF service

In the previous chapter, we hosted our `HelloWorldService` in IIS Express. In addition to this we have several other options for hosting a WCF service. In this section we will explore them one by one.

Hosting the service in ASP.NET Development Server

Prior to Visual Studio 2012, the built-in hosting web server for Visual Studio was the ASP.NET Development Server (in Visual Studio 2010 SP1, you could also manually configure IIS Express as the hosting server). Just like IIS Express, the ASP.NET Development Server is intended for development only and has functionality similar to IIS, but with a lot more limitations compared to IIS Express. For example, the ASP.NET Development Server associates the incoming requests with the context of the currently logged in user while IIS associates a security context with the machine account unless otherwise authenticated. Another major difference is in servicing static content. When using the ASP.NET Development Server, every request is processed by the ASP.NET runtime, but when using IIS, a request is processed by the ASP.NET runtime only if the request comes from an ASP.NET resource (like an ASP.NET web page).

In Visual Studio 2012, you can still choose to use the ASP.NET Development Server to host your WCF services. Just right-click on the hosting application project, and select **Use Visual Studio Development Server...** from the context menu. Then next time when you start your hosting application, the service will be hosted within the ASP.NET Development Server. The following diagram shows this context menu:

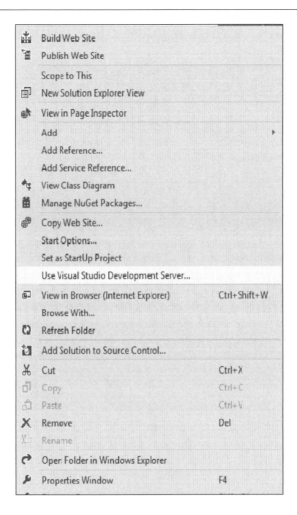

Hosting the service in a managed application

Besides using IIS Express or the ASP.NET Development Server for hosting WCF services, you may also create a .NET managed application and host a WCF service within that application. The hosting application can be, for example, a command-line application, a Windows Forms application, or a web application. This hosting method gives you full control over the lifetime of the WCF service. It is very easy to debug and deploy, and supports all bindings and transports. The major drawbacks of this hosting method are that you have to start the hosting application manually and that it provides only limited support for high availability, easy manageability, robustness, recoverability, versioning, and deployment scenarios. (You could implement a hosting environment that provides all of these. But it would cost you a lot in terms of effort and money to build something that is comparable to IIS.)

Hosting the service in a console application

Following are the steps to host `HelloWorldService` in a command-line application. Note that these steps are very similar to the steps in one of the previous sections where we hosted a WCF service in IIS Express. However, the configuration file is called `app.config` and not `web.config`. Refer to the specific previous section for diagrams. If you want to host a WCF service in a Windows Forms application or a web application, you can follow the same steps that we have listed here simply by creating the project, using the appropriate project template.

1. Add a console application project to the solution:

    In **Solution Explorer**, right-click on the solution file and select **Add | New Project...** from the context menu. The **Add New Project** dialog box should appear. Select **Visual C# | Console Application** as the template. Then change the name from `ConsoleApplication1` to `HostCmdLineApp` and click on the **OK** button. A new project is added to the solution.

2. Set the `HostCmdLineApp` project as the startup project:

    In **Solution Explorer**, right-click on the project **HostCmdLineApp** and select **Set as StartUp Project** from the context menu. You can also select the project in the **Solution Explorer** and then select the menu item **Project | Set as StartUp Project** to do this.

3. Add a reference to the `HelloWorldService` project:

    In **Solution Explorer**, right-click on the project **HostCmdLineApp** and select **Add Reference...** from the shortcut menu. The **Reference Manager** dialog box will appear. Click on **Projects** under the the **Solution** tab, select and check the **HelloWorldService** project, and then click on **OK**. Now, **HelloWorldService** is under the **References** folder of this project.

4. Add a reference to `System.ServiceModel`:

    This reference is required as we will manually create a service host application, and start and stop it in the steps that follow. In the **Solution Explorer** window, right-click on the **HostCmdLineApp** project and select **Add Reference...** from the context menu. You can also select the menu item **Project | Add Reference...** to do this. Check **System.ServiceModel** from **Framework** under the **Assemblies** tab and click on **OK**.

5. Modify the configuration file to define the behavior of the service. We need to add a `serviceModel` node to enable the metadata for all services hosted within this application.

6. The following is the full content of the `app.config` file:

```xml
<?xml version="1.0" encoding="utf-8" ?>
<configuration>
    <startup>
        <supportedRuntime version="v4.0"
        sku=".NETFramework,Version=v4.5" />
    </startup>

  <system.serviceModel>
    <behaviors>
      <serviceBehaviors>
        <behavior>
          <serviceMetadata httpGetEnabled="true"/>
        </behavior>
      </serviceBehaviors>
    </behaviors>
  </system.serviceModel>

</configuration>
```

7. Now we need to modify the `Program.cs` file to write some code to start and stop the WCF service inside the `Program.cs file`.

8. First, add a `using` statement as follows:

```
using System.ServiceModel;
```

9. Then add the following lines of code within the static `Main` method:

```
ServiceHost host =
new ServiceHost(typeof(MyWCFServices.HelloWorldService),
new Uri("http://localhost:1054/HostCmdLineApp/HelloWorldService.
svc"));
host.Open();
Console.WriteLine("HelloWorldService is now running. ");
Console.WriteLine("Press any key to stop it ...");
Console.ReadKey();
host.Close();
```

10. As you can see, we get the type of `HelloWorldService`, construct a base address for the WCF service, create a service host passing the type and base address, and call the `Open` method of the host to start the service. To stop the service, we just call the `Close` method of the service host.

11. The following code snippet shows the full content of the `Program.cs` file:

```
using System;
using System.Collections.Generic;
using System.Linq;
using System.Text;
using System.Threading.Tasks;
using System.ServiceModel;

namespace HostCmdLineApp
{
  class Program
  {
    static void Main(string[] args)
    {
      ServiceHost host =
      new ServiceHost(typeof
      (MyWCFServices.HelloWorldService),
      new Uri("http://localhost:1054/
      HostCmdLineApp/HelloWorldService.svc"));
      host.Open();
      Console.WriteLine("HelloWorldService is
      now running. ");
      Console.WriteLine("Press any key to stop it
      ...");
      Console.ReadKey();
      host.Close();
    }
  }
}
```

12. After the project has been successfully built, you can press *Ctrl + F5* to start the service. You will see a command-line window indicating that `HelloWorldService` is available and is waiting for requests.

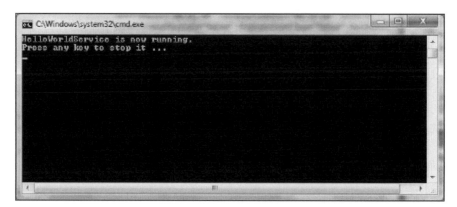

Note that when you run the program you may get an error message of `System.ServiceModel.AddressAccessDeniedException, Your process does not have access rights to this namespace`. This is because Visual Studio has to register the namespace for the `HelloWorld` service and, by default, Windows runs applications under a limited-rights user account even when you are logged in to the computer as an administrator. You have to run Visual Studio as an administrator to solve this issue. Just right-click on the Visual Studio executable file `devenv.exe` and select `Run as administrator`, or change the property **Privilege Level** to **Run this program as an administrator**, so you can always run Visual Studio as an administrator.

Alternatively, if you don't want to run Visual Studio as an administrator, you can manually register the namespace, using tools such as `HttpSysConfig`. You can search for "Your process does not have access rights to this namespace" on the Internet, using your preferred search provider to see various options for this issue. However, it seems to me that no matter which option is taken, the process to manually register a namespace for .NET is a little bit too complex and is beyond the context of this chapter, so I would simply run Visual Studio as an administrator.

Consuming the service hosted in a console application

To consume the service hosted in the previous console application, you can follow the same steps described in the *Creating a client to consume the WCF service* section in *Chapter 2, Implementing a Basic HelloWorld WCF Servics*, except that you pass `http://localhost:1054/HostCmdLineApp/HelloWorldService.svc?wsdl` instead of `http://localhost:1054/HostDevServer/HelloWorldService.svc?wsdl` to the `SvcUtil.exe` when you generate the proxy class and the configuration file.

In fact you can re-use the same client project because the contract is the same as it is the same service, just hosted differently. To re-use the same client, inside the `app.config` file, you just have to change the following line:

```
<endpoint address=
    "http://localhost:1054/HostDevServer/HelloWorldService.svc"
```

Into the following line:

```
<endpoint address=
    "http://localhost:1054/HostCmdLineApp/HelloWorldService.svc"
```

Now, when you run the client program, it will use the WCF service hosted in the newly created command-line application and not the previously-created `HostDevServer` application. You will get the same result as before when IIS Express was used to host the WCF service.

Hosting the service in a Windows service

If you don't want to manually start the WCF service, you can host it in a Windows service. In addition to the automatic start, Windows service hosting gives you some other features such as recovery ability when failures occur, security identity under which the service is running, and some degree of manageability. Just like the self-hosting method, this hosting method also supports all bindings and transports. However, it also has some limitations. For example, you have to deploy it with an installer and it doesn't fully support high availability, easy manageability, versioning, or deployment scenarios.

The steps to create such a hosting application are very similar to what we did to host a WCF service in a command-line application, except that you have to create an installer to install the Windows service in the Service Control Manager (or you can use the .NET Framework `Installutil.exe` utility). However, how to create such an installer is outside the context of this chapter and we will not discuss it further (there is a lot of information on this topic and there is no difference for a WCF service installer).

Hosting the service in the Internet Information Services server using the HTTP protocol

It is a better option to host a WCF service within the **Internet Information Services (IIS)** server because IIS provides a robust, efficient, and secure host for WCF services. IIS also has better thread and process execution boundaries handling (in addition to many other features) compared to a regular managed application. Actually, web service development on IIS has been the domain of ASP.NET for a long time. When ASP.NET 1.0 was released, a web service framework was part of it. Microsoft leveraged the ASP.NET HTTP pipeline to make web services a reality on the Windows platform.

The main drawback of hosting the service within IIS prior to version 7.0 is the tight coupling between ASP.NET and web services, which limits the transport protocol to HTTP/HTTPS. However, with IIS 7.0 and beyond, in addition to HTTP, you can now host a WCF service with TCP, named pipe, or MSMQ. You are no longer limited to HTTP.

Another thing you need to pay particular attention to when hosting WCF in IIS is that the process and/or application domain may be recycled if certain conditions are met. By default, the WCF service session state is saved in memory so that all such information will be lost in each recycle. This will be a big problem if you run a website in a load-balanced or web-farm (web-garden) environment. In this case, you should save the session state in a SQL Server database or in the ASP.NET State Server.

Next, we will learn how to host `HelloWorldService` in IIS, using the HTTP protocol. After this section, we will learn how to host it using the TCP protocol so that you can choose the appropriate protocol for your service according to your specific needs.

Preparing the folders and files

First, we need to prepare the folders and files for the host application. Follow these steps to create the folders and copy the required files:

1. Create the folders:

   In Windows Explorer, create a new folder called `HostIIS` under `c:\SOAwithWCFandLINQ\Projects\HelloWorld` and a new subfolder called `bin` under this `HostIIS` folder. You should now have the following new folders:

   ○ `C:\SOAwithWCFandLINQ\Projects\HelloWorld\HostIIS`

   ○ `C:\SOAwithWCFandLINQ\Projects\HelloWorld\HostIIS\bin`

2. Copy the files:

   Now copy the files `HelloWorldService.dll` and `HelloWorldService.pdb` from the `HelloWorldService` project folder `C:\SOAwithWCFandLINQ\Projects\HelloWorld\HelloWorldService\bin\Debug` to the new folder `C:\SOAwithWCFandLINQ\Projects\HelloWorld\HostIIS\bin`.

3. Copy the `config` file:

   Copy `Web.config` from the `HostDevServer` project folder `C:\SOAwithWCFandLINQ\Projects\HelloWorld\HostDevServer` to the new folder `C:\SOAwithWCFandLINQ\Projects\HelloWorld\HostIIS`.

   The files under the two new directories should now be like the following:

   ○ **Parent Folder**: `C:\SOAwithWCFandLINQ\Projects\HelloWorld\`

Folder	HostIIS	HostIIS\bin
Files	Web.config	HelloWorldService.dll
		HelloWorldService.pdb

4. Create the Visual Studio solution folder:

   To make it easier to view and manage from Visual Studio Solution Explorer, you can add a new solution folder, HostIIS, to the solution and add the file web.config to this folder. Add another new solution folder, bin, under HostIIS, and add the files HelloWorldService.dll and HelloWorldService.pdb under this bin folder. Your **Solution Explorer** should be as shown in the following screenshot:

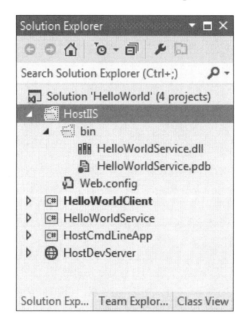

5. Add the following post-built event to the HelloWorldService project, so next time all files will be copied automatically when the service project is built:

   ```
   xcopy "$(AssemblyName).dll" "C:\SOAwithWCFandLINQ\Projects\
   HelloWorld\HostIIS\bin" /Y
   xcopy "$(AssemblyName).pdb" "C:\SOAwithWCFandLINQ\Projects\
   HelloWorld\HostIIS\bin" /Y
   ```

6. Modify the web.config file:

   The web.config file that we have copied from HostDevServer has a relative address HostDevServer/HelloWorldService.svc. For IIS hosting, we need to get rid of HostDevServer from the path. Just open the web.config file under the HostIIS\bin folder and change the relative path from ./HostDevServer/HelloWorldService.svc to ./HelloWorldService.svc.

Turn on Internet Information Services

By default, IIS is not turned on in Windows 7. You can follow these steps to turn it on if it has not been turned on:

1. Go to **Control Panel | Programs | Turn Windows features on or off**.

2. From the **Windows Features** dialog box, check **Internet Information Services**.

3. Click on **OK**.

IIS is now turned on but since Visual Studio was installed before IIS was turned on, at this point IIS does not have any ASP.NET features enabled. This means if you create an ASP.NET website within IIS now, when you try to access it, you will get an error.

There are two ways to enable WCF support from within IIS. The first one is to run `aspnet_regiis.exe` to enable `aspnet_isapi` as a web service extension, then to run `ServiceModelReg.exe` to register the required script maps in IIS, and manually create the Application Extension Mapping and the Managed Handlers for SVC files inside IIS.

The second and the much easier way is to reinstall the .NET Framework. After you have turned on the IIS features, as we just did previously in this section, uninstall and then reinstall .NET Framework 4.5. ASP.NET 4.5 will automatically be supported by IIS, once .NET 4.5 is reinstalled. I used this method as it is much easier.

Creating the IIS application

Next, we need to create an IIS application named `HelloWorldService`. Follow these steps to create this application in IIS:

1. Open the IIS Manager through the menu options **Control Panel | Administrative Tools** (or just type `start inetmgr` in the command prompt).

2. Expand the nodes of the tree in the left-hand pane until the node named **Default Web Site** becomes visible.

3. Right-click on that node and choose **New | Add Application...** from the context menu.

4. In the **Add Application** window, enter `HelloWorldService` in the **Alias** field.

5. Choose or enter `C:\SOAWithWCFandLINQ\Projects\HelloWorld\HostIIS` is the **Physical path** field.

6. Leave **DefaultAppPool** as the **Application pool**. You can click on the **Select...** button to verify if this application pool is a .NET 4.0.30319 application pool. If it is not, you need to enable IIS to support .NET 4.0.30319, as described in the previous section. If you create your own application pool, make sure it is a .NET 4.0.30319 pool.

7. Click on the **OK** button.

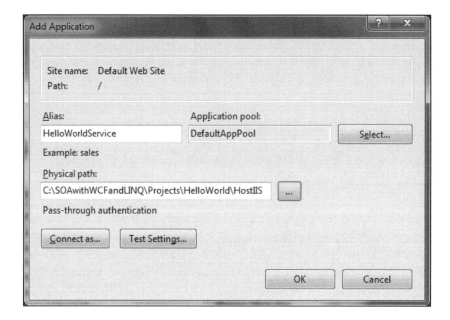

Starting the WCF service in IIS

Once you have copied the files to the `HostIIS` folder and you have created the IIS application or virtual directory, the WCF service is ready to be called by the clients. When a WCF service is hosted within IIS, we don't need to explicitly start the service. As with other normal web applications, IIS will control the lifetime of the service. As long as the IIS service is started, client programs can access it.

Testing the WCF service hosted in IIS

To test the WCF service, open an Internet browser and enter the following URL in the address bar of the browser. You will get an almost identical screen to the one you got previously:

```
http://localhost/HelloWorldService/HelloWorldService.svc
```

You don't need to add a port after the host because it is now hosted in IIS with the default HTTP port 80. This also means that you can access the service, using your real computer (host) name and even outside of your computer if your computer is in a network. Two example URLs are as follows:

- `http://[your_pc_name]/HelloWorldService/HelloWorldService.svc`
- `http://[your_pc_name].[your_company_domain].com/HelloWorldService/HelloWorldService.svc`

We can re-use the client program that we created earlier to consume this WCF service hosted within IIS. Just change the endpoint address from the following:

```
<endpoint address=
    "http://localhost:1054/HostCmdLineAPP/HelloWorldService/"
```

To the following:

```
<endpoint address=
    "http://localhost/HelloWorldService/HelloWorldService.svc"
```

Now, when you run this client program, it will use the WCF service hosted within IIS instead of the previously-created `HostCmdLineApp` application. You will get the same result as before, when it was hosted in our own host application.

Hosting the service in the Internet Information Services server using the TCP protocol

Hosting WCF services in IIS using the HTTP protocol gives the best interoperability to the service. However, sometimes interoperability might not be an issue. For example, the service may be invoked only within your network with all Microsoft clients. In this case hosting the service by using the TCP protocol might be a better solution.

Benefits of hosting a WCF service using the TCP protocol

Compared to HTTP, there are a few benefits in hosting a WCF service using the TCP protocol:

- It supports connection-based, stream-oriented delivery services with end-to-end error detection and correction
- It is the fastest WCF binding for scenarios that involve communication between different machines

- It supports duplex communication and so it can be used to implement duplex contracts

- It has reliable data delivery capability (applies between two TCP/IP nodes, and is not the same thing as WS-ReliableMessaging, which applies between endpoints)

Preparing the folders and files

First, we need to prepare the folders and files for the host application, just as we did for hosting the service, using the HTTP protocol. We will use the previous HTTP hosting application as the base to create the new TCP hosting application:

1. Create the folders:

   In Windows Explorer, create a new folder called `HostIISTcp` under `c:\SOAwithWCFandLINQ\Projects\HelloWorld` and a new subfolder called `bin` under this `HostIISTcp` folder. You should now have the following new folders:

   ° `C:\SOAwithWCFandLINQ\Projects\HelloWorld\HostIISTcp`
   ° `C:\SOAwithWCFandLINQ\Projects\HelloWorld\HostIISTcp\bin`

2. Copy the files:

   Now copy all the files from the `HostIIS` hosting application folder at `C:\SOAwithWCFandLINQ\Projects\HelloWorld\HostIIS` to the new folder that we created at `C:\SOAwithWCFandLINQ\Projects\HelloWorld\HostIISTcp`.

3. Create the Visual Studio solution folder:

   To make it easier to be viewed and managed from the Visual Studio Solution Explorer, you can add a new solution folder `HostIISTcp` to the solution and add the `web.config` file to this folder. Add another new solution folder `bin` under `HostIISTcp` and add the `HelloWorldService.dll` and `HelloWorldService.pdb` files under this `bin` folder.

> Add the following post-build events to the `HelloWorldService` project, so next time all files will be copied automatically when the service project is built:
>
> ```
> xcopy "$(AssemblyName).dll" "C:\SOAwithWCFandLINQ\
> Projects\HelloWorld\HostIISTcp\bin" /Y
>
> xcopy "$(AssemblyName).pdb" "C:\SOAwithWCFandLINQ\
> Projects\HelloWorld\HostIISTcp\bin" /Y
> ```

4. Modify the `web.config` file:

   The `web.config` file that we have copied from `HostIIS` is using the default `basicHttpBinding` as the service binding. To make our service use the TCP binding, we need to change the binding to TCP and add a TCP base address. Open the `web.config` file and add the following node to it:

   ```
   <services>
     <service name="MyWCFServices.HelloWorldService">
       <endpoint address="" binding="netTcpBinding"
       contract="MyWCFServices.IHelloWorldService"/>
       <host>
         <baseAddresses>
           <add baseAddress=
           "net.tcp://localhost/HelloWorldServiceTcp/"/>
         </baseAddresses>
       </host>
     </service>
   </services>
   ```

5. In this new services node, we have defined one service called `MyWCFServices.HelloWorldService`. This service's base address is `net.tcp://localhost/HelloWorldServiceTcp/`. Remember we have defined the host activation relative address as `./HelloWorldService.svc`, so we can invoke this service from the client application with the following URL:

   `http://localhost/HelloWorldServiceTcp/HelloWorldService.svc`

6. For the file-less WCF activation, if no endpoint is defined explicitly, HTTP and HTTPS endpoints will be defined by default. In this example, we would like to expose only one TCP endpoint, so we have added an endpoint explicitly (as soon as this endpoint is added explicitly, the default endpoints will not be added). If you don't add this TCP endpoint explicitly here, the TCP client that we will create in the next section will still work, but on the client `config` file, you will see three endpoints instead of one, and you will have to specify which endpoint you are using in the client program.

7. Following is the full content of the `web.config` file:

   ```
   <?xml version="1.0"?>
   <!--
     For more information on how to configure your ASP.NET
     application, please visit
     http://go.microsoft.com/fwlink/?LinkId=169433
     -->
   ```

```xml
<configuration>
  <system.web>
    <compilation debug="true" targetFramework="4.5"/>
    <httpRuntime targetFramework="4.5" />
  </system.web>

  <system.serviceModel>
    <serviceHostingEnvironment >
      <serviceActivations>
        <add factory="System.ServiceModel.
        Activation.ServiceHostFactory"
         relativeAddress="./HelloWorldService.svc"
         service="MyWCFServices.HelloWorldService"/>
      </serviceActivations>
    </serviceHostingEnvironment>

    <behaviors>
      <serviceBehaviors>
        <behavior>
          <serviceMetadata httpGetEnabled="true"/>
        </behavior>
      </serviceBehaviors>
    </behaviors>

    <services>
      <service name="MyWCFServices.HelloWorldService">
        <endpoint address="" binding="netTcpBinding"
        contract="MyWCFServices.IHelloWorldService"/>
        <host>
          <baseAddresses>
            <add baseAddress=
            "net.tcp://localhost/HelloWorldServiceTcp/"/>
          </baseAddresses>
        </host>
      </service>
    </services>
  </system.serviceModel>

</configuration>
```

Enabling the non-HTTP WCF activation for the hosting machine

By default, the non-HTTP WCF activation service is not enabled on your machine. This means your IIS server won't be able to host a WCF service with the non-HTTP protocols. You can follow these steps to enable the non-HTTP service:

1. Go to **Control Panel | Programs | Turn Windows features on or off**.

2. Expand the node **Microsoft .Net Framework 3.5.1**.

3. Check **Windows Communication Foundation Non-HTTP Activation**:

4. Repair .NET 4.0 Framework. After you have turned on the non-HTTP WCF activation, you have to repair .NET. Just go to **Control Panel**, click **Uninstall a Program**, select Microsoft .NET Framework 4.5, and Repair.

Creating the IIS application

Next, we need to create an IIS application named `HelloWorldServiceTcp` to host the WCF service, using the TCP protocol. Follow these steps to create this application in IIS.

1. Open IIS Manager.

2. Add a new IIS application `HelloWorldServiceTcp`, pointing to the physical folder `HostIISTcp` under your project's folder.

3. Choose **DefaultAppPool** as the application pool for the new application. Again make sure your **DefaulAppPool** is a .NET 4.0.30319 application pool.

4. Enable the TCP protocol for the application. Right-click on **HelloWorldServiceTcp**, select **Advanced Settings**, and then add `net.tcp` to **Enabled Protocols**. Make sure you use all lowercase and separate it from the existing HTTP protocol with a comma.

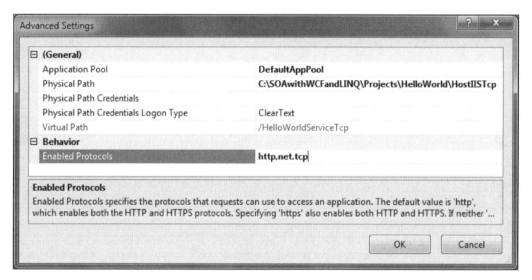

Now the service is hosted in IIS, using the TCP protocol. To view the WSDL of the service, browse to `http://localhost/HelloWorldServiceTcp/HelloWorldService.svc` and you should see the service description and a link to the WSDL of the service.

Testing the WCF service hosted in IIS using the TCP protocol

Now we have the service hosted in IIS using the TCP protocol, let's create a new test client to test it:

1. Add a new console application project to the solution named `HelloWorldClientTcp`.

2. Add a reference to `System.ServiceModel` to the new project.

3. Add a service reference to the WCF service to the new project, naming the reference as `HelloWorldServiceRef` and using the URL `http://localhost/HelloWorldServiceTcp/HelloWorldService.svc?wsdl`:

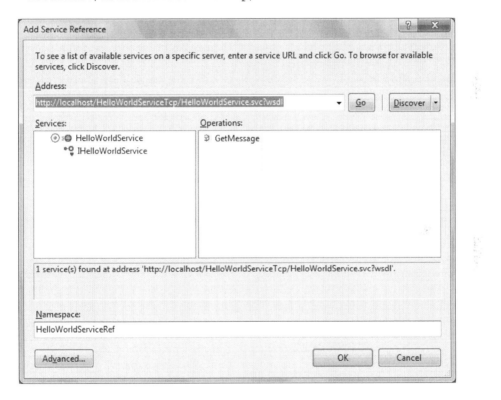

4. You can still use the command-line tool `SvcUtil.exe` to generate the proxy and config files for the service hosted with TCP, just like we did in previous sections. Actually, behind the scenes Visual Studio is also calling `SvcUtil.exe` to generate the proxy and config files.

5. Add the following code to the `Main` method of the new project:

```
HelloWorldServiceRef.HelloWorldServiceClient client =
new HelloWorldServiceRef.HelloWorldServiceClient ();
Console.WriteLine(client.GetMessage("Mike Liu"));
```

6. And finally set the new project as the Startup project.

Now if you run the program, you will get the same result as before, but this time the service is hosted in IIS, using the TCP protocol. To know more about how this client is now communicating with the server using the TCP protocol, you can run a specific tool such as a network traffic debugger and see what is going on under the hood. However, this is beyond the context of this chapter and won't be discussed here.

Other WCF service hosting options

From previous sections, we know that a WCF service can be hosted in IIS Express, in the ASP.NET Development Server, in a website, in a Windows Service application, in a command-line application, or in IIS. Besides these options, there are some other ways to host a WCF service.

First, in Visual Studio, there is a built-in, general-purpose WCF service host (`WcfSvcHost.exe`), which makes the WCF host and development test much easier. This host will be used by default if you create a WCF service, using a WCF Service Library template. We will cover this new feature in the next chapter.

Another option is to create a WCF service, using a WCF Service Application template, in which case the WCF service project itself is a website and is ready to be run within its own project folder. We will also cover this new feature in the next chapter.

Debugging the HelloWorld WCF service

Now that we have a fully working WCF service, let us have a look at the debugging options of this service. We will use our original client `HelloWorldClient` to discuss the debugging options, so in the following sections whenever you see the client, the client program, or the client application, please treat it as `HelloWorldClient`.

Debugging from the client application

The first and most common scenario is to debug from the client program. This means that you start a client program in debug mode and then step into your WCF service.

Starting the debugging process

Follow these steps to start the debugging process from the client application:

1. Change the client program's configuration file to call `HelloWorldService` hosted within IIS Express. Open the `app.config` file inside the `HelloWorldClient` project and set the address of the endpoint to `http://localhost:1054/HostDevServer/HelloWorldService.svc`.

2. In Solution Explorer, right-click on the **HelloWorldClient** project and select **Set as Startup Project** from the context menu.

3. Open the `Program.cs` file inside the `HelloWorldClient` project and set a breakpoint at the following line:

   ```
   HelloWorldServiceClient client = new HelloWorldServiceClient();
   ```

   Your screen will look as follows:

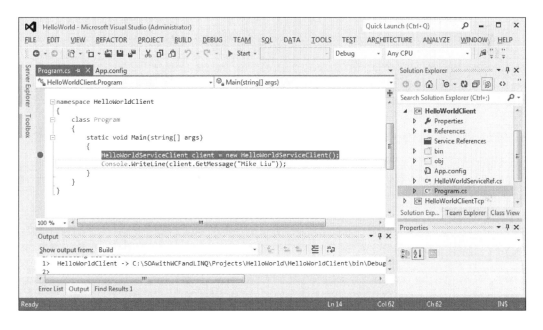

4. You can set a breakpoint by clicking on the gray strip to the left of the code (the little ball in the preceding screenshot), pressing *F9* while the cursor is on the line, or selecting the menu items **Debug | Toggle Breakpoint**. You should ensure that the breakpoint line is highlighted, and if you hover your mouse over the red breakpoint dot, an information line will pop up.

5. Now press *F5* or select menu options **Debug | Start Debugging** to start the debugging process.

Debugging on the client application

The cursor should have stopped on the breakpoint line, as you can see in the following **HelloWorld (Debugging)** screenshot. The active line is highlighted and you can examine the variables just as you do for any other C# applications.

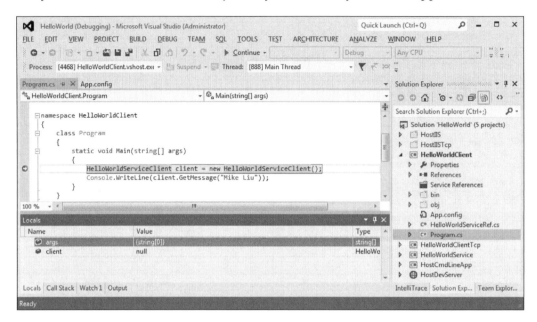

At this point, the channel between the client and the hosting server (`HostDevServer`) has not been created. Press *F10* or select menu options **Debug | Step Over** to skip over this line. If you don't have the menu options **Debug | Step Over**, you may have to reset your development environment settings through the menu options **Tools | Import and Export Settings...** (check appropriate options in **Import and Export Settings Wizard**).

Now, the following line to the source code should be active and highlighted. At this point, we have a valid client object, which contains all of the information related to the WCF service such as the channel, the endpoint, the members, and the security credentials. The following screenshot shows the details of the **Endpoint** local variable:

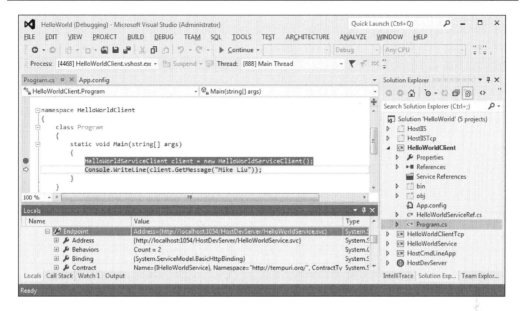

Stepping into the WCF service

Now press *F11* to step into the service code. The cursor now resides on the opening bracket of the `GetMessage` method of `HelloWorldService`. You can now examine the variables and their values inside `HelloWorldService` just as you would for any other program. Keep pressing *F10* and you should eventually come back to the client program.

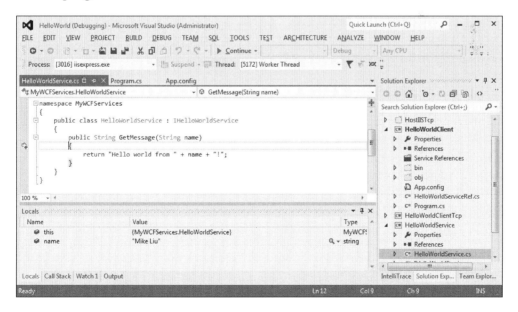

However, if you stay inside `HelloWorldService` for too long, when you come back to `HelloWorldClient` you will get an exception saying that it has timed out. This is because by default `HelloWorldClient` will call `HelloWorldService` and wait for a response for a maximum time of one minute. You can change this to a longer value in the `app.config` configuration file, depending on your own needs.

You may also have noticed that you don't see the output window of `HelloWorldClient`. This is because, in debug mode, once a console application finishes, the console window is closed. You have to add one line at the end of `Program.cs` to wait for a keystroke so that you can look at the output before it closes. You can do this by adding the following line of code:

```
Console.ReadKey();
```

 This can only be done if you are the owner of the source—for example, you can't step into a web service on a remote host.

Directly debugging the WCF service

In the previous section, we started debugging from the client program and then stepped into the service program. Sometimes we may not want to run the client application in the debug mode. For example, if the client application is a third-party product, we won't have the source code or the client application may be a BPM product that runs on a different machine. In this case, if we need to, we can run the service in debugging mode and debug only the service.

Starting the WCF service in debugging mode

To start `HelloWorldService` in debug mode, first set `HostDevServer` as the startup project. Then, open `HelloWorldService.cs` from the `HelloWorldService` project and set a breakpoint on a line inside the `GetMessage` method.

Now press *F5* to start the service in debugging mode, and the WCF service will be running in debugging mode, waiting for requests. A browser will open, displaying the `403.14` error page. If you go back to the Visual Studio IDE, you may find that a new solution folder **Script Documents** has been added to the solution. This folder is the actual content of the web page being displayed in the browser. Because its content is dynamically generated, this folder will only be included in the solution when `HostDevServer` is being debugged. Whenever you stop the debugging session, this folder will go away automatically.

Starting the client application

Now that we have the WCF service running in debugging mode, we need to start the client application so that we can step inside the WCF service that is being debugged.

There are two ways to start the `HelloWorldClient` program. The first one is to start it within the same instance of the Visual Studio. While leaving `HelloWorldService` running in debugging mode, from the **Solution Explorer** of the Visual Studio, right-click on the project **HelloWorldClient**, select **Debug | Start new instance**, and `HelloWorldClient` will also start running in debugging mode. Because we have set a breakpoint on the first line of the `Program.cs` file, the cursor should stop on that line now. Press *F10* to step over it, then press *F11* and you will step inside the WCF service, stopping on the first line of the `GetMessage` method within `HelloWorldService`. From this point onwards you can keep debugging the service as you would do to any other program.

Another way to start `HelloWorldClient` is to start it from Windows Explorer. Go to the `C:\SOAwithWCFandLINQ\Projects\HelloWorld\HelloWorldClient\bin\Debug` directory and double-click on the `HelloWorldClient.exe` file. You will then get the same result as you did when you started it from within Visual Studio.

Attaching to a running WCF service process

Another common scenario for debugging is when attaching to a running WCF service. Suppose that `HelloWorldService` is hosted and running outside Visual Studio, either in IIS or in a managed application such as `HostCmdLineApp`. In this case, the client application is also running outside of Visual Studio. At a certain point, you may want to start debugging the running WCF service. In this case, we can attach to the running WCF service process and start debugging from the middle of a process.

Running the WCF service and client applications in non-debugging mode

To test this scenario, change the `app.config` file in the client program project to use the IIS hosting `HelloWorldService`. This means that we use the following address for the endpoint in the `app.config` file for the `HelloWorldClient` project:

```
http://localhost/HelloWorldService/HelloWorldService.svc
```

Build the solution and set a breakpoint inside the `GetMessage` method of the `HelloWorldService` project. Then run `HelloWorldClient` in non-debugging mode by pressing *Ctrl + F5*. You will see the breakpoint that we had previously set within the `HelloWorldService` is not hit at this time. This is because the service is now hosted by IIS and it is not available for debugging by any Visual Studio.

Debugging the WCF service hosted in IIS

To debug the service hosted by IIS, we can attach to the IIS process. But before we can debug it, we have to enable debugging for the web application. Just open the `web.config` file under the `HostIIS` folder and change the debug value to `True`.

Now start Visual Studio and select menu options **Debug | Attach to Process...**. The **Attach to Process** window should now appear. If you can't see the **Debug** menu from Visual Studio, just open any project or create an empty new project.

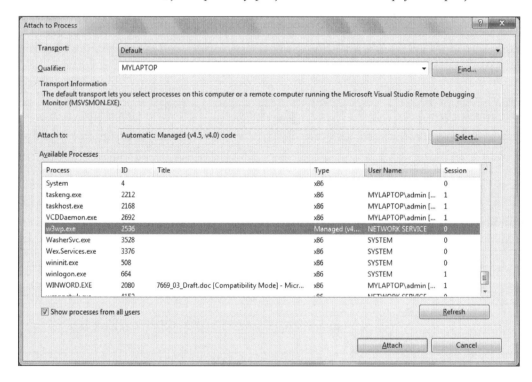

Select the process `w3wp.exe` from the list of available processes and click on the **Attach** button. Note that you need to check **Show processes from all users** in order to see **w3wp.exe** in the available processes list. If it is still not there, run `HelloWorldClient` once and hit the **Refresh** button. **w3wp.exe** will appear in the list.

Now you will find the IIS worker process attached to the debugger. Open the `HelloWorldService.cs` file and set a breakpoint if you haven't done so already. Now run the `HelloWorldClient` program in non-debugging mode (use *Ctrl + F5*) from Visual Studio or from Windows Explorer and you will see that the breakpoint is now hit.

If you are not able to set a breakpoint inside the `HelloWorldService.cs` file (or the breakpoint is disabled after you attach to the `w3wp.exe` process), make sure you have enabled debugging for the `HostIIS` application (as we did at the beginning of this section), and the `HostIIS\bin` folder contains the latest binary files from the `HelloWorldService` folder.

If you didn't start Visual Studio as an administrator, you will get a dialog window asking you to restart Visual Studio, using different credentials. Select **Restart under different credentials** and you will be able to continue.

When you have finished debugging `HelloWorldService` using this method, you can select menu options **Debug | Detach All** or **Debug | Stop Debugging** to exit debugging mode.

You may also have noticed that when you attach to `w3wp.exe`, IIS Express is also started, even though we have not used it at all at this time. This is because the **Always Start When Debugging** property of `HostDevServer` is set to `True`. You can turn it off if you feel it is annoying.

Summary

In this chapter, we have hosted the `HelloWorld` WCF service in several different ways and explored different scenarios for debugging a WCF service. Now that we have the basic skills for the WCF service development, in the next chapter we will start developing a three-layered WCF service following the best practice of WCF service development.

4
Implementing a WCF Service in the Real World

In the previous chapter we created a basic WCF service. The WCF service we have created, `HelloWorldService`, has only one method, named `GetMessage`. As this was just an example, we implemented this WCF service in one layer only. Both the service interface and implementation are within one deployable component.

Now in the following two chapters, we will implement a WCF service, which will be called `RealNorthwindService`, to reflect a real-world service. In this chapter, we will separate the service interface layer from the business logic layer, and in the following chapter, we will add a data access layer to the service.

Note that the service we will create in the next two chapters is only a simplified version of a real-world WCF service. In a real-world situation, there is no doubt that the WCF service would contain more custom scenarios, more business logics, and more data constraints. For learning purposes, here we will just create a WCF service in three layers, with minimum business logic and some basic functionality. After you have acquired the basic skills to create the framework for a layered WCF service, you can customize this solution to your own needs.

We should also mention here that the design pattern that the next two chapters will talk about is exactly what the Microsoft Service Software Factory is doing. After you have finished following these two chapters, you will have a solid understanding of the layered WCF service structures, and should then go to the Microsoft Service Factory website (http://www.codeplex.com/servicefactory) to adopt the Service Factory to create your WCF service structures.

In this chapter, we will create and test the WCF service by following these steps:

- Creating the WCF service project, using a WCF Service Library template
- Creating the service operation contracts
- Creating the data contracts
- Adding a Product **Business Domain Object (BDO)** project
- Adding a business logic layer project
- Calling the business logic layer from the service interface layer
- Testing the service

Why layer a service?

An important aspect of SOA design is that service boundaries should be explicit (being technology neutral, or agnostic), which means hiding all the details of the implementation behind the service boundary. This includes revealing or dictating which particular technology was used.

Furthermore, inside the implementation of a service, the code responsible for the data manipulation should be separated from the code responsible for the business logic. Therefore, in the real world, it is always a good practice to implement a WCF service in three or more layers. The three layers are the service interface layer, the business logic layer, and the data access layer:

- **Service interface layer**: This layer will include the service contracts and operation contracts that are used to define the service interfaces that will be exposed at the service boundary. Data contracts are also defined to pass data in and out of the service. If any exception is expected to be thrown outside of the service, Fault contract will also be defined at this layer.

- **Business logic layer**: This layer will apply the actual business logic to the service operations. It will check the preconditions of each operation, perform business activities, and return any necessary results to the interface layer of the service.

- **Data access layer**: This layer will take care of all of the tasks needed to access the underlying databases. It will use a specific data adapter to query and update the databases. This layer will handle connections to databases, transaction processing, and concurrency controlling. Neither the service interface layer nor the business logic layer needs to worry about these things.

Layering provides separation of concerns and better factoring of code, which gives you better maintainability. The data access code should be separated into its own project that focuses on performing translation services between the databases and the application domain. Services should be placed in a separate service layer that focuses on performing translation services between the service-oriented external world and the application domain.

The service interface layer will be compiled into a separate class assembly and hosted in a service host environment. The outside world will only know about and have access to this layer. Whenever a request is received by the service interface layer on the hosting server, the request will be dispatched to the business logic layer, and the business logic layer will get the actual work done. If any database support is needed by the business logic layer, it will always go through the data access layer.

Creating a new solution and project using WCF templates

To start with, we will first create a new solution for the layered service and then add a new WCF service project to this solution. This time we will use the built-in Visual Studio WCF template for the new project.

Creating the WCF service project

There are a few built-in WCF service templates within Visual Studio. In this section, we will use the service library template to create our WCF service project. If you are interested in other templates, you can try each of them yourself and choose the appropriate one for your own developments.

Follow these steps to create the `RealNorthwind` solution and the project, using the service library template:

1. Start Visual Studio, select the menu options **File | New | Project...**, and you will see the **New Project** dialog box. Do not open the `HelloWorld` solution (from the previous chapter) as from this point onwards, we will create a completely new solution and save it in a different location.

2. In the **New Project** window, specify **Visual C# | WCF | WCF Service Library** as the project template, **RealNorthwindService** as the (project) name, and change the solution name from the defaulted **RealNorthwindService** to **RealNorthwind**. Make sure that the checkbox **Create directory for solution** is selected.

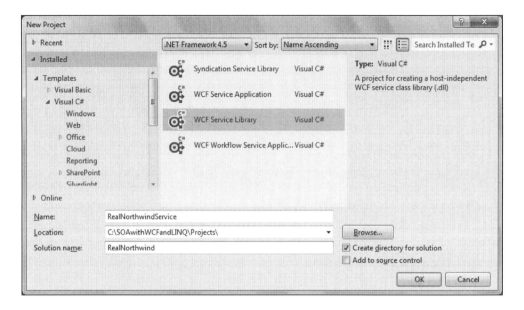

3. Click on the **OK** button, and the solution is created with a WCF project inside it. The project already has an `IService1.cs` file to define a service interface and `Service1.cs` to implement the service. It also has an `app.config` file, which we will cover shortly.

Now we have created the WCF service project. This project is actually an application containing a WCF service, a hosting application (`WcfSvcHost`), and a WCF Test Client. This means that we don't need to write any other code to host it, and as soon as we have implemented a service, we can use the built-in WCF Test Client to invoke it. This makes it very convenient for WCF development.

Creating the service interface layer

In the previous section, we created a WCF project by using the WCF Service Library template. In this section, we will create the service interface layer contracts.

As two sample files have already been created for us, we will try to re-use them as much as possible. Then we will start customizing these two files to create the service contracts.

Creating the service interfaces

To create the service interfaces, we need to open the `IService1.cs` file and do the following:

1. Change its namespace from `RealNorthwindService` to `MyWCFServices.RealNorthwindService`.

2. Right-click on the class name **IService1**, select **Refactor | Rename**, and then change the interface name from **IService1** to **IProductService** as shown in the following screenshot:

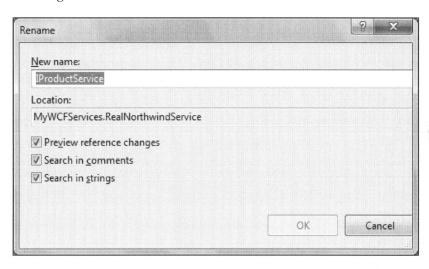

3. Change the first operation contract definition from the following line:

```
string GetData(int value);
```

To this line:

```
Product GetProduct(int id);
```

4. Change the second operation contract definition from the following line:

```
CompositeType GetDataUsingDataContract(CompositeType composite);
```

To this line:

```
bool UpdateProduct(Product product, ref string message);
```

5. Change the filename from **IService1.cs** to **IProductService.cs**.

With these changes, we have defined two service contracts. The first one can be used to get the product details for a specific product ID, while the second one can be used to update a specific product. The product type, which we used to define these service contracts, is still not defined. We will define it right after this section.

The changed part of the service interface for `RealNorthwindService.ProductService` should look now look as follows:

```
using System;
using System.Collections.Generic;
using System.Linq;
using System.Runtime.Serialization;
using System.ServiceModel;
using System.Text;

namespace MyWCFServices.RealNorthwindService
{
    [ServiceContract]
    public interface IProductService
    {
        [OperationContract]
        Product GetProduct(int id);

        [OperationContract]
        bool UpdateProduct(Product product, ref string message);

        // TODO: Add your service operations here
    }
//Unchanged part omitted
}
```

This is not the whole content of the `IProductService.cs` file. The bottom part of this file should still have the class `CompositeType`, which we will change to our product type in the next section.

Creating the data contracts

Another important aspect of SOA design is that you should not assume that the consuming application supports a complex object model. One part of the service boundary definition is the data contract definition for the complex types that will be passed as operation parameters or return values.

For maximum interoperability and alignment with SOA principles, you should not pass any .NET-specific types such as DataSet or Exceptions across the service boundary, as your service could be called by clients under different operating systems other than Windows, which might not understand .NET-specific types. You should stick to fairly simple data structure objects with only primitive properties. You can pass objects that have nested complex types such as "Customer with an Order collection". However, you should not make any assumption about the consumer being able to support object-oriented constructs such as inheritance or base classes for interoperable web services.

In our example, we will create a complex datatype to represent a product object. This data contract will have five properties:

- ProductID
- ProductName
- QuantityPerUnit
- UnitPrice
- Discontinued

These will be used to communicate with the client applications. For example, a supplier may call the web service to update the price of a particular product or to mark a product for discontinuation.

It is preferable to put data contracts in separate files within a separate assembly, but to simplify our example, we will put DataContract in the same file as the service contract. We will modify the IProductService.cs file as follows:

1. Open the IProductService.cs file if it is not open.
2. Delete existing DataContract CompositeType.
3. Add a new DataContract Product.

The data contract part of the finished service contract file IProductService.cs should now look as follows:

```
[DataContract]
public class Product
{
        [DataMember]
        public int ProductID { get; set; }
        [DataMember]
        public string ProductName { get; set; }
```

```
[DataMember]
public string QuantityPerUnit { get; set; }
[DataMember]
public decimal UnitPrice { get; set; }
[DataMember]
public bool Discontinued { get; set; }
}
```

Implementing the service contracts

To implement the two service interfaces that we defined in the previous section, open the `Service1.cs` file and do the following:

1. Change the filename from `Service1.cs` to `ProductService.cs`.

2. Change its namespace from `RealNorthwindService` to `MyWCFServices.RealNorthwindService`.

3. Change the class name from `Service1` to `ProductService` (if it is not already done for you). Make it inherit from the `IProductService` interface, instead of `IService1`. The class definition line should be as follows:

    ```
    public class ProductService : IProductService
    ```

4. Delete the `GetData` and `GetDataUsingDataContract` methods.

5. Add the following method to get a product:

    ```
    public Product GetProduct(int id)
    {
      // TODO: call business logic layer to retrieve product
      Product product = new Product();
      product.ProductID = id;
      product.ProductName =
        "fake product name from service layer";
      product.UnitPrice = 10.0m;
      product.QuantityPerUnit = "fake QPU";
      return product;
    }
    ```

 In this method, we created a fake product and returned it to the client. Later, we will remove the hardcoded product from this method and call the business logic to get the real product.

6. Add the following method to update a product:

```
public bool UpdateProduct(Product product,
  ref string message)
{
  bool result = true;

  // first check to see if it is a valid price
  if (product.UnitPrice <= 0)
  {
    message = "Price cannot be <= 0";
    result = false;
  }
  // ProductName can't be empty
  else if (string.IsNullOrEmpty(product.ProductName))
  {
    message = "Product name cannot be empty";
    result = false;
  }
  // QuantityPerUnit can't be empty
  else if (string.IsNullOrEmpty(product.QuantityPerUnit))
  {
    message = "Quantity cannot be empty";
    result = false;
  }
  else
  {
    // TODO: call business logic layer to update product
    message = "Product updated successfully";
    result = true;
  }

  return result;
}
```

7. Also, in this method, we don't update anything. Instead, we always return `true` if a valid product is passed in. In one of the following sections, we will implement the business logic to update the product and apply some business logic to the update.

Now we have finished implementing the service interface. The content of the ProductService.cs file should look as follows:

```csharp
using System;
using System.Collections.Generic;
using System.Linq;
using System.Runtime.Serialization;
using System.ServiceModel;
using System.Text;

namespace MyWCFServices.RealNorthwindService
{
  public class ProductService : IProductService
  {
    public Product GetProduct(int id)
    {
      // TODO: call business logic layer to retrieve
      // product
      Product product = new Product();
      product.ProductID = id;
      product.ProductName =
        "fake product name from service layer";
      product.UnitPrice = 10.0m;
      product.QuantityPerUnit = "fake QPU";
      return product;
    }

    public bool UpdateProduct(Product product,
    ref string message)
    {
      bool result = true;

      // first check to see if it is a valid price
      if (product.UnitPrice <= 0)
      {
        message = "Price cannot be <= 0";
        result = false;
      }
      // ProductName can't be empty
      else if
      (string.IsNullOrEmpty(product.ProductName))
      {
        message = "Product name cannot be empty";
```

```
        result = false;
      }
      // QuantityPerUnit can't be empty
      else if
      (string.IsNullOrEmpty(product.QuantityPerUnit))
      {
        message = "Quantity cannot be empty";
        result = false;
      }
      else
      {
        // TODO: call business logic layer to update
        // product
        message = "Product updated successfully";
        result = true;
      }

      return result;
    }
  }
}
```

Modifying the app.config file

As we have changed the service name, we have to make the appropriate changes
to the configuration file. Note that when you rename the service, if you have used
the refactor feature of Visual Studio, some of the following tasks may have been
done by Visual Studio.

Follow these steps to change the configuration file:

1. Open the `app.config` file from Solution Explorer.

2. Change all instances of the `RealNorthwindService` string except the one
   in `baseAddress` to `MyWCFServices.RealNorthwindService`. This is for
   the namespace change.

3. Change the `RealNorthwindService` string in `baseAddress` to
   `MyWCFServices/RealNorthwindService`.

4. Change all instances of the `Service1` string to `ProductService`, including
   the one in the endpoint node. This is for the actual service name change.

5. Change the service address port from the default one to 8080 (the default port might be 8731 or some other number). This is to prepare for the client application, which we will create soon.

6. Remove Design_Time_Addresses from baseAddress of the service.

The content of the app.config file should now look as follows (all the comments are removed):

```xml
<?xml version="1.0" encoding="utf-8" ?>
<configuration>

  <appSettings>
    <add key="aspnet:UseTaskFriendlySynchronizationContext"
    value="true" />
  </appSettings>

  <system.web>
    <compilation debug="true" />
  </system.web>
  <system.serviceModel>
    <services>
      <service
      name="MyWCFServices.RealNorthwindService.ProductService">
        <host>
          <baseAddresses>
            <add baseAddress =
            "http://localhost:8080/MyWCFServices/
            RealNorthwindService/ProductService/" />
          </baseAddresses>
        </host>
        <endpoint address="" binding="basicHttpBinding"
          contract=
          "MyWCFServices.RealNorthwindService.IProductService">
          <identity>
            <dns value="localhost"/>
          </identity>
        </endpoint>
        <endpoint address="mex" binding="mexHttpBinding"
                  contract="IMetadataExchange"/>
      </service>
    </services>
    <behaviors>
      <serviceBehaviors>
```

```
        <behavior>
          <serviceMetadata httpGetEnabled="True"
          httpsGetEnabled="True"/>
          <serviceDebug includeExceptionDetailInFaults="False" />
        </behavior>
      </serviceBehaviors>
    </behaviors>
  </system.serviceModel>

</configuration>
```

Testing the service using WCF Test Client

Because we are using the WCF Service Library template in this example, we are now ready to test this web service. As we pointed out when creating this project, this service will be hosted in the Visual Studio WCF Service Host environment.

To start the service, press *F5* or *Ctrl + F5*. WcfSvcHost will be started and WCF Test Client will also start. This is a Visual Studio built-in test client for the WCF Service Library projects.

 In order to run the WCF Test Client, you have to log in to your machine as a local administrator. You also have to start Visual Studio as an administrator because we have changed the service port from the default one to 8080, and running Visual Studio as an administrator will automatically register this port.

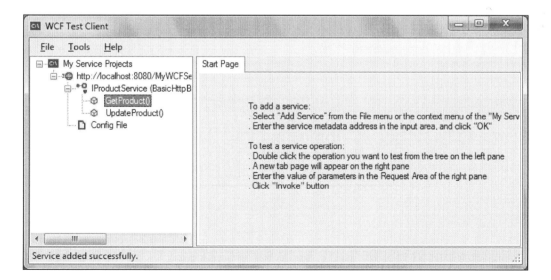

Again, if you get an `Access is denied` error, make sure you run Visual Studio as an administrator.

Now from this WCF Test Client, we can double-click on an operation to test it. First, let us test the `GetProduct` operation:

1. In the left panel of the client, double-click on the **GetProduct()** operation; `GetProduct` Request will be shown on the right-hand side panel.

2. In this **Request** panel, specify an integer for the product ID and click on the **Invoke** button to let the client call the service. You may get a dialog box to warn you about the security of sending information over the network. Click on the **OK** button to acknowledge this warning (you can check the **In the future, do not show this message** option so that it won't be displayed again).

Now the message **Invoking Service...** will be displayed in the status bar as the client is trying to connect to the server. It may take a while for this initial connection to be made as several things need to be done in the background. Once the connection has been established, a channel will be created and the client will call the service to perform the requested operation. Once the operation has been completed on the server side, the response package will be sent back to the client, and the WCF Test Client will display this response in the bottom panel.

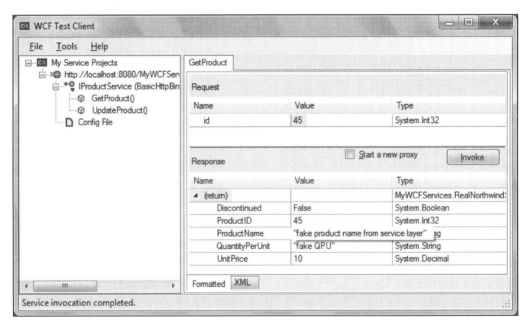

If you start the test client in debugging mode (by pressing *F5*), you can set a breakpoint at a line inside the `GetProduct` method in the `RealNorthwindService.cs` file, and when the **Invoke** button is clicked, the breakpoint will be hit so that you can debug the service as we learned earlier.

Note that the response is always the same, no matter what product ID you use to retrieve the product. Specifically, the product name is hardcoded, as shown in the diagram for testing purposes. Moreover, from the client response panel, we can see that several properties of the `Product` object have been assigned the default values.

Also, because the product ID is an integer value from the WCF Test Client, you can only enter an integer for it. If a non-integer value is entered, when you click on the **Invoke** button, you will get an error message box to warn you that you have entered a value with the wrong type.

Now let's test the operation `UpdateProduct`:

1. Double-click on the **UpdateProduct()** operation in the left panel, and **UpdateProduct** will be shown in the right-side panel in a new tab.

2. Enter a decimal value for the **UnitPrice** input parameter and then click on the **Invoke** button to test it. Depending on the value you enter in the **UnitPrice** column, you will get a **True** or **False** response package back.

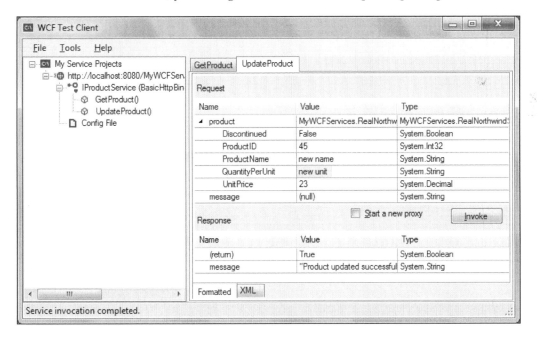

The **Request/Response** packages are displayed in grids by default but you have the option of displaying them in the XML format. Just select the **XML** tab at the bottom of the right-side panel, and you will see the XML-formatted **Request/Response** packages. From these XML strings, you can see that they are SOAP messages.

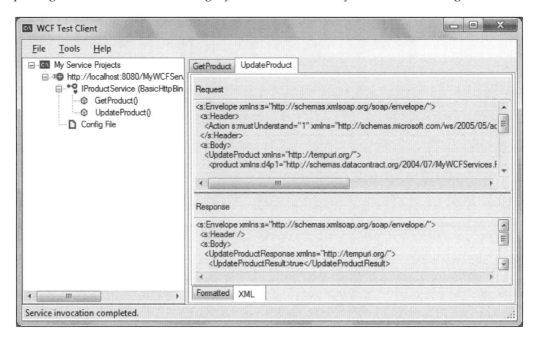

Besides testing operations, you can also look at the configuration settings of the web service. Just double-click on **Config File** from the left-side panel and the configuration file will be displayed in the right-side panel. This will show you the bindings for the service, the addresses of the service, and the contract for the service.

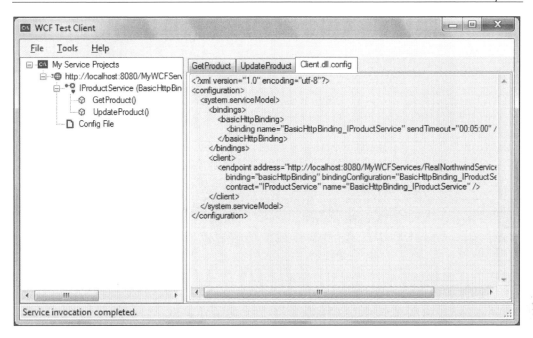

If you are satisfied with the test results, just close the WCF Test Client, and you will go back to Visual Studio IDE. Note that as soon as you close the client, the WCF Service Host is stopped. This is different from hosting a service inside IIS Express, where IIS Express still stays active even after you close the client.

Testing the service using our own client

It is very convenient to test a WCF service using the built-in WCF Test Client, but sometimes it is desirable to test a WCF service using your own test client. The built-in WCF Test Client is limited to test only simple WCF services. For complex WCF services, for example, one where the parameter is an object, we have to create our own test client.

To create our own client to consume the WCF service, we first need to host the WCF service in a host application. For this purpose, we can use the methods that we learned in previous chapter to host the WCF service in IIS, IIS Express, the ASP.NET Development Server, or a managed .NET application.

In addition to the previous methods we learned, we can also use the built-in WCF Service Host to host the WCF service. So we don't need to create a host application, but just need to create a client. In this section, we will use this hosting method to save us some time.

First, let us find a way to get the metadata for the service. From the Visual Studio built-in WCF Test Client, you cannot examine the WSDL of the service, although the client itself must have used the WSDL to communicate with the service. To see the WSDL outside of the WCF Service Test Client, just copy the address of the service from the configuration file and paste it into a web browser. In our example, the address of the service is http://localhost:8080/MyWCFServices/RealNorthwindService/ ProductService/. So copy and paste this address to a web browser, and we will see the WSDL languages of the service, just as we have seen many times before.

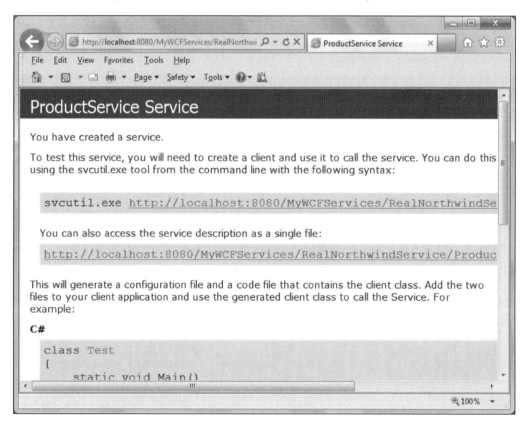

To get the metadata for the service, the service host application must run. The easiest way to start RealNorthwindService in the WCF Service Host is to start the WCF Test Client and leave it running.

Now that we know how to get the metadata for our service, we can start building the test client. We can leave the host application running, and manually generate the proxy classes by using the same method that we used earlier. But this time we will let Visual Studio do it for us.

Follow these steps to build your own client to test the WCF service:

1. Add a new **Console Application** project to the RealNorthwind solution. Let's call it RealNorthwindClient.

2. Add a reference to the WCF service. In Visual Studio Solution Explorer, right-click on the **RealNorthwindClient** project, select **Add Service Reference...** from the context menu, and you will see the **Add Service Reference** dialog box. Be sure to choose the **Add Service Reference...** and not the **Add Reference...** from the context menu, as they are completely different from each other.

3. In the **Add Service Reference** dialog box, type the following address into the **Address** box, and then click on the **Go** button to connect to the service:

    http://localhost:8080/MyWCFServices/RealNorthwindService/
    ProductService/

4. You can also simply click on the **Discover** button (or click on the little arrow next to the **Discover** button and select **Services** in **Solution**) to find this service.

In order to connect to or discover a service in the same solution, you don't have to start the host application for the service. The WCF Service Host will be automatically started for this purpose. However, if it is not started in advance, it may take a while for the **Add Service Reference** window to download the required metadata information for the service.

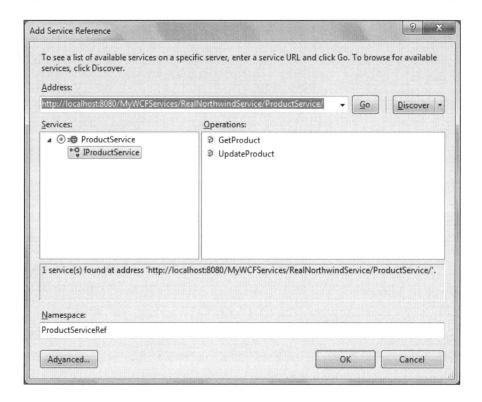

5. **ProductService** should now be listed on the left-hand side of the window. You can expand it and select the service contract to view its details.

6. Next, let's change the namespace of this service from `ServiceReference1` to `ProductServiceRef`. This will make the reference meaningful in the code.

7. If you have a Legacy Asmx web service and would like to call it from your application, you can still add a web reference through the **Add Service Reference** dialog window. Just click on the **Advanced...** button in the **Add Service Reference** window, and in the **Service Reference Settings** pop-up dialog box, click on the **Add Web Reference...** button. This will cause the proxy code to be generated based on the .NET 2.0 web service standards.

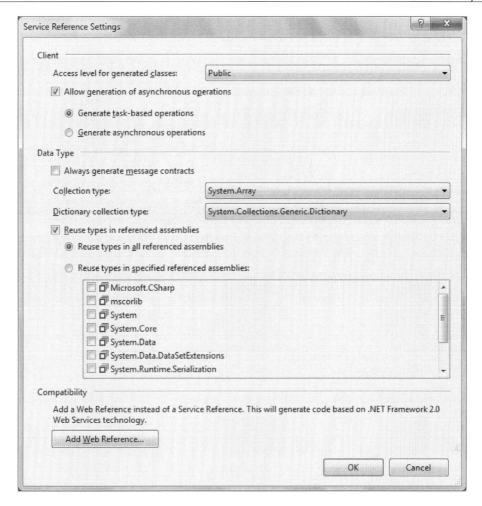

8. In this example, we won't do this, so click on the **Cancel** button to discard these changes.

9. Now click on the **OK** button in the **Add Service Reference** dialog box to add the service reference. You will see that a new folder named **ProductServiceRef** is created under **Service References** in **Solution Explorer** for the **RealNorthwindClient** project. This folder contains lots of files including the WSDL file, the service map, and the actual proxy code. If you can't see them, click on **Show All Files** in **Solution Explorer**.

10. The config file `App.config` is also modified to include the service details.

11. At this point, the proxy code to connect to the WCF service has been created and added to the project for us without us having to enter a single line of code. What we need to do next is to write just a few lines of code to call the service.

12. Just as we did earlier, we will modify the `Program.cs` file to call the WCF service.

13. First, open the `Program.cs` file, and add the following `using` line to the file:

```
using RealNorthwindClient.ProductServiceRef;
```

14. Then inside the `Main` method, add the following line of code to create a `client` object:

```
ProductServiceClient client = new ProductServiceClient();
```

15. Finally, add the following lines of code to the file and to call the WCF service to get and update a product:

```
Product product = client.GetProduct(23);
Console.WriteLine("product name is " +
        product.ProductName);
Console.WriteLine("product price is " +
        product.UnitPrice.ToString());
product.UnitPrice = 20.0m;
string message = "";
bool result = client.UpdateProduct(product,
    ref message);
Console.WriteLine("Update result is " +
        result.ToString());
Console.WriteLine("Update message is " +
        message);
Console.ReadLine();
```

The content of the `Program.cs` file is as follows:

```
using System;
using System.Collections.Generic;
using System.Linq;
using System.Text;
using System.Threading.Tasks;
using RealNorthwindClient.ProductServiceRef;

namespace RealNorthwindClient
{
    class Program
```

```
    {
        static void Main(string[] args)
        {
            ProductServiceClient client =
                new ProductServiceClient();
            Product product = client.GetProduct(23);
            Console.WriteLine("product name is " +
                product.ProductName);
            Console.WriteLine("product price is " +
                    product.UnitPrice.ToString());
            product.UnitPrice = 20.0m;
            string message = "";
            bool result = client.UpdateProduct(product,
                ref message);
            Console.WriteLine("Update result is " +
                            result.ToString());
            Console.WriteLine("Update message is " +
                            message);
            Console.ReadLine();
        }
    }
}
```

Now you can run the client application to test the service. Remember that you need to run Visual Studio as an administrator.

- If you want to start it in debugging mode (*F5*), you need to add a `Console.ReadLine();` statement to the end of the program so that you can see the output of the program. Also remember to set the `RealNorthwindClient` application as the startup project. The WCF Service Host application will be started automatically before the client is started (but the WCF Test Client won't be started).

- If you want to start the client application in non-debugging mode (*Ctrl + F5*), you need to start the WCF Service Host application (and the WCF Test Client application) in advance, as there will be no service for the client to call otherwise. You can start the WCF Service Host application (and the WCF Test Client) from another Visual Studio IDE instance, or you can set `RealNorthwindService` as the startup project, start it in non-debugging mode (*Ctrl + F5*), leave it running, and then change `RealNorthwindClient` to be the startup project, and start it in non-debugging mode. Also, you can set the solution to start with multiple projects with `RealNorthwindService` as the first project to be run and `RealNorthwindClient` as the second project to be run.

In my environment, I set the solution to start with multiple projects, so I am sure that the WCF service is always started before the client application, no matter whether it is in debugging mode or not.

The output of this client program is as shown in the following screenshot:

```
C:\Windows\system32\cmd.exe
product name is fake product name from service layer
product price is 10
Update result is True
Update message is Product updated successfully
```

Adding a business logic layer

Until now the WCF service has contained only one layer. In this section, we will add a business logic layer and define some business rules in this layer.

Adding the business domain object project

Before we add the business logic layer, we need to add a project for the business domain objects. The business domain object project will hold definitions such as products, customers, and orders. These domain objects will be used across the business logic layer, the data access layer, and the service layer. They will be very similar to the data contracts we defined in the previous section, but will not be seen outside of the service. The product business domain object will have the same properties as the product contract data, plus some extra properties such as UnitsInStock and ReorderLevel. These properties will be used internally and shared by all layers of the service. For example, when an order is placed, UnitsInStock should be updated as well. Also, if the updated UnitsInStock is less than ReorderLevel, an event should be raised to trigger the reordering process.

The business domain data objects by themselves do not act as a layer. They are just pure C# classes—also called **POCO (Plain Old CLR Objects)**—representing internal data within the service implementations. There is no logic inside these business domain objects. Also, in our example, these business domain objects are very similar to the data contracts (with only two extra fields in the business domain object class). In reality, the business domain object classes could be very different from the data contracts, from property names and property types to data structures.

As with the data contracts, the business domain object classes should be in their own assembly. Therefore, we first need to create a project for them. Just add a new C# class library `RealNorthwindBDO` to the solution. Then, modify the `Class1.cs` file, which has been auto-created by Visual Studio, as follows:

1. Rename it to `ProductBDO.cs`.

2. Change its namespace from `RealNorthwindBDO` to `MyWCFServices.RealNorthwindBDO`.

3. Change the class name from `Class1` to `ProductBDO`.

4. Add the following properties to this class:

   - `ProductID`
   - `ProductName`
   - `QuantityPerUnit`
   - `UnitPrice`
   - `Discontinued`
   - `UnitsInStock`
   - `UnitsOnOrder`
   - `ReorderLevel`

 Five of the above properties are also present in the product service data contract. The last three properties are used inside the service implementations. For example, `UnitsOnOrder` may be used to trigger business logic when discontinuing a product.

The following is the code list of the `ProductBDO` class:

```
using System;
using System.Collections.Generic;
using System.Linq;
using System.Text;
using System.Threading.Tasks;
namespace MyWCFServices.RealNorthwindBDO
{
    public class ProductBDO
    {
        public int ProductID { get; set; }
        public string ProductName { get; set; }
        public string QuantityPerUnit { get; set; }
        public decimal UnitPrice { get; set; }
```

```
        public int UnitsInStock { get; set; }
        public int ReorderLevel { get; set; }
        public int UnitsOnOrder { get; set; }
        public bool Discontinued { get; set; }
    }
}
```

Adding the business logic project

Next, let us create the business logic layer project. Again, we just need to add a new C# class library project `RealNorthwindLogic` to the solution. Then, modify the file `Class1.cs` as follows:

1. Rename the file from `Class1.cs` to `ProductLogic.cs`.

2. Change its namespace from `RealNorthwindLogic` to `MyWCFServices.RealNorthwindLogic`.

3. Change the class name from `Class1` to `ProductLogic`.

4. Add a reference to the project `RealNorthwindBDO` as shown in the following **Reference Manager** screenshot:

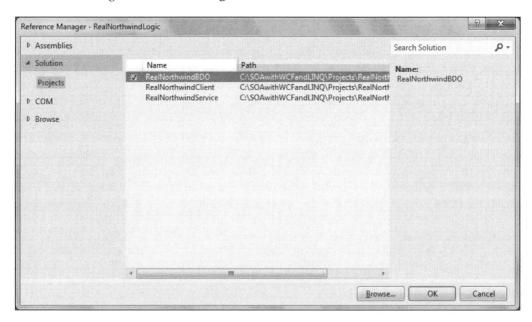

Now we need to add some code to the `ProductLogic` class:

1. Add the following `using` line:

    ```
    using MyWCFServices.RealNorthwindBDO;
    ```

2. Add the `GetProduct` method. It should look as follows:

    ```
    public ProductBDO GetProduct(int id)
    {
        // TODO: call data access layer to retrieve product
        ProductBDO p = new ProductBDO();
        p.ProductID = id;
        p.ProductName =
            "fake product name from business logic layer";
        p.UnitPrice = 20.00m;
        p.QuantityPerUnit = "fake QPU";
        return p;
    }
    ```

3. In this method, we create a `ProductBDO` object, assign values to some of its properties, and return it to the caller. Everything is still hardcoded so far.

> We hardcode the product name as `fake product name from business logic layer` so that we know this is a different product from the one that is returned directly from the service layer.

4. Add the `UpdateProduct` method as follows:

    ```
    public bool UpdateProduct(ProductBDO product,
        ref string message)
    {
        ProductBDO productInDB =
            GetProduct(product.ProductID);
        // invalid product to update
        if (productInDB == null)
        {
            message = "cannot get product for this ID";
            return false;
        }
        // a product can't be discontinued
        // if there are non-fulfilled orders
        if (product.Discontinued == true
            && productInDB.UnitsOnOrder > 0)
    ```

```
        {
            message = "cannot discontinue this product";
            return false;
        }
        else
        {
            // TODO: call data access layer to update product
            message = "Product updated successfully";
            return true;
        }
    }
```

5. Add test logic to the `GetProduct` method.

   We still have not updated anything in a database, but this time we have added several pieces of logic to the `UpdateProduct` method. First, we tried to retrieve the product to see if it was a valid product to update. If not we will return `false` and stop here. We also added a check to make sure that a supplier cannot discontinue a product if there are unfulfilled orders for this product. However, at this stage, we cannot truly enforce this logic because when we check the `UnitsOnOrder` property of a product it is always `0` as we didn't assign a value to it in the `GetProduct` method. For test purposes, we can change the `GetProduct` method to include the following line of code:

   ```
   if(id > 50) p.UnitsOnOrder = 30;
   ```

   Now, when we test the service, we can select a product with an ID that is greater than `50`, and try to update its `Discontinued` property to see what result we will get.

After you put all of this together the content of the `ProductLogic.cs` file should be as follows:

```
using System;
using System.Collections.Generic;
using System.Linq;
using System.Text;
using System.Threading.Tasks;
using MyWCFServices.RealNorthwindBDO;

namespace MyWCFServices.RealNorthwindLogic
{
    public class ProductLogic
    {
        public ProductBDO GetProduct(int id)
```

```
    {
        // TODO: call data access layer to retrieve product
        ProductBDO p = new ProductBDO();
        p.ProductID = id;
        p.ProductName =
            "fake product name from business logic layer";
        p.UnitPrice = 20.00m;
        p.QuantityPerUnit = "fake QPU";
        if (id > 50) p.UnitsOnOrder = 30;
        return p;
    }


    public bool UpdateProduct(ProductBDO
        product, ref string message)
    {

        ProductBDO productInDB =
            GetProduct(product.ProductID);
        // invalid product to update
        if (productInDB == null)
        {
            message = "cannot get product for this ID";
            return false;
        }
        // a product can't be discontinued
        // if there are non-fulfilled orders
        if (product.Discontinued == true
            && productInDB.UnitsOnOrder > 0)
        {
            message = "cannot discontinue this product";
            return false;
        }
        else
        {
            // TODO: call data access layer to update product
            message = "Product updated successfully";
            return true;
        }
    }
    }
}
```

Calling the business logic layer from the service interface layer

We now have the business logic layer ready and can modify the service contracts to call this layer so that we can enforce some business logic.

First, we want to make it very clear that we are going to change the service implementations and not the interfaces. Therefore, we will only change the `ProductService.cs` file.

We will not touch the `IProductService.cs` file. All of the existing clients (if there are any) that are referencing our service will not notice that we are changing the implementation.

Follow these steps to customize the service interface layer (the `RealNorthwindService` project):

1. In order to call a method inside the business logic layer we need to add a reference to the assembly that the business logic is included in. We will also use the `ProductBDO` class. So we need a reference to `RealNorthwindBDO` as well.

2. To add the references, from **Solution Explorer** right-click on the project **RealNorthwindService**, select **Add Reference...** from the context menu, and check **RealNorthwindLogic** from the **Solution\Projects** tab. Also, check **RealNorthwindBDO**, as we will need a reference to `ProductBDO` inside it. Click on the **OK** button to add references to the selected projects.

3. Now we have added two references. We then add the following two `using` statements to the `ProductService.cs` file so that we don't need to type the full names for their classes:

   ```
   using MyWCFServices.RealNorthwindBDO;
   using MyWCFServices.RealNorthwindLogic;
   ```

4. Next, inside the `GetProduct` method, we can use the following statements to get the product from our business logic layer:

   ```
   ProductLogic productLogic = new ProductLogic();
   ProductBDO productBDO = productLogic.GetProduct(id);
   ```

5. However, we cannot return this product back to the caller because this product is of the type `ProductBDO`, which is not the type that the caller is expecting. The caller is expecting a return value of the type `Product`, which is a data contract defined within the service interface. We need to translate this `ProductBDO` object to a `Product` object. To do this, we add the following new method to the `ProductService` class:

```
private void TranslateProductBDOToProductDTO(
    ProductBDO productBDO,
    Product product)
{
    product.ProductID = productBDO.ProductID;
    product.ProductName = productBDO.ProductName;
    product.QuantityPerUnit = productBDO.QuantityPerUnit;
    product.UnitPrice = productBDO.UnitPrice;
    product.Discontinued = productBDO.Discontinued;
}
```

6. Inside this translation method, we copy all of the properties from the ProductBDO object to the service contract data object, but not the last three properties—UnitsInStock, UnitsOnOrder, and ReorderLevel. These three properties are used only inside the service implementations. Outside callers cannot see them at all.

7. The GetProduct method should now look as follows:

```
public Product GetProduct(int id)
{
    ProductLogic productLogic = new ProductLogic();
    ProductBDO productBDO = productLogic.GetProduct(id);
    Product product = new Product();
    TranslateProductBDOToProductDTO(productBDO, product);
    return product;
}
```

8. We can modify the UpdateProduct method in the same way, making it look as shown in the following code snippet:

```
public bool UpdateProduct(Product product,
    ref string message)
{
    bool result = true;

    // first check to see if it is a valid price
    if (product.UnitPrice <= 0)
    {
        message = "Price cannot be <= 0";
        result = false;
    }
    // ProductName can't be empty
    else if (string.IsNullOrEmpty(product.ProductName))
```

```
                {
                    message = "Product name cannot be empty";
                    result = false;
                }
                // QuantityPerUnit can't be empty
                else if
                (string.IsNullOrEmpty(product.QuantityPerUnit))
                {
                    message = "Quantity cannot be empty";
                    result = false;
                }
                else
                {
                    ProductLogic productLogic = new ProductLogic();
                    ProductBDO productBDO = new ProductBDO();
                    TranslateProductDTOToProductBDO(product,
                    productBDO);

                    return productLogic.UpdateProduct(productBDO, ref
                    message);
                }
                return result;
            }
```

9. Note that we have to create a new method to translate a product contract data object to a `ProductBDO` object. In translation, we leave the three extra properties unassigned in the `ProductBDO` object because we know a supplier won't update these properties.

10. Since we have to create a `ProductLogic` variable in both the methods, let's make it a class member:

    ```
    ProductLogic productLogic = new ProductLogic();
    ```

The final content of the `ProductService.cs` file is as follows:

```
using System;
using System.Collections.Generic;
using System.Linq;
using System.Runtime.Serialization;
using System.ServiceModel;
using System.Text;
using MyWCFServices.RealNorthwindBDO;
using MyWCFServices.RealNorthwindLogic;
```

```
namespace MyWCFServices.RealNorthwindService
{
    public class ProductService : IProductService
    {
        ProductLogic productLogic = new ProductLogic();
        public Product GetProduct(int id)
        {
            ProductBDO productBDO = productLogic.GetProduct(id);
            Product product = new Product();
            TranslateProductBDOToProductDTO(productBDO, product);
            return product;
        }

        public bool UpdateProduct(Product product,
            ref string message)
        {
            bool result = true;

            // first check to see if it is a valid price
            if (product.UnitPrice <= 0)
            {
                message = "Price cannot be <= 0";
                result = false;
            }
            // ProductName can't be empty
            else if (string.IsNullOrEmpty(product.ProductName))
            {
                message = "Product name cannot be empty";
                result = false;
            }
            // QuantityPerUnit can't be empty
            else if
            (string.IsNullOrEmpty(product.QuantityPerUnit))
            {
                message = "Quantity cannot be empty";
                result = false;
            }
            else
            {
                ProductBDO productBDO = new ProductBDO();
                TranslateProductDTOToProductBDO(product,
                productBDO);
```

```
            return productLogic.UpdateProduct(
                productBDO, ref message);
        }
        return result;
    }

    private void TranslateProductBDOToProductDTO(
        ProductBDO productBDO,
        Product product)
    {
        product.ProductID = productBDO.ProductID;
        product.ProductName = productBDO.ProductName;
        product.QuantityPerUnit = productBDO.QuantityPerUnit;
        product.UnitPrice = productBDO.UnitPrice;
        product.Discontinued = productBDO.Discontinued;
    }

    private void TranslateProductDTOToProductBDO(
        Product product,
        ProductBDO productBDO)
    {
        productBDO.ProductID = product.ProductID;
        productBDO.ProductName = product.ProductName;
        productBDO.QuantityPerUnit = product.QuantityPerUnit;
        productBDO.UnitPrice = product.UnitPrice;
        productBDO.Discontinued = product.Discontinued;
    }
  }
}
```

Testing the WCF service with a business logic layer

We can now compile and test the new WCF service with a business logic layer. We will use the WCF Test Client to simplify the process.

1. Make the project RealNorthwindService as the startup project.

2. Start the WCF Service Host application and WCF Service Test Client by pressing *F5* or *Ctrl + F5*.

3. In the WCF Service Test Client, double-click on the **GetProduct()** operation to bring up the GetProduct test screen.

4.   Enter a value of 56 for the ID field and then click on the **Invoke** button.

5.   You will see that this time the product is returned from the business logic layer, instead of the service layer. Also note that the UnitsOnOrder property is not displayed as it is not part of the service contract datatype. However, we know that a product has a UnitsOnOrder property, and we will use this for our next test.

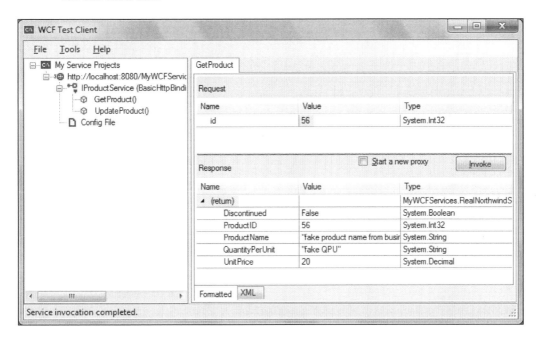

Now let us try to update a product:

1.   In the WCF Service Test Client, double-click on the **UpdateProduct()** operation to bring up the **UpdateProduct** test screen.

2.   Enter -10 as the price and click on the **Invoke** button. You will see that the **Response** result is **False**.

3.   Enter a valid price, say 25.6, a name, and a quantity per unit, and leave the **Discontinued** property set to **False**, and then click on the **Invoke** button. You will see that the **Response** result is now **True**.

4. Change the **Discontinued** value from **False** to **True** and click on the **Invoke** button again. The **Response** result is still **True**. This is because we didn't change the product ID and it has been defaulted to 0. Remember in our business logic layer in GetProduct operation, for a product with ID less than or equal to 50, we didn't set the property UnitsOnOrder, thus it defaults to 0, and in our business logic in the UpdateProduct operation, it is ok to set the **Discontinued** property to be **True**, if UnitsOnOrder is less than or equal to 0.

5. Change the product ID to **51**, leave the **Discontinued** value as **True** and the product price as **25.6**, and click on the **Invoke** button again. This time you will see that the **Response** result is **False**. This is because the business logic layer has checked the **UnitsOnOrder** and **Discontinued** properties and did not allow us to make the update.

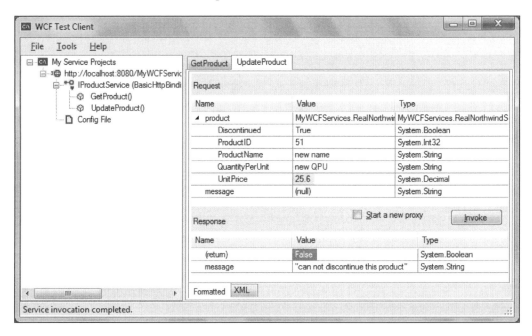

Summary

In this chapter, we created a real world WCF service that has a service contract layer and a business logic layer. We used the built-in WCF Service Library template to create the service, and followed the WCF service development best practice to separate the service interfaces from the business logics.

In the next chapter, we will add one more layer, the data access layer, to the service, and add error handling to the service.

5
Adding Database Support and Exception Handling

In the previous chapter we created a WCF service with two layers. We didn't add the third layer, that is, the data access layer. Therefore, all of the service operations just returned a fake result from the business logic layer.

In this chapter we will add the third layer to the WCF service. We will also introduce fault contracts for service error handling.

We will accomplish the following tasks in this chapter:

- Creating the data access layer project
- Modifying the business logic layer to call the data access layer
- Preparing the Northwind database for the service
- Connecting the WCF service to the Northwind database
- Testing the service with the data access layer
- Adding a fault contract to the service
- Throwing a fault contract exception to the client
- Catching the fault contract exception in the client program
- Testing the service fault contract

Adding a data access layer

We have two layers—the service interface layer and the business logic layer—in our solution now. We need to add one more layer—the data access layer. Within this third layer, we will query a real database to get the product information and update the database for a given product.

Creating the data access layer project

First, we will create the project for the data access layer. As we did for the business logic layer, what we need to do is add a C# class library project named RealNorthwindDAL (where **DAL** stands for **Data Access Layer**) to the solution. Then we need to change the default class file to be our **Data Access Object (DAO)** file.

Now modify the Class1.cs file as follows:

1. Rename it to ProductDAO.cs.

2. Change its namespace from RealNorthwindDAL to MyWCFServices. RealNorthwindDAL.

3. Change the class name from Class1 to ProductDAO.

4. Add a RealNorthwindBDO reference to the project.

Next, let's modify ProductDAO.cs for our product service:

1. Add the following using statement:

   ```
   using MyWCFServices.RealNorthwindBDO;
   ```

2. Add two new methods to the ProductDAO class. The first method is GetProduct, which should be as follows:

   ```
   public ProductBDO GetProduct(int id)
   {
       // TODO: connect to DB to retrieve product
       ProductBDO p = new ProductBDO();
       p.ProductID = id;
       p.ProductName =
           "fake product name from data access layer";
       p.UnitPrice = 30.00m;
       p.QuantityPerUnit = "fake QPU";
       return p;
   }
   ```

   In this method, all the product information is still hardcoded, though we have changed the product name to be specific to the data access layer. We will soon modify this method to retrieve the actual product information from a real Northwind database.

3. Add the second method `UpdateProduct`, as shown in the following code snippet:

```
public bool UpdateProduct(ProductBDO product, ref string message)
{
    // TODO: connect to DB to update product
    message = "product updated successfully";
    return true;
}
```

4. Again, we didn't update any database in this method. We will also modify this method soon to update to the real `Northwind` database.

5. The content of the `ProductDAO.cs` file should now be as follows:

```
using System;
using System.Collections.Generic;
using System.Linq;
using System.Text;
using System.Threading.Tasks;
using MyWCFServices.RealNorthwindBDO;

namespace MyWCFServices.RealNorthwindDAL
{
    public class ProductDAO
    {
        public ProductBDO GetProduct(int id)
        {
            // TODO: connect to DB to retrieve product
            ProductBDO p = new ProductBDO();
            p.ProductID = id;
            p.ProductName =
            "fake product name from data access layer";
            p.UnitPrice = 30.00m;
            p.QuantityPerUnit = "fake QPU";
            return p;
        }

        public bool UpdateProduct(ProductBDO product,
         ref string message)
        {
            // TODO: connect to DB to update product
            message = "product updated successfully";
            return true;
        }
    }
}
```

Calling the data access layer from the business logic layer

Before we modify these two methods to interact with a real database, we will first modify the business logic layer to call them, so that we know that the three-layer framework is working:

1. Add a reference of this new layer to the business logic layer project. From **Solution Explorer**, just right-click on the **RealNorthwindLogic** project item, select **Add Reference...** from the context menu, select **RealNorthwindDAL** from **Projects** under the **Solutions** tab, and then click on the **OK** button.

2. Open the **ProductLogic.cs** file under the **RealNorthwindLogic** project and add a using statement:

   ```
   using MyWCFServices.RealNorthwindDAL;
   ```

3. Add a new class member:

   ```
   ProductDAO productDAO = new ProductDAO();
   ```

4. Modify the GetProduct method to contain only the following line:

   ```
   return productDAO.GetProduct(id);
   ```

   We will use the data access layer to retrieve the product information. At this point, we will not add any business logic to this method.

5. Modify the last two lines of the UpdateProduct method to call the data access layer. The method call should look as follows:

   ```
   return productDAO.UpdateProduct(product, ref message);
   ```

6. In this method, we have replaced the last return statement to call the data access layer method UpdateProduct. This means that all of the business logic is still enclosed in the business logic layer and the data access layer should be used only to update the product in the database.

Here is the full content of the ProductLogic.cs file:

```
using System;
using System.Collections.Generic;
using System.Linq;
using System.Text;
using System.Threading.Tasks;
using MyWCFServices.RealNorthwindBDO;
using MyWCFServices.RealNorthwindDAL;
```

```
namespace MyWCFServices.RealNorthwindLogic
{
  public class ProductLogic
  {
    ProductDAO productDAO = new ProductDAO();
    public ProductBDO GetProduct(int id)
    {
      return productDAO.GetProduct(id);
    }

    public bool UpdateProduct(ProductBDO
    product, ref string message)
    {
      ProductBDO productInDB =
      GetProduct(product.ProductID);
      // invalid product to update
      if (productInDB == null)
      {
        message = "cannot get product for this ID";
        return false;
      }
      // a product can't be discontinued
      // if there are non-fulfilled orders
      if (product.Discontinued == true
      && productInDB.UnitsOnOrder > 0)
      {
        message = "cannot discontinue this product";
        return false;
      }
      else
      {
        return productDAO.UpdateProduct(product,
        ref message);
      }
    }
  }
}
```

If you run the program and test it using the WCF Test Client, you will get exactly the same result as before, although now it is a three-layer application and you will see a different, but obviously still fake, product name.

Preparing the database

As we have the three-layer framework ready, we will now implement the data access layer to actually communicate with a real database.

In this book, we will use the Microsoft sample `Northwind` database. This database is not installed by default in SQL Server, so we need to install it first (you can use any version's SQL Server database, but in this book we will use SQL Server 2008 for all screenshots):

1. Download the database package. Just search for *Northwind Sample Databases download* on the Internet or go to `http://www.microsoft.com/download/en/details.aspx?id=23654`.

2. Download the `SQL2000SampleDb.msi` file. Note that this sample database was designed for SQL Server 2000, but it can also be used with more recent versions of SQL Server.

3. Install (extract) it to `C:\SQL Server 2000 Sample Databases`.

4. Change the security of both `Northwnd.mdf` and `Northwnd.ldf` to be read/write-able to your SQL Server service account user.

5. Open SQL Server Management Studio.

6. Connect to your database engine.

7. Right-click on the **Databases** node and select **Attach...** from the context menu, as shown in the following **SQL Server Management Studio** screenshot:

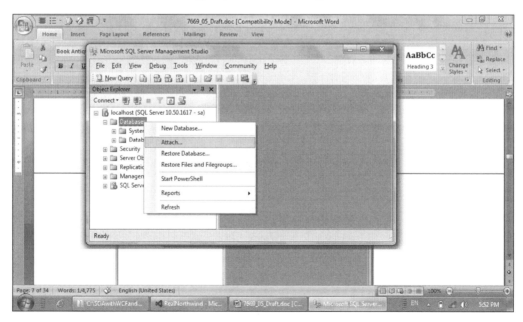

8. In the pop-up **Attach Databases** dialog box, click on **Add**, browse to the file `C:\SQL Server 2000 Sample Databases\NORTHWND.MDF`, click on `OK`, and you now have the `Northwind` database attached to your SQL Server 2005 or 2008 engine.

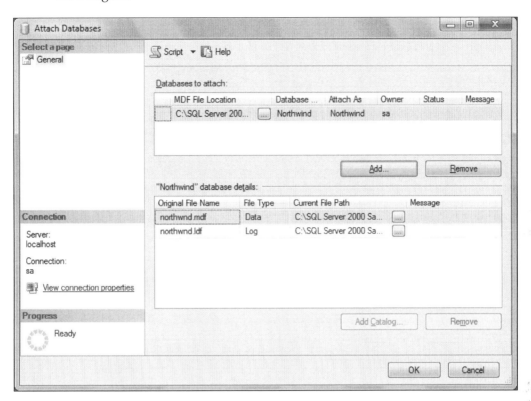

Adding the connection string to the configuration file

Now that we have the `Northwind` database attached, we will modify our data access layer to use this actual database. At this point, we will use a raw `SqlClient` adapter to do the database work. We will replace this layer with LINQ to Entities in a later chapter.

Before we start coding, we need to add a connection string to the configuration file. We don't want to hardcode the connection string in our project. Instead, we will set it in the `App.config` file so that it can be changed on the fly.

You can open the App.config file under the RealNorthwindService project and add a new configuration node connectionStrings as a child node of the root configuration node, configuration. You can choose Windows integrated security or SQL Server login as the security mode for your connection. The following code snippet shows my connection string with integrated security:

```
<connectionStrings>
  <add name ="NorthwindConnectionString"
    connectionString="server=localhost;Integrated
    Security=SSPI;database=Northwind" />
</connectionStrings>
```

Querying the database (GetProduct)

As we have added the connection string as a new key to the configuration file, we need to retrieve this key in the DAO class so that we can use it when we want to connect to the database. Follow these steps to get and use this new key from within the DAO class:

1. Add a reference to System.Configuration to the RealNorthwindDAL project. We need this reference to read the connection string in the configuration file.

2. Open the file ProductDAO.cs in the RealNorthwindDAL project and first add two using statements:

   ```
   using System.Data.SqlClient;
   using System.Configuration;
   ```

3. Add a new class member to the ProductDAO class (note the following code should be in one line in Visual Studio; we have broken them into three lines just for printing purposes):

   ```
   string connectionString = ConfigurationManager.
       ConnectionStrings["NorthwindConnectionString"].
       ConnectionString;
   ```

   We will use this connection string to connect to the Northwind database for both the GetProduct and UpdateProduct methods.

4. Modify the GetProduct method to get the product from the database as follows:

   ```
   public ProductBDO GetProduct(int id)
   {
     ProductBDO p = null;
   ```

```
using (SqlConnection conn =
new SqlConnection(connectionString))
{
  using (SqlCommand cmd = new SqlCommand())
  {
    cmd.CommandText =
    "select * from Products where ProductID=@id";
    cmd.Parameters.AddWithValue("@id", id);
    cmd.Connection = conn;
    conn.Open();
    using (SqlDataReader reader =
    cmd.ExecuteReader())
    {
      if (reader.HasRows)
      {
        reader.Read();
        p = new ProductBDO();
        p.ProductID = id;
        p.ProductName =
        (string)reader["ProductName"];
        p.QuantityPerUnit =
        (string)reader["QuantityPerUnit"];
        p.UnitPrice =
        (decimal)reader["UnitPrice"];
        p.UnitsInStock =
        (short)reader["UnitsInStock"];
        p.UnitsOnOrder =
        (short)reader["UnitsOnOrder"];
        p.ReorderLevel =
        (short)reader["ReorderLevel"];
        p.Discontinued =
        (bool)reader["Discontinued"];
      }
    }
  }
}
return p;
}
```

In this method, we first create a `SqlConnection` to the `Northwind` database and then issue a SQL query to get product details for the ID. Remember we will change this ADO.NET code to LINQ to Entities in a later chapter.

Testing the GetProduct method

If you now set `RealNorthwindService` as the startup project and run the application, you can get the actual product information from the database, as seen in the following screenshot:

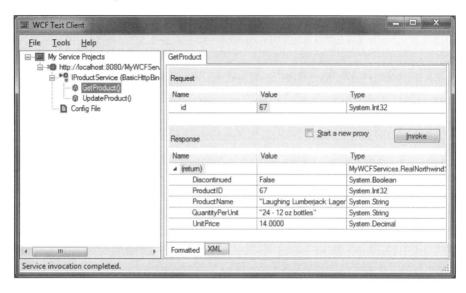

If you get an error screen, it is probably because you have set your connection string incorrectly. Double-check the new connection string node in your `App.config` file and try again until you can connect to your database.

Instead of the connection error message, you might see the following error message:

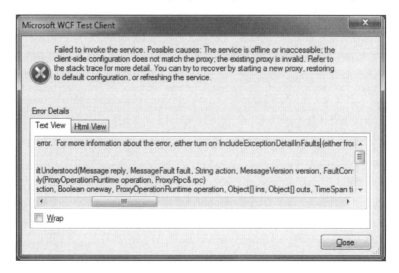

This error will happen when you try to get the product information for a product with a product ID of 0. The error message does not give much detail about what went wrong here because we did not let the server reveal the details of any error. Let's follow the instructions in the error message to change the setting `IncludeExceptionDetailInFaults` to `True` in the `App.config` file and run it again. Now you will see that the error detail has changed to **Object reference not set to an instance of an object**.

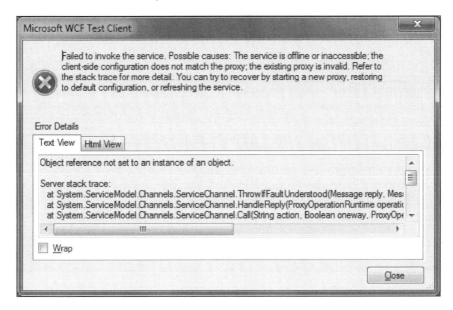

A little investigation will tell us that there is a bug in our `ProductService` class. Inside the `ProductService` `GetProduct` method, after we call the business logic layer to get the product detail for an ID, we will get a null product if the ID is not a valid product ID in the database. When we pass this null object to the next method (`TranslateProductBDOToProductDTO`), we get the above error message. Actually, this will happen whenever you enter a product ID outside the range of 1 to 77. This is because, in the sample `Northwind` database, there are only 77 products, with product IDs ranging from 1 to 77. To fix this problem we can add the following statement inside the `GetProduct` method right after the call to the business logic layer:

```
if (productBDO == null)
    throw new Exception("No product found for id " + id);
```

In the `ProductService.cs` file, the `GetProduct` method will now be as follows:

```
public Product GetProduct(int id)
{
  ProductBDO productBDO = productLogic.GetProduct(id);
  if (productBDO == null)
  throw new Exception("No product found for id " + id);
  Product product = new Product();
  TranslateProductBDOToProductDTO(productBDO, product);
  return product;
}
```

For now, we will raise an exception if an invalid product ID is entered. Later, we will convert this exception to a `FaultContract` so that the caller will be able to catch and process the fault properly.

Now run the application again, and if you enter an invalid product ID, say 0, you will get an error message **No product found for id 0**. This is much clearer than the previous **Object reference not set to an instance of an object** error message.

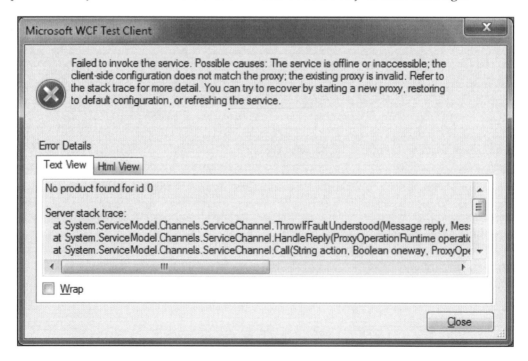

Updating the database (UpdateProduct)

Next, we will modify the UpdateProduct method to update the product record in the database. UpdateProduct in the RealNorthwindDAL project should be modified as follows:

```
public bool UpdateProduct(ProductBDO product,
  ref string message)
{
  message = "product updated successfully";
  bool ret = true;
  using (SqlConnection conn =
  new SqlConnection(connectionString))
  {
    string cmdStr = @"UPDATE products
    SET ProductName=@name,
    QuantityPerUnit=@unit,
    UnitPrice=@price,
    Discontinued=@discontinued
    WHERE ProductID=@id";
    using (SqlCommand cmd = new SqlCommand(cmdStr, conn))
    {
      cmd.Parameters.AddWithValue("@name",
      product.ProductName);
      cmd.Parameters.AddWithValue("@unit",
      product.QuantityPerUnit);
      cmd.Parameters.AddWithValue("@price",
      product.UnitPrice);
      cmd.Parameters.AddWithValue("@discontinued",
      product.Discontinued);
      cmd.Parameters.AddWithValue("@id",
      product.ProductID);
      conn.Open();
      if (cmd.ExecuteNonQuery() != 1)
      {
        message = "no product was updated";
        ret = false;
      }
    }
  }
  return ret;
}
```

Inside this method, we have used parameters to specify arguments to the update command. This is a good practice because it will prevent SQL Injection attacks, as the SQL statement is precompiled instead of being dynamically built.

We can follow these steps to test it:

1. Start the WCF service by pressing *Ctrl + F5* or *F5*. WCF Test Client should also start automatically.

2. Double-click on the **UpdateProduct()** operation in the WCF Test Client.

3. Enter a valid product ID, name, price, and quantity per unit.

4. Click on **Invoke**.

You should get a True response. To prove it, just go to the **GetProduct()** page, enter the same product ID, click on **Invoke**, and you will see that all of your updates have been saved to the database.

The content of the ProductDAO.cs file is now as follows:

```
using System;
using System.Collections.Generic;
using System.Linq;
using System.Text;
using System.Threading.Tasks;
using MyWCFServices.RealNorthwindBDO;
using System.Data.SqlClient;
using System.Configuration;

namespace MyWCFServices.RealNorthwindDAL
{
  public class ProductDAO
{
  //Note put following three lines in one line in your code
    string connectionString = ConfigurationManager.
    ConnectionStrings["NorthwindConnectionString"].
    ConnectionString;

    public ProductBDO GetProduct(int id)
    {
      ProductBDO p = null;
      using (SqlConnection conn =
      new SqlConnection(connectionString))
      {
        using(SqlCommand cmd = new SqlCommand())
        {
          cmd.CommandText =
          "select * from Products where ProductID=@id";
```

```csharp
      cmd.Parameters.AddWithValue("@id", id);
      cmd.Connection = conn;
      conn.Open();
      using(SqlDataReader reader = cmd.ExecuteReader())
      {
        if (reader.HasRows)
        {
          reader.Read();
          p = new ProductBDO();
          p.ProductID = id;
          p.ProductName =
          (string)reader["ProductName"];
          p.QuantityPerUnit =
          (string)reader["QuantityPerUnit"];
          p.UnitPrice =
          (decimal)reader["UnitPrice"];
          p.UnitsInStock =
          (short)reader["UnitsInStock"];
          p.UnitsOnOrder =
          (short)reader["UnitsOnOrder"];
          p.ReorderLevel =
          (short)reader["ReorderLevel"];
          p.Discontinued =
          (bool)reader["Discontinued"];
        }
      }
    }
  }
  return p;
}

public bool UpdateProduct(ProductBDO product,
ref string message)
{
  message = "product updated successfully";
  bool ret = true;
  using (SqlConnection conn =
  new SqlConnection(connectionString))
  {
    string cmdStr = @"UPDATE products
    SET ProductName=@name,
    QuantityPerUnit=@unit,
    UnitPrice=@price,
    Discontinued=@discontinued
```

```
                    WHERE ProductID=@id";
            using(SqlCommand cmd = new SqlCommand(cmdStr, conn))
            {
                cmd.Parameters.AddWithValue("@name",
                product.ProductName);
                cmd.Parameters.AddWithValue("@unit",
                product.QuantityPerUnit);
                cmd.Parameters.AddWithValue("@price",
                product.UnitPrice);
                cmd.Parameters.AddWithValue("@discontinued",
                product.Discontinued);
                cmd.Parameters.AddWithValue("@id",
                product.ProductID);
                conn.Open();
                if (cmd.ExecuteNonQuery() != 1)
                {
                    message = "no product is updated";
                    ret = false;
                }
            }
        }
        return ret;
    }
  }
}
```

Adding error handling to the service

In the previous sections, when we were trying to retrieve a product but the
product ID passed in was not a valid one, we just threw an exception. Exceptions
are technology-specific and therefore are not suitable for crossing the service
boundary of SOA-compliant services. Thus, for WCF services, we should not
throw normal exceptions.

What we need are SOAP faults that meet industry standards for seamless
interoperability.

The service interface layer operations that may throw `FaultExceptions` must
be decorated with one or more `FaultContract` attributes, defining the exact
`FaultException`.

On the other hand, the service consumer should catch specific `FaultExceptions`
to be in a position to handle the specified fault exceptions.

Adding a fault contract

We will now wrap the exception in the GetProduct operation with a FaultContract.

Before we implement our first FaultContract, we need to modify the App.config file in the RealNorthwindService project. We will change the includeExceptionDetailInFaults setting back to False so that every unhandled, non-fault exception will be a violation. In this way, client applications won't know the details of those exceptions, so that the service technology and the hosting environment won't be revealed to them.

 You can set includeExceptionDetailInFaults to True while debugging, as this can be very helpful in diagnosing problems during the development stage. In production, it should always be set to False.

Open the App.config file in the RealNorthwindService project, change includeExceptionDetailInFaults from True to False, and save it.

Next, we will define a FaultContract. For simplicity, we will define only one FaultContract and leave it inside the IProductService.cs file, although in a real system you can have as many FaultContracts as you want, and they should also normally be in their own files.

FaultContract should be as follows:

```
[DataContract]
public class ProductFault
{
    public ProductFault(string msg)
    {
        FaultMessage = msg;
    }

    [DataMember]
    public string FaultMessage;
}
```

We then decorate the service operations GetProduct and UpdateProduct with the following attribute:

```
[FaultContract(typeof(ProductFault))]
```

This is to tell the service consumers that these operations may throw a fault of the type ProductFault.

The content of IProductService.cs should now be as follows:

```
using System;
using System.Collections.Generic;
using System.Linq;
using System.Runtime.Serialization;
using System.ServiceModel;
using System.Text;

namespace MyWCFServices.RealNorthwindService
{
    [ServiceContract]
    public interface IProductService
    {
        [OperationContract]
        [FaultContract(typeof(ProductFault))]
        Product GetProduct(int id);

        [OperationContract]
        [FaultContract(typeof(ProductFault))]
        bool UpdateProduct(Product product, ref string message);

        // TODO: Add your service operations here
    }

    [DataContract]
    public class Product
    {
        [DataMember]
        public int ProductID;

        [DataMember]
        public string ProductName;

        [DataMember]
        public string QuantityPerUnit;

        [DataMember]
        public decimal UnitPrice;

        [DataMember]
        public bool Discontinued;
    }
```

```
[DataContract]
public class ProductFault
{
    public ProductFault(string msg)
    {
        FaultMessage = msg;
    }
    [DataMember]
    public string FaultMessage;
}
}
```

Throwing a fault contract exception

Once we have modified the interface, we need to modify the implementation.
Open the `ProductService.cs` file and change `GetProduct` to be as follows:

```
public Product GetProduct(int id)
{
    ProductBDO productBDO = null;
    try
    {
        productBDO = productLogic.GetProduct(id);
    }
    catch (Exception e)
    {
        string msg = e.Message;
        string reason = "GetProduct Exception";
        throw new FaultException<ProductFault>
            (new ProductFault(msg), reason);
    }

    if (productBDO == null)
    {
        string msg =
            string.Format("No product found for id {0}",
            id);
        string reason = "GetProduct Empty Product";
        if (id == 999)
        {
            throw new Exception(msg);
        }
        else
        {
            throw new FaultException<ProductFault>
                (new ProductFault(msg), reason);
```

```
            }
        }
        Product product = new Product();
        TranslateProductBDOToProductDTO(productBDO, product);
        return product;
    }
```

In this modified method, we have wrapped the call to the business logic method, hence to the data access layer method, in a try/catch block. If anything goes wrong when the product is being retrieved from the database, such as the login is invalid, the database server is down, or the network is broken, we will throw a fault exception, so the client will be able to catch the exception and display a proper message to the end user, should they wish to.

We will also throw a `ProductFault` exception if an invalid ID is passed into the `GetProduct` operation. However, we will throw a normal C# exception if the passed ID is `999`. Later, we will use this special ID to compare a normal C# exception with a Fault exception.

For the `UpdateProduct` method, we need to do the same thing as with the `GetProduct` method, that is wrapping the call to the business logic method within a try/catch block. In a sum, we need to change the following code in the `UpdateProduct` method:

```
return productLogic.UpdateProduct(
        productBDO, ref message);
To be like this:
try
{
    result = productLogic.UpdateProduct(
        productBDO, ref message);
}
catch (Exception e)
{
    string msg = e.Message;
    string reason = "UpdateProduct Exception";
    throw new FaultException<ProductFault>
        (new ProductFault(msg), reason);
}
```

Now build the `RealNorthwindService` project. After it has been successfully built, we will use the client that we built earlier to test this service. We will examine the fault message and the exception details after a normal exception has been thrown and a fault exception has been thrown.

We can't do this with the WCF Service Test Client because in WCF Test Client, each request will create a new channel and we don't have a way to examine the channel status after the service call.

Updating the client program to catch the fault exception

Now let's update the client program so that the fault exception is handled:

1. First, we need to update the service reference because we have changed the contracts for the service. From the `RealNorthwindClient` project, expand the **Service References** node and right-click on **ProductServiceRef**. Select **Update Service Reference** from the context menu and the **Updating Service Reference** dialog box will pop up. The WCF Service Host will be started automatically, and the updated metadata information will be downloaded to the client side. Proxy code will be updated with modified and new service contracts.

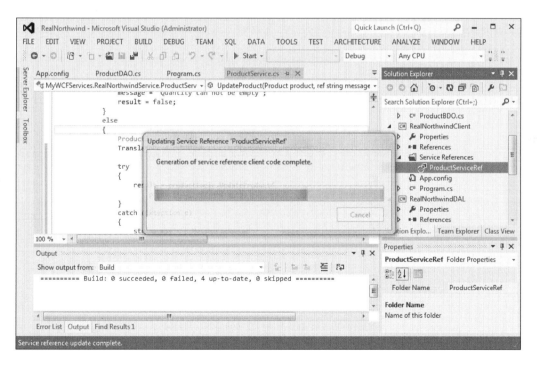

2. Then open `Program.cs` under the `RealNorthwindClient` project and add the following `using` statement:

```
using System.ServiceModel;
```

3. Add the following method to the `Program` class:

```
static void TestException(ProductServiceClient client,
    int id)
{
    if (id != 999)
        Console.WriteLine("\n\nTest Fault Exception");
    else
        Console.WriteLine("\n\nTest normal Exception");

    try
    {
        Product product = client.GetProduct(id);
    }
    catch (TimeoutException ex)
    {
        Console.WriteLine("Timeout exception");
    }
    catch (FaultException<ProductFault> ex)
    {
        Console.WriteLine("ProductFault. ");
        Console.WriteLine("\tFault reason:" +
            ex.Reason);
        Console.WriteLine("\tFault message:" +
            ex.Detail.FaultMessage);
    }
    catch (FaultException ex)
    {
        Console.WriteLine("Unknown Fault");
        Console.WriteLine(ex.Message);
    }
    catch (CommunicationException ex)
    {
        Console.WriteLine("Communication exception");
    }
    catch (Exception ex)
    {
        Console.WriteLine("Unknown exception");
    }
}
```

4. Inside this method, we first call `GetProduct` with a passed-in ID. If the ID is an invalid product ID the service will throw a `ProductFault` exception. So we have to add the `catch` statement to catch the `ProductFault` exception. We will print the reason and the message of the fault exception. We have also added several other exceptions such as timeout exception, communication exception, and general fault exception, so that we can handle every situation. Note that the order of the `catch` statements is very important and should not be changed.

5. If `999` is passed to this method as the ID, the service will throw a normal C# exception instead of a fault exception. As you can see, with this exception we don't have a way to find the reason and details of the exception, so we will just print out the raw exception message.

6. Now add the following statements to the end of the `Main` function in this class:

```
// FaultException
TestException(client, 0);
// regular C# exception
TestException(client, 999);
```

So we will first test the `ProductFault` exception, and then the regular C# exception.

7. Finally, set the solution to start with multi-projects `RealNorthwindService` and `RealNorthwindClient` (make sure the service project is started before the client project).

The full content of `Program.cs` is now as follows:

```
using System;
using System.Collections.Generic;
using System.Linq;
using System.Text;
using System.Threading.Tasks;
using RealNorthwindClient.ProductServiceRef;
using System.ServiceModel;

namespace RealNorthwindClient
{
    class Program
    {
        static void Main(string[] args)
        {
            ProductServiceClient client =
```

```
            new ProductServiceClient();
        Product product = client.GetProduct(23);
        Console.WriteLine("product name is " +
            product.ProductName);
        Console.WriteLine("product price is " +
                product.UnitPrice.ToString());
        product.UnitPrice = 20.0m;
        string message = "";
        bool result = client.UpdateProduct(product,
            ref message);
        Console.WriteLine("Update result is " +
                            result.ToString());
        Console.WriteLine("Update message is " +
                            message);

        // FaultException
        TestException(client, 0);
        // regular C# exception
        TestException(client, 999);

        Console.WriteLine("Press any key to continue ...");
        Console.ReadLine();
    }

    static void TestException(ProductServiceClient client,
        int id)
    {
        if (id != 999)
            Console.WriteLine("\n\nTest Fault Exception");
        else
            Console.WriteLine("\n\nTest normal Exception");

        try
        {
            Product product = client.GetProduct(id);
        }
        catch (TimeoutException ex)
        {
            Console.WriteLine("Timeout exception");
        }
        catch (FaultException<ProductFault> ex)
        {
            Console.WriteLine("ProductFault. ");
            Console.WriteLine("\tFault reason:" +
                ex.Reason);
```

```
                    Console.WriteLine("\tFault message:" +
                        ex.Detail.FaultMessage);
            }
            catch (FaultException ex)
            {
                Console.WriteLine("Unknown Fault");
                Console.WriteLine(ex.Message);
            }
            catch (CommunicationException ex)
            {
                Console.WriteLine("Communication exception");
            }
            catch (Exception ex)
            {
                Console.WriteLine("Unknown exception");
            }
        }
    }
}
```

Testing the fault exception

Now you can press *Ctrl* + *F5* to run the client program (remember to set
RealNorthwindService and RealNorthwindClient to be the startup projects).
You will get the output shown in the following screenshot:

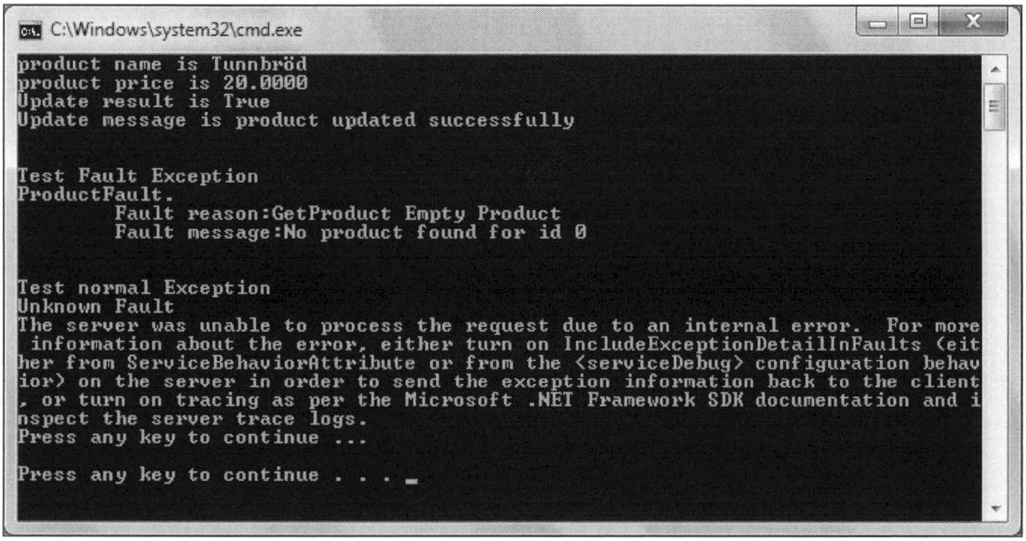

As you can see from the output, the client has the full details of the customized fault exception, such as fault reason and fault message. On the other hand, for the regular C# exception, the client does not have the fault details, except the raw fault message, which is a generic error message to all un-handled service faults.

If you turn on the flag, like the generic fault error message suggested, the client will be able to get the exception messages from the service side, but meanwhile a lot of other details will also be revealed, such as the call stack and language specification of the service. As we said earlier, this is against the SOA principal, and it is not recommended for production.

 A big difference between WCF 4.0 and 4.5 is, with WCF 4.0, after a regular C# exception is thrown, the communication channel is faulted and thus will not be able to be re-used afterwards. While with WCF 4.5, the channel is still open and can be re-used afterwards.

Summary

In this chapter, we have added the third layer — the data access layer — to `RealNorthwindService`. We have also added exception handling to the service we have finished implementing the three-layered WCF service, according to the WCF service development best practices.

In the next three chapters, we will learn LINQ and Entity Framework, and then apply LINQ to Entities to our WCF service.

6
LINQ: Language Integrated Query

In the previous chapters of this book, we created a WCF service with three layers. In the data access layer, we used the raw ADO.NET SQL adapters to communicate with the `Northwind` database. In one of the following chapters, we will change the service to use LINQ to Entities in the data access layer.

Before using LINQ to Entities in our data access layer, we need to understand what LINQ or LINQ to Entities actually mean. Before understanding LINQ, we first need to understand some of the C# features related to LINQ. In this chapter, we will first explore these C# features related to LINQ and then we will explore LINQ. In the next two chapters, we will explore LINQ to Entities, and after that, we will apply LINQ to Entities to our WCF service data access layer.

In this chapter we will cover:

- What is LINQ?
- Datatype `var`
- Automatic properties
- Object initializer and collection initializer
- Anonymous types
- Extension methods
- Lambda expressions
- Built-in LINQ extension methods and method syntax
- LINQ query syntax and query expression
- Built-in LINQ operators

What is LINQ?

Language Integrated Query (LINQ) is a set of extensions to the .NET Framework that encompass language-integrated query, set, and transform operations. It extends C# and Visual Basic with native language syntax for queries from object, XML, and databases, and provides class libraries to take advantage of these capabilities.

Let us see an example first. Suppose there is a list of integers as follows:

```
var list = new List<int>() { 1, 2, 3, 4, 5, 6, 100 };
```

To find all the even numbers in this list, you might write some code as follows:

```
var list1 = new List<int>();
foreach (var num in list)
{
    if (num % 2 == 0)
        list1.Add(num);
}
```

Now with LINQ, you can select all of the even numbers from this list and assign the query result to a variable in just one-sentence expression like this:

```
var list2 = from number in list
            where number % 2 == 0
            select number;
```

In this example, `list2` and `list1` are equivalent. `list2` contains the same numbers as `list1` does. As you can see, you don't write a `foreach` loop. Instead, you write a SQL statement.

But what do `from`, `where`, and `select` mean here? Where are they defined? How and when can they be used? Let us start the exploration now.

Creating the test solution and project

To show these LINQ-related features, we will need a test project to demonstrate what they are and how to use them. Therefore, we first need to create the test solution and the project.

Follow these steps to create the solution and the project:

1. Start Visual Studio.
2. Select menu options **File | New | Project...** to create a new solution.

3. In the **New Project** window, select **Visual C# | Console Application** as the **Template**.

4. Enter `TestLINQ` as the **Solution Name** and `TestLINQFeaturesApp` as the (project) **Name**.

5. Click on **OK** to create the solution and the project.

Datatype var

The first feature that is very important for LINQ is the datatype `var`. This is a keyword of C# 3.0 that can be used to declare a variable and this variable can be initialized to any valid C# datatype. It is basically an un-typed object or an object without type until it is initialized.

In the C# 3.0 specification, such variables are called implicitly-typed local variables.

A `var` variable must be initialized when it is declared. The compile-time type of the `initializer` expression must not be of the `null` type, but the runtime expression can be `null`. Once it is initialized, its datatype is fixed to the type of the initial data.

The following statements are valid uses of the `var` keyword:

```
// valid var statements
var x = "1";
var n = 0;
string s = "string";
var s2 = s;
s2 = null;
string s3 = null;
var s4 = s3;
```

At compile time, the above `var` statements are compiled to **Intermediate Language (IL)**, as follows:

```
string x = "1";
int n = 0;
string s2 = s;
string s4 = s3;
```

The `var` keyword is only meaningful to the Visual Studio compiler. The compiled assembly is actually a valid .NET assembly. It doesn't need any special instructions or libraries to support this feature.

The following statements are invalid usages of the var keyword:

```
// invalid var statements
var v;
var nu = null;
var v2 = "12"; v2 = 3;
```

The first example is illegal because it does not have an initializer.

The second example initializes variable nu to null, which is not allowed, although once defined, a var type variable can be assigned null. If you think that at compile time the compiler needs to create a variable using this type of initializer, you have understood why the initializer cannot be null at compile time.

The third example is illegal because, once defined, an integer cannot be converted to a string implicitly (v2 is of type string).

Automatic properties

In the past, if we wanted to define a class member as a property member, we had to define a private member variable first. For example, for the Product class, we can define a property called productName as follows:

```
private string productName;
public string ProductName
{
    get { return productName; }
    set { productName = value; }
}
```

This may be useful if we need to add some logic inside the get or set methods. However, if we don't need to, the above format gets tedious, especially if there are many members.

Now, with C# 3.0 and above, the previous property can be simplified into one statement:

```
public string ProductName { get; set; }
```

For this property, the accessors' scope of the inner get; and set; methods can also be overridden, as shown in the following example:

```
public string ProductName
{
    get;
    private set;
}
```

When Visual Studio compiles this statement, it will automatically create a private member variable and use the old style's `get` or `set` methods to define the property. This could save lots of typing.

Just as with the type `var`, the automatic properties are only meaningful to the Visual Studio compiler. The compiled assembly is actually a valid .NET assembly.

Interestingly, later on, if you find you need to add logic to the `get` or `set` methods, you can still convert this automatic property to the old style's property.

Now let us create this class in the test project:

```
public class Product
{
    public int ProductID { get; set; }
    public string ProductName { get; set; }
    public decimal UnitPrice { get; set; }
}
```

We can put this class inside the `Program.cs` file within the namespace `TestLINQFeaturesApp`. We will use this class throughout this chapter to test the C# features related to LINQ.

Object initializer

In the past, we could not initialize an object without using a constructor. For example, we could create and initialize a `Product` object as follows, if the `Product` class had a constructor with three parameters:

```
Product p = new product(1, "first candy", 100.0m);
```

Or we could create the object and then initialize it later, as follows:

```
Product p = new Product();
p.ProductID = 1;
p.ProductName = "first candy";
p.UnitPrice=100.0m;
```

Now with the **object initializer** feature, we can do it as follows:

```
var product = new Product
{
    ProductID = 1,
    ProductName = "first candy",
    UnitPrice = 100.0m
};
```

At compile time, the compiler will automatically insert the necessary property setter code. So again, this feature is a Visual Studio compiler feature. The compiled assembly is actually a valid .NET assembly.

We can also define and initialize a variable with an array, as follows:

```
var arr = new[] { 1, 10, 20, 30 };
```

This array is called an **implicitly typed array**.

Collection initializer

Similar to the object initializer, we can also initialize a collection when we declare it, as follows:

```
var products = new List<Product> {
    new Product {
        ProductID = 1,
        ProductName = "first candy",
        UnitPrice = (decimal)10.0m },
    new Product {
        ProductID = 2,
        ProductName = "second candy",
        UnitPrice = (decimal)35.0m },
    new Product {
        ProductID = 3,
        ProductName = "first vegetable",
        UnitPrice = (decimal)6.0m },
    new Product {
        ProductID = 4,
        ProductName = "second vegetable",
        UnitPrice = (decimal)15.0m },
    new Product {
        ProductID = 5,
        ProductName = "another product",
        UnitPrice = (decimal)55.0m }
};
```

Here we created a list and initialized it with five new products. For each new product, we used the object initializer to initialize its value.

Just as with the object initializer, this feature called the collection initializer, is also a Visual Studio compiler feature and the compiled assembly is a valid .NET assembly.

Anonymous types

With the feature of the object initializer and the `var` datatype, we can create anonymous datatypes easily in C#.

For example, we can define a variable as follows:

```
var a = new { Name = "name1", Address = "address1" };
```

At compile time, the compiler will actually create an anonymous type, as follows:

```
class __Anonymous1
{
    private string name;
    private string address;
    public string Name {
        get{
            return name;
        }
        set {
            name=value
        }
    }
    public string Address {
        get{
            return address;
        }
        set{
            address=value;
        }
    }
}
```

The name of the anonymous type is automatically generated by the compiler and cannot be referenced in the program text.

If two variables that are defined by anonymous types have the same members with the same datatypes in their initializers, these two variables have the same anonymous types. For example, if there is another variable defined as follows:

```
var b = new { Name = "name2", Address = "address2" };
```

Then we can assign a to b as in the following example:

```
b = a;
```

The anonymous type is particularly useful for LINQ when the result of LINQ can be shaped to be whatever you like. We will give more examples of this when we discuss LINQ.

As mentioned earlier, this feature is again a Visual Studio compiler feature and the compiled assembly is a valid .NET assembly.

Extension methods

Extension methods are static methods that can be invoked using the instance method syntax. In effect, extension methods make it possible for us to extend existing types and constructed types with additional methods.

For example, we can define an extension method as follows:

```
public static class MyExtensions
{
    public static bool IsCandy(this Product p)
    {
        if (p.ProductName.IndexOf("candy") >= 0)
            return true;
        else
            return false;
    }
}
```

In this example, the static method IsCandy takes a this parameter of the Product type and searches for the string candy inside the product name. If it finds a match, it assumes this is a candy product and returns true. Otherwise, it returns false, meaning this is not a candy product.

Because all extension methods must be defined in top-level static classes, here to simplify the example, we put this class inside the same namespace as our main test application TestLINQFeaturesApp, and defined this class on the same level as the Program class so that it is a top-level class. Now, in the program, we can call this extension method as follows:

```
if (product.IsCandy())
    Console.WriteLine("yes, it is a candy");
else
    Console.WriteLine("no, it is not a candy");
```

It looks as if `IsCandy` is a real instance method of the `Product` class. Actually, it is a real method of the `Product` class, but it is not defined inside the `Product` class. Instead, it is defined in another static class to extend the functionality of the `Product` class. This is why it is called an extension method.

Not only does it look like a real instance method, but this new extension method actually pops up when a dot is typed by using IntelliSense on the `product` variable. The following screenshot shows the possible options when using IntelliSense on the product variable within Visual Studio:

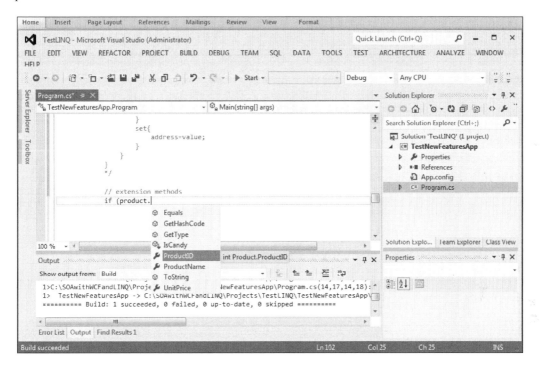

Under the hood in Visual Studio, when a method call on an instance is being compiled, the compiler first checks to see if there is an instance method in the class for this method. If there is no matching instance method, it looks for an imported static class or any static class within the same namespace. It also searches for an extension method with the first parameter that is the same as the instance type (or is a super type of the instance type). If it finds a match, the compiler will call that extension method. This means that instance methods take precedence over extension methods, and extension methods that are imported in inner namespace declarations take precedence over extension methods that are imported in outer namespaces.

In our example, when `product.IsCandy()` is being compiled, the compiler first checks the `Product` class and doesn't find a method named `IsCandy`. It then searches the static class `MyExtensions` and finds an extension method with the name `IsCandy`, and due to that it has a first parameter of the type `Product`.

At compile time, the compiler actually changes the `product.IsCandy()` call to this call:

```
MyExtensions.IsCandy(product)
```

Surprisingly, extension methods can be defined for sealed classes. As we all know a sealed class, by definition, is a class that cannot be modified in any way, for example, being inherited or overridden. However with extension methods, we can add as much functionality to a sealed class as we like. This gives us an opportunity to improve a class that we don't have ownership of. In our example, you can change the `Product` class to be sealed and it still runs without any problem. This gives us great flexibility to extend system types because many of the system types are sealed.

On the other hand, extension methods are less discoverable and are harder to maintain, so they should be used with great caution. If your requirements can be achieved with an instance method, you should not define an extension method to do the same work.

Not surprisingly, this feature is again a Visual Studio compiler feature and the compiled assembly is a valid .NET assembly.

Extension methods are the basis of LINQ. We will discuss the various LINQ extension methods defined by .NET Framework in the `System.Linq` namespace later (the actual LINQ extension methods are defined in the `System.Core` assembly, which is added to every project by default).

Now the `Program.cs` file should be as follows:

```
using System;
using System.Collections.Generic;
using System.Linq;
using System.Text;

namespace TestLINQFeaturesApp
{
    class Program
    {
        static void Main(string[] args)
        {
            // valid var statements
```

```
var x = "1";
var n = 0;
string s = "string";
var s2 = s;
s2 = null;
string s3 = null;
var s4 = s3;
/*
string x = "1";
int n = 0;
string s2 = s;
string s4 = s3;
*/

// invalid var statements
/*
var v;
var nu = null;
var v2 = "12"; v2 = 3;
*/

// old way to create and initialize an object
/*
Product p = new product(1, "first candy", 100.0m);
Product p = new Product();
p.ProductID = 1;
p.ProductName = "first candy";
p.UnitPrice=100.0m;
*/
//object initializer

var product = new Product
{
    ProductID = 1,
    ProductName = "first candy",
    UnitPrice = (decimal)100.0m
};
var arr = new[] { 1, 10, 20, 30 };

// collection initializer
var products = new List<Product> {
    new Product {
```

```
        ProductID = 1,
        ProductName = "first candy",
        UnitPrice = (decimal)10.0m },
    new Product {
        ProductID = 2,
        ProductName = "second candy",
        UnitPrice = (decimal)35.0m },
    new Product {
        ProductID = 3,
        ProductName = "first vegetable",
        UnitPrice = (decimal)6.0m },
    new Product {
        ProductID = 4,
        ProductName = "second vegetable",
        UnitPrice = (decimal)15.0m },
    new Product {
        ProductID = 5,
        ProductName = "third product",
        UnitPrice = (decimal)55.0m }
};
// anonymous types
var a = new { Name = "name1", Address = "address1" };
var b = new { Name = "name2", Address = "address2" };
b = a;
/*
class __Anonymous1
{
    private string name;
    private string address;
    public string Name {
        get{
            return name;
        }
        set {
            name=value
        }
    }
    public string Address {
        get{
            return address;
        }
        set{
```

```
                address=value;
            }
        }
    }
    */

    // extension methods
    //if(MyExtensions.IsCandy(product))
    if (product.IsCandy())
        Console.WriteLine("yes, it is a candy");
    else
        Console.WriteLine("no, it is not a candy");
    }
}


public sealed class Product
{
    public int ProductID { get; set; }
    public string ProductName { get; set; }
    public decimal UnitPrice { get; set; }
}

public static class MyExtensions
{
    public static bool IsCandy(this Product p)
    {
        if (p.ProductName.IndexOf("candy") >= 0)
            return true;
        else
            return false;
    }
}
}
```

So far in `Program.cs`, we have carried out the following:

- Defined several `var` type variables
- Defined a sealed class called `Product`
- Created a product with the name of "first candy"
- Created a product list containing five products

- Defined a static class and added a static method called IsCandy with a this parameter of the Product type to it, making this method an extension method

- Called the extension method on the candy product and printed out a message according to its name

If you run the program, the output will look like the one shown in the following screenshot:

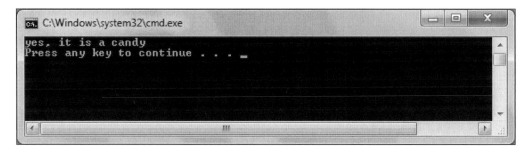

Lambda expressions

With extension methods and anonymous methods (or inline methods), Visual Studio introduces an expression called the lambda expression.

A **lambda expression** is actually a syntax change for anonymous methods. It is just another way of writing anonymous methods.

Now, let's learn what a lambda expression is, step by step.

First we need to understand what a delegate is. A delegate is a type that references a method, which means you can define a delegate and then assign a method to it. Once a delegate is assigned a method, it behaves exactly like that method. The delegate method can be used like any other method, with parameters and a return value.

In C# there is a generic delegate type, Func<A,R>, which represents a function taking an argument of type A and returning a value of type R:

```
delegate R Func<A,R> (A Arg);
```

In fact there are several overloaded versions of Func, of which Func<A,R> is one.

Now we will use this generic delegate type to define an extension method in our extension class MyExtensions:

```
public static IEnumerable<T> Get<T>(this IEnumerable<T> source,
Func<T, bool> predicate)
{
    foreach (T item in source)
    {
      if (predicate(item))
          yield return item;
    }
}
```

This extension method will apply to any object that extends the IEnumerable interface and has one parameter of type Func, which you can think of as a pointer to a function. This parameter function is the predicate to specify the criteria for the selection. This method will return a list of objects that match the predicate criteria.

 Make sure you define this method within the extension class MyExtensions, not within the main class Program.

Now we can create a new function as the predicate in our main class, just after the Main method:

```
public static bool IsVege(Product p)
{
    return p.ProductName.Contains("vegetable");
}
```

Then we can use the extension method Get, to retrieve all of the vegetable products, as follows:

```
var veges1 = products.Get(IsVege);
```

In previous sections, we created a products list with five products, of which two are vegetables. So veges1 is actually of the IEnumerable<Product> type and should contain two products. We can write the following test statements to print out the results:

```
Console.WriteLine("\nThere are {0} vegetables:", veges1.Count());
foreach (var p in veges1)
{
    Console.WriteLine("Product ID: {0}  Product name: {1}",
                      p.ProductID, p.ProductName);
}
```

The output will be as follows:

Or we can first create a new variable of type `Func`, assign the function pointer of `IsVege` to this new variable, and then pass this new variable to the `Get` method as shown in the following code snippet:

```
Func<Product, bool> predicate = IsVege;
var veges2 = products.Get(predicate);
```

The `veges2` variable will contain the same products as `veges1`.

Now let us use the `Contains` anonymous method to rewrite the above statement, which will now become the following:

```
var veges3 = products.Get(
    delegate (Product p)
    {
        return p.ProductName.Contains("vegetable");
    }
);
```

At this time, we put the body of the predicate method `IsVege` inside the extension method call with the keyword `delegate`. In order to get the vegetables from the products list, we don't have to define a specific predicate method. We can specify the criteria on the spot when we need it.

The lambda expression comes into play right after the preceding step. In C# 3.0 and above, using a lambda expression, we can actually write the following one-line statement to retrieve all of the vegetables from the `products` list:

```
var veges4 = products.Get(p => p.ProductName.Contains("vegetable"));
```

In the preceding statement, the parameter of the Get method is a lambda expression. The first p is the parameter of the lambda expression, just like the parameter p in the anonymous method when we get veges3. This parameter is implicitly typed and in this case it is of the type Product, because this expression is applied to a Products object, which contains a list of the Product objects. This parameter can also be explicitly typed as follows:

```
var veges5 = products.Get((Product p) => p.ProductName.
Contains("vegetable"));
```

The parameter is followed by the => token and then followed by an expression or a statement block, which will be the predicate.

The => token here is called the lambda operator. It is used in lambda expressions to separate the input variables on the left side from the lambda body on the right side. This operator is read as "goes to".

So now, we can easily write the following statement to get all of the candy products:

```
var candies = products.Get(p => p.ProductName.Contains("candy"));
```

At compile time, all lambda expressions are translated into anonymous methods according to the lambda expression conversion rules. So again, this feature is only a Visual Studio compiler feature. We don't need any special .NET runtime libraries or instructions to run an assembly containing lambda expressions.

In short, lambda expressions are just another way of writing anonymous methods in a more concise, functional syntax.

Built-in LINQ extension methods and method syntax

The .NET Framework defines lots of extension methods in the System.Linq namespace, including Where, Select, SelectMany, OrderBy, OrderByDescending, ThenBy, ThenByDescending, GroupBy, Join, and GroupJoin. But remember the assembly that the namespace exists in is System.Core.

We can use these extension methods just as we would use our own extension methods. For example, we can use the Where extension method to get all vegetables from the Products list, as follows:

```
var veges6 = products.Where(p => p.ProductName.Contains("vegetable"));
```

This will give us the same result as `veges1` through `veges5`.

As a matter of fact, the definition of the built-in LINQ extension method `Where` is just like our extension method `Get`, but in a different namespace:

```
namespace System.Linq
{
    public static class Enumerable
    {
        public static IEnumerable<T> Where<T>(this IEnumerable<T>
                            source, Func<T, bool> predicate)
        {
            foreach (T item in source)
            {
                if (predicate(item))
                    yield return item;
            }
        }
    }
}
```

The statements that use LINQ extension methods are called by using the LINQ method syntax.

Unlike the other C# features that we have talked about in previous sections, these LINQ-specific extension methods are defined in .NET Framework. Therefore, to run an assembly containing any of these LINQ extension methods, you need to have .NET Framework 3.5 or above installed.

LINQ query syntax and query expression

With built-in LINQ extension methods and lambda expressions, Visual Studio allows us to write SQL-like statements in C# when invoking these methods. The syntax of these statements is called **LINQ query syntax** and the expression in query syntax is called a **query expression**.

For example, we can change the following statement:

```
var veges6 = products.Where(p => p.ProductName.Contains("vegetable"));
```

To the following query statement by using the LINQ query syntax:

```
var veges7 = from p in products
            where p.ProductName.Contains("vegetable")
            select p;
```

In the above C# statement, we can directly use the SQL keywords `select`, `from`, and `where` to "query" an in-memory collection list. In addition to the in-memory collection lists, we can use the same syntax to manipulate data in XML files, in the dataset, and in the database. In the following chapters, we will see how to query a database, using LINQ to Entities.

Combined with the anonymous datatype, we can shape the result of the query in the following statement:

```
var candyOrVeges = from p in products
                   where p.ProductName.Contains("candy")
                       || p.ProductName.Contains("vegetable")
                   orderby p.UnitPrice descending, p.ProductID
                   select new { p.ProductName, p.UnitPrice };
```

As you have seen, the query syntax is a very convenient, declarative shorthand for expressing queries using the standard LINQ query operators. It offers a syntax that increases the readability and clarity of expressing queries in code and is easy to read and write correctly.

Not only is query syntax easy to read and write, Visual Studio actually provides complete IntelliSense and compile-time checking support for the query syntax. For example, when typing in `p` and the following dot, we get all of the `Product` members listed in the IntelliSense list, as shown in the following screenshot:

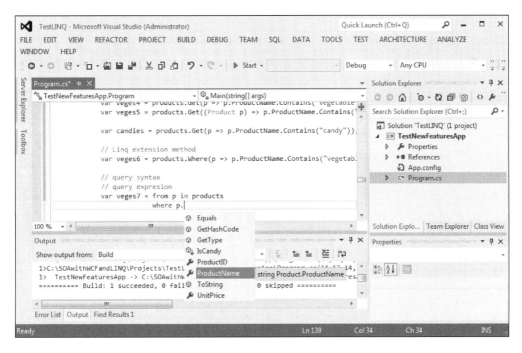

If there is a typing mistake in the syntax (as is the case in the `where p.productName.Contains("vegetable")` statement), the compiler will tell you exactly where the mistake is and why it is wrong. There won't be any runtime error such as `invalid SQL statement`. The following screenshot shows the error message when there is a typing mistake in the statement:

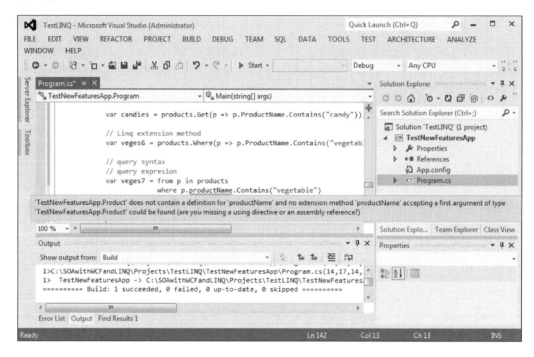

As you can see, you can write a LINQ statement in the query syntax, much like when you are working with a database in Query Analyzer. However, the .NET **Common Language Runtime (CLR)** has no notion itself of the query syntax. Therefore, at compile time, query expressions are translated to something that the CLR does understand—method calls. Under the cover, the compiler takes the query syntax expressions and translates them into explicit method-invocation code that utilizes the LINQ extension method and lambda expression language features in C#.

For example, the `candyOrVeges` query expression will be translated to the following method invocation call:

```
var candyOrVeges2 = products.Where(p => p.ProductName.
Contains("candy") || p.ProductName.Contains("vegetable")).
OrderByDescending(p => p.UnitPrice).ThenBy(p=>p.ProductID).
Select(p=>new { p.ProductName, p.UnitPrice });
```

You can print out and compare the results of using query syntax and method syntax to make sure they are equivalent. The following statements will print out the product name and unit price for the products in the query result, using query syntax:

```
foreach (var p in candyOrVeges)
{
    Console.WriteLine("{0} {1}", p.ProductName, p.UnitPrice);
}
```

Do the same for the results using method syntax and you will get a printout as shown in the following screenshot:

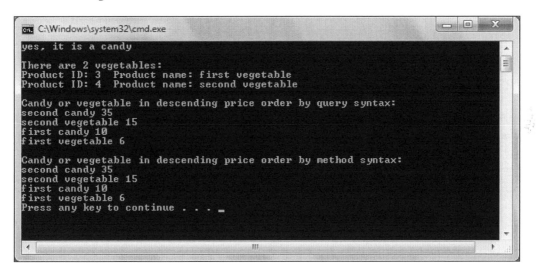

In general, query syntax is recommended over method syntax because it is usually simpler and more readable. However, there is no semantic difference between method syntax and query syntax.

Built-in LINQ operators

As we have seen in previous sections, there are no semantic differences between method syntax and query syntax. In addition, some queries such as those that retrieve the number of elements matching a specified condition or those that retrieve the element that has the maximum value in a source sequence can be expressed only as method calls. These kinds of methods are sometimes referred to as .NET standard query operators and include the following:

- Take
- ToList

- FirstOrDefault

- Max

- Min

In addition to those methods that can only be expressed as method calls, all the extension methods that can be used in either query syntax or method syntax are also defined as standard query operators such as select, where, and from. Therefore, the .NET standard query operators contain all of the LINQ-related methods.

A complete list of these operators can be found in the Microsoft MSDN library for the System.Linq.Enumerable class (http://msdn.microsoft.com/en-us/library/ system.linq.enumerable(v=vs.110).aspx).

To have a quick look at all those operators, open the program.cs file in Visual Studio and type in System.Linq.Enumerable. Then type in a dot after Enumerable. You will see the whole list of operators in the IntelliSense menu.

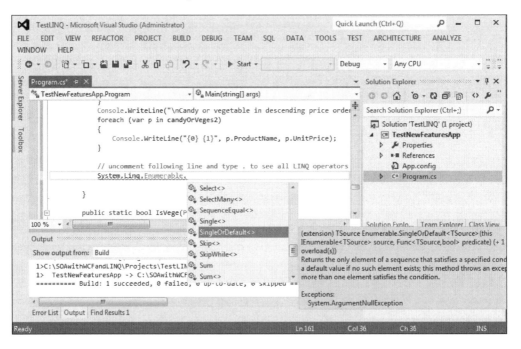

The methods in this static class provide an implementation of the standard query operators for querying data sources that implement IEnumerable<(Of <(T>)>). The standard query operators are general-purpose methods that follow the LINQ pattern and enable you to express traversal, filter, and projection operations over data in any .NET-based programming language.

The majority of the methods in this class are defined as extension methods that extend `IEnumerable<(Of <(T>)>)`. This means that they can be called like an instance method on any object that implements `IEnumerable<(Of <(T>)>)`.

Summary

In this chapter, we learned features related to LINQ including the new datatype `var`, object and collection initializers, extension methods, lambda expressions, LINQ syntax, and query expressions. Now that we have the required knowledge for LINQ, we are ready to try LINQ to Entities, which will be discussed in the next chapters.

7

LINQ to Entities: Basic Concepts and Features

In the previous chapter, we learned a few features related to LINQ. In the next two chapters, we will learn how to use LINQ to query a database, or in other words, how to use LINQ to Entities in C#. After reading these two chapters, we will have a good understanding of LINQ to Entities so that we can rewrite the data access layer of our WCF Service with LINQ to Entities, to securely and reliably communicate with the underlying database.

In this chapter, we will cover the basic concepts and features of LINQ to Entities:

- What is an ORM?
- What is LINQ to Entities?
- What is LINQ to SQL?
- Comparing LINQ to Entities with LINQ to Objects and LINQ to SQL
- Modeling the `Northwind` database with LINQ to Entities
- Querying and updating a database table
- Deferred execution
- Lazy loading and eager loading
- Joining two tables
- Querying with a view

In the next chapter, we will cover the advanced concepts and features of LINQ to Entities such as stored procedure support, inheritance, simultaneous updating, and transaction processing.

ORM: Object-Relational Mapping

LINQ to Entities is considered to be Microsoft's preferred ORM product. So before we start learning LINQ to Entities, let's first understand what an ORM is.

ORM stands for **Object-Relational Mapping**. Sometimes it is called O/RM or O/R mapping. It is a programming technique that contains a set of classes that map relational database entities to objects in a specific programming language.

Initially, applications could call specified, native database APIs to communicate with a database. For example, `Oracle Pro*C` is a set of APIs supplied by Oracle to query, insert, update, or delete records in an Oracle database from the C applications. The `Pro*C` pre-compiler translates embedded SQL into calls to the Oracle runtime library (`SQLLIB`).

Then **ODBC (Open Database Connectivity)** was developed to unify all of the communication protocols for various **relational database management systems (RDBMS)**. ODBC was designed to be independent of programming languages, database systems, and operating systems. So with ODBC, one application can communicate with different RDBMS by using the same code simply by replacing the underlying ODBC drivers.

No matter which method is used to connect to a database, the data returned from a database has to be presented in some format in the application. For example, if an `Order` record is returned from the database, there has to be a variable to hold the `Order` number and a set of variables to hold the `Order` details. Alternatively, the application may create a class for `Orders` and another class for `Order` details. When another application is developed, the same set of classes may have to be created again, or, if it is designed well, they can be put into a library and re-used by various applications.

This is exactly where an ORM fits in. With an ORM, each database is represented by an ORM context object in the specific programming language and database entities such as tables are represented by classes with relationships between these classes. For example, an ORM may create an `Order` class to represent the `Order` table and an `OrderDetail` class to represent the `Order Details` table. The `Order` class will contain a collection member to hold all of its details. The ORM is responsible for the mappings and the connections between these classes and the database. So to the application, the database is now fully represented by these classes. The application only needs to deal with these classes, instead of with the physical database. The application does not need to worry about how to connect to the database, how to construct the SQL statements, how to use the proper locking mechanism to ensure concurrency, or how to handle distributed transactions. These database-related activities are handled by the ORM.

Entity Framework

As LINQ to Entities is part of the Entity Framework, let's now learn what that is.

ADO.NET **Entity Framework (EF)** is an addition to the Microsoft ADO.NET family. It enables developers to create data access applications by programming against a conceptual application model instead of programming directly against a relational storage schema. The goal is to decrease the amount of code and maintenance required for the data-oriented applications. The Entity Framework applications provide the following benefits:

- Applications can work in terms of a more application-centric conceptual model including types with inheritance, complex members, and relationships
- Applications are freed from hardcoded dependencies on a particular data engine or storage schema
- Mappings between the conceptual model and the storage-specific schema can change without changing the application code
- Developers can work with a consistent application object model that can be mapped to various storage schemas, possibly implemented in different database management systems
- Multiple conceptual models can be mapped to a single storage schema
- The **Language Integrated Query (LINQ)** support provides compile-time syntax validation for queries against a conceptual model

With Entity Framework, developers work with a conceptual data model, an **Entity Data Model (EDM)**, instead of the underlying databases. The conceptual data model schema is expressed in the **Conceptual Schema Definition Language (CSDL)**, the actual storage model is expressed in the **Storage Schema Definition Language (SSDL)**, and the mapping in between is expressed in the **Mapping Schema Language (MSL)**. A new data-access provider, `EntityClient`, is created for this new framework, but under the hood, the ADO.NET data providers are still being used for communicating with the databases.

The following diagram shows the high-level architectures of Entity Framework:

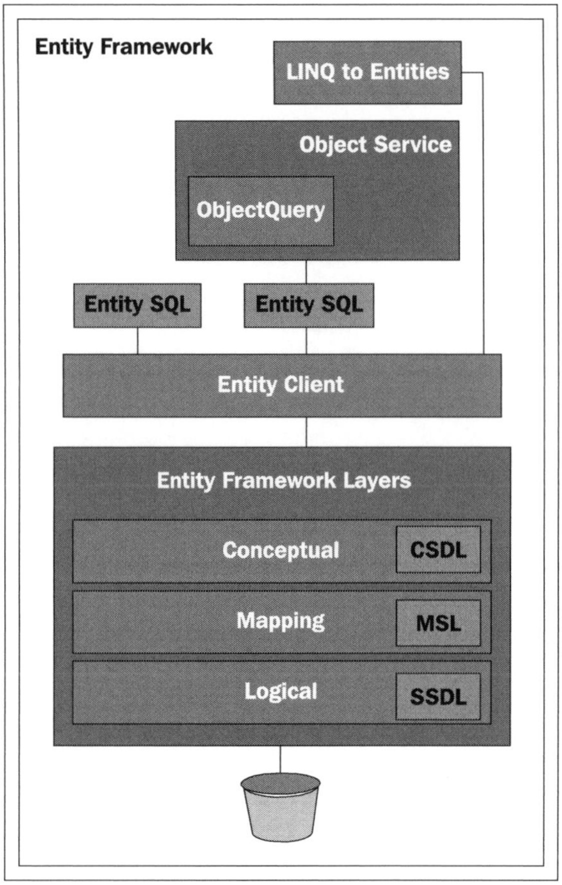

LINQ to Entities

Now let's have a look at what LINQ to Entities is.

LINQ to Entities provides the LINQ support that enables developers to write queries against an Entity Framework conceptual model using Visual Basic or Visual C#. Queries against the Entity Framework are represented by command-tree queries, which execute against the object context. LINQ to Entities converts the LINQ queries to the command-tree queries, executes the queries against Entity Framework, and returns objects that can be used by both Entity Framework and LINQ.

LINQ to Entities allows developers to create flexible, strongly-typed queries against the EDM by using the LINQ expressions and standard LINQ query operators. To a certain degree, LINQ to Entities is similar to LINQ to SQL, but LINQ to Entities is a true ORM product from Microsoft and it supports more features than LINQ to SQL, such as multiple-table inheritance. LINQ to Entities also supports many other mainstream RDBMS databases such as Oracle, DB2, and MySQL, in addition to Microsoft SQL Server.

Comparing LINQ to Entities with LINQ to Objects

In the previous chapter, we used LINQ to query in-memory objects. Before we dive further into the world of LINQ to Entities, we first need to look at the relationships between LINQ to Entities and LINQ to Objects.

Some key differences between LINQ to Entities and LINQ to Objects are as follows:

- LINQ to Entities needs an Object Context/Db Context object. The `ObjectContext/DbContext` object is the bridge between LINQ and the database (we will learn more about `ObjectContext/DbContext` later). LINQ to Objects doesn't need any intermediate LINQ provider or API.

- LINQ to Entities returns data of type `IQueryable<T>`, whereas LINQ to Objects returns data of type `IEnumerable<T>`.

- LINQ to Entities queries are translated to SQL using Expression Trees, which allow them to be evaluated as a single unit and translated to appropriate and optimal SQL Statements. LINQ to Objects queries do not need to be translated.

- LINQ to Entities queries are translated to SQL calls and executed on the specified database, while LINQ to Objects queries are executed in the local machine memory.

The similarities shared by all aspects of LINQ are the syntax. They all use the same SQL-like syntax and share the same groups of standard query operators. From the language syntax perspective, working with a database is the same as working with in-memory objects.

LINQ to SQL

Before LINQ to Entities, Microsoft released another ORM product, LINQ to SQL. Both LINQ to SQL and LINQ to Entities can be used in the data access layer to interact with databases, but they are quite different. In this section, we will learn what LINQ to SQL is, and in the next section we will compare these two technologies.

In short, LINQ to SQL is a component of the .NET framework that provides a runtime infrastructure for managing relational data as objects.

In LINQ to SQL, the data model of a relational database is mapped to an object model expressed in the programming language of the developer. When the application runs, LINQ to SQL translates the language-integrated queries in the object model into SQL and sends them to the database for execution. When the database returns the results, LINQ to SQL translates the results back to objects that you can work with in your own programming language.

Unlike LINQ to Entities, with LINQ to SQL developers don't need to create an extra data model between their applications and the underlying database. Under the hood of LINQ to SQL, the ADO.NET `SqlClient` adapters are used to communicate with the actual SQL Server databases.

The following diagram shows the use of LINQ to SQL in a .NET application:

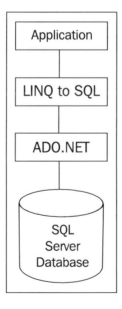

Comparing LINQ to SQL with LINQ to Entities

Now we know what LINQ to Entities is and what LINQ to SQL is. Next in this section, let's compare these two technologies.

As described earlier, LINQ to Entities applications work against a conceptual data model (EDM). All mappings between the languages and the databases go through the new `EntityClient` mapping provider. The application no longer connects directly to a database or sees any database-specific constructs. The entire application operates in terms of the higher level EDM.

This means that you can no longer use the native database query language. Not only will the database not understand the EDM model, but also current database query languages do not have the constructs required to deal with the elements introduced by EDM such as inheritance, relationships, complex types, and so on.

On the other hand, for developers who do not require mapping to a conceptual model, LINQ to SQL enables developers to experience the LINQ programming model directly over the existing database schema.

LINQ to SQL allows developers to generate the .NET classes that represent data. Rather than mapping to a conceptual data model, these generated classes are mapped directly to database tables, views, stored procedures, and user-defined functions. Using LINQ to SQL, developers can write code directly against the storage schema, using the same LINQ programming pattern as was previously described for in-memory collections, entities, or the dataset, as well as for other data sources such as XML.

Compared to LINQ to Entities, LINQ to SQL has some limitations, mainly because of its direct mapping against the physical relational storage schema. For example, you cannot map two different database entities into one single C# or VB object and if the underlying database schema changes, this might require significant client application changes.

To summarize, if you want to work against a conceptual data model, use LINQ to Entities. If you want to have a direct mapping to the database from your programming languages, use LINQ to SQL.

The following table lists some of the features supported by these two data access methodologies:

Features	LINQ to SQL	LINQ to Entities
Conceptual data model	No	Yes
Storage schema	No	Yes
Mapping schema	No	Yes
New data access provider	No	Yes
Non-SQL Server database support	No	Yes
Direct database connection	Yes	No
Language extensions support	Yes	Yes
Stored procedures	Yes	Yes
Single-table inheritance	Yes	Yes
Multiple-table inheritance	No	Yes
Single entity from multiple tables	No	Yes
Lazy loading support	Yes	Yes

 Interestingly, some people say LINQ to SQL was an intermediate solution. The fact is that LINQ to SQL was created by the C# team instead of the ADO.NET team. It was of great importance for the C# team to release an O/RM mapper together with their new LINQ technology. Without a LINQ to databases implementation, the C# team would have had a hard time evangelizing LINQ.

Creating a LINQ to Entities test application

Now that we have learned some of the basic concepts of LINQ to Entities, let's start exploring LINQ to Entities with some real examples. We will apply the skills we are going to learn in the following two chapters, to the data access layer of our WCF service, so that from the WCF service we can communicate with the database, using LINQ to Entities instead of the raw ADO.NET data adapter.

First, we need to create a new project to test LINQ to Entities. Just follow these steps to add this test application to the solution:

1. Open the `TestLINQ` solution.

2. From **Solution Explorer**, right-click on the **Solution** item and select **Add | New Project...** from the context menu.

3. Select **Visual C# | Console Application** as the project template, enter `TestLINQToEntitiesApp` as the (project) **Name**, and leave the default value `C:\SOAWithWCFandLINQ\Projects\TestLINQ` as the **Location**.

4. Click on the **OK** button to create the project.

Creating the data model

To use LINQ to Entities, we need to add a conceptual data model — EDM — to the project. There are two ways to create the EDM — create from a database or create manually. Here we will create the EDM from the `Northwind` database. We will add two tables and one view from the `Northwind` database into our project so that later on we can use them to demonstrate LINQ to Entities.

Adding a LINQ to Entities item to the project

To start with, let's add a new item to our test project `TestLINQToEntitiesApp`. The new item added should be the ADO.NET Entity Data Model type and named `Northwind.edmx`, as shown in the following **Add New Item** dialog window:

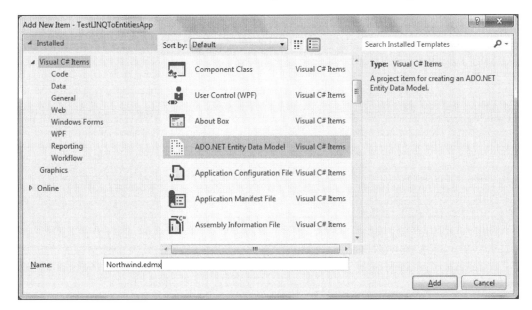

After you click on the **Add** button, the **Entity Data Model Wizard** window will pop up. Follow these steps to finish this wizard:

1. On the **Choose Model Contents** page, select **Generate from database**. Later we will connect to the Northwind database and let Visual Studio generate the conceptual data model for us. If you choose the **Empty model** option here, you will have to manually create the data model, which may be applicable in certain circumstances such as when you do not have a physical database while you do the modeling. You can even create your physical database from your model later if you have chosen this option and have finished your model.

2. Click on the **Next** button in this window.

3. Now the **Choose Your Data Connection** window should be displayed. As this is our first LINQ to Entities application, there is no existing data connection to choose from, so let's click on the **New Connection...** button and set up a new data connection.

a. The **Connection Properties** window should be displayed on the screen. First, make sure the **Data source** is **Microsoft SQL Server** (SqlClient). If it is not, click on the **Change...** button to bring up the **Change Data Source** window. On this window, you can choose Microsoft SQL Server as the data source and leave **.NET Framework Data Provider for SQL Server** as the data provider. Click on the **OK** button to close this window.

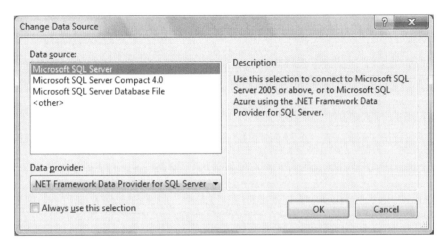

b. Now in the **Connection Properties** window, enter your database server name together with your database instance name if your database instance is not the default one on your server. If it is on your machine, you can enter localhost as the server name.

c. Then, specify the login details to your database.

d. Click on the **Test Connection** button to test your database connection settings. You should get the **Test connection succeeded** message. If not, modify your server name or login details and make sure your SQL Server service is started. If your SQL Server is on another computer and your firewall is turned on, remember to verify/change your firewall settings to enable the SQL Server port on the SQL Server machine.

e. Now select **Northwind** as the database name. If you don't see **Northwind** in the database list, you need to mount/restore it to your SQL Server (refer to the previous chapter for installation details).

f.   Now, the **Connection Properties** window should be as shown in the following screenshot:

g.   Click on the **OK** button in the **Connection Properties** window to go back to the **Entity Data Model Wizard** window.

h. The **Entity Data Model Wizard** window should be as shown in the following screenshot:

i. Click on the **Next** button in this window to go to the next page.

4. On the **Choose Your Database Objects and Settings** page, select the tables **Products** and **Categories** and view **Current Product List**, and then click on the **Finish** button:

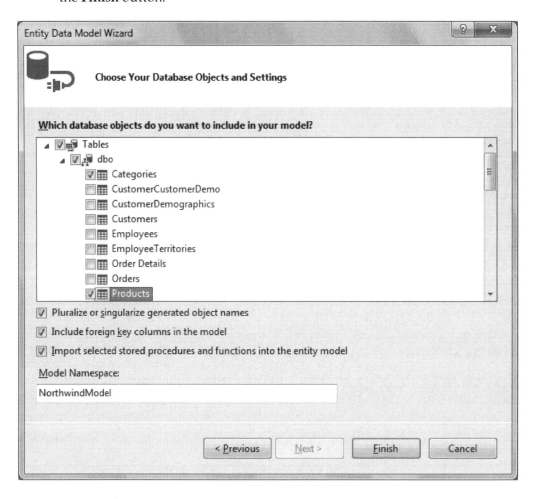

After you click on the **Finish** button, you will get a security warning dialog box. This is because Visual Studio will now run a custom template to generate the **POCO (Plain Old CLR/C# Object)** classes for your data model. Just click on **OK** to dismiss this dialog box (you can check the **Do not show this message again** checkbox to dismiss it forever).

At this point, the Visual Studio LINQ to Entities designer should be open, as shown in the following screenshot:

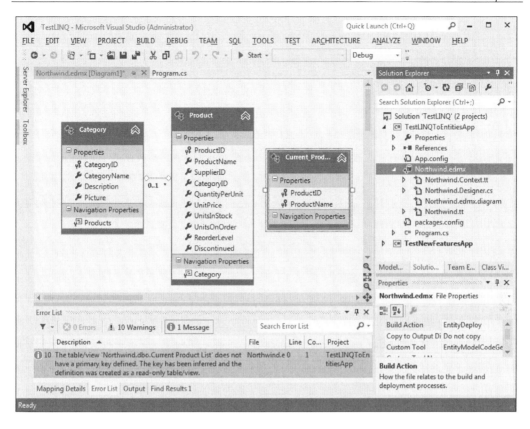

Generated LINQ to Entities classes

If you browse in **Solution Explorer**, you will find that the following classes have been generated for the project:

```
public partial class NorthwindEntities : DbContext
public partial class Product
public partial class Category
public partial class Current_Product_List
```

In the previous four classes, the `NorthwindEntities` class is the main conduit through which we'll query entities from the database as well as apply changes back to it. It contains three properties of type `DbSet<>`, one for each table/view that we will be working with. It inherits from the `DbContext` class, which represents the main entry point for the LINQ to Entities framework.

The next two classes are for the two tables that we are interested in. They are all POCO classes with a few properties. Note `Products` has a navigation property `Category` and `Category` has a collection property `Products`. We can use these properties to get the category of a product or the product list of a category.

The last class is for the view. This is a simple class with only two property members.

 These classes are generated through the T4 templating system and should not be manually altered in any way. If any of them is modified, the changes will be overwritten when the files are re-generated.

Besides these generated classes, a few references are added to the project for you. Among these references, `EntityFramework` and `System.Data.Entity` are particularly important, as they are required for us to use LINQ to Entities in the code. If any of these two references is not added for you automatically, you need to double-check your Visual Studio installation or add them manually.

Querying and updating a database table

Now that we have the entity classes created, we will use them to interact with the database. We will first work with the `products` table to query and update records as well as to insert and delete records.

Querying records

First we will query the database to get some products.

To query a database by using LINQ to Entities, we first need to construct a `DbContext` object, as follows:

```
NorthwindEntities NWEntities = new NorthwindEntities();
```

We can then use the LINQ query syntax to retrieve records from the database:

```
IEnumerable<Product> beverages = from p in NWEntities.Products
                where p.Category.CategoryName == "Beverages"
                orderby p.ProductName
                select p;
```

The preceding code will retrieve all of the products in the `Beverages` category sorted by product name.

You can use this statement to print out the total number of beverage products in the `Northwind` database:

```
Console.WriteLine("There are {0} Beverages", beverages.Count());
```

After we have finished working with this context object, we need to dispose of it as follows:

```
NWEntities.Dispose();
```

Alternatively, we can wrap all preceding code in a `using` statement, so the code will be as follows:

```
using (NorthwindEntities NWEntities = new NorthwindEntities())
{
    // retrieve all Beverages products
    IEnumerable<Product> beverages =
        from p in NWEntities.Products
        where p.Category.CategoryName == "Beverages"
        orderby p.ProductName
        select p;
    Console.WriteLine("There are {0} Beverages",
        beverages.Count());
}
```

Updating records

We can update any of the products that we have just retrieved from the database, as follows:

```
// update a product
Product bev1 = beverages.ElementAtOrDefault(10);
if (bev1 != null)
{
    decimal newPrice = (decimal)bev1.UnitPrice + 10.00m;
    Console.WriteLine("The price of {0} is {1}. Update to {2}",
                bev1.ProductName, bev1.UnitPrice, newPrice);
    bev1.UnitPrice = newPrice;
    // submit the change to database
    NWEntities.SaveChanges();
}
```

We used the `ElementAtOrDefault` method, not the `ElementAt` method, just in case there was no `Beverages` product at element 10 (`ElementAt` will throw an exception if the index is out of range while `ElementAtOrDefault` will return the default value of the list type, which is `null` in this example). We know that there are 12 beverage products in the sample database so we increased the eleventh product's price by 10.00 and called `NWEntities.SaveChanges()` to update the record in the database. After you run the program, if you query the database, you will find that the eleventh beverage's price is increased by 10.00.

Inserting records

We can also create a new product and then insert this new product into the database by using the following code:

```
// add a product
Product newProduct = new Product {ProductName="new test product" };
NWEntities.Products.Add(newProduct);
NWEntities.SaveChanges();
Console.WriteLine("Added a new product with name
                'new test product'");
```

Deleting records

To delete a product we first need to retrieve it from the database and then call the `Remove` method, as shown in the following code snippet:

```
// delete a product
IQueryable<Product> productsToDelete =
                    from p in NWEntities.Products
                    where p.ProductName == "new test product"
                    select p;
  if (productsToDelete.Count() > 0)
  {
      foreach (var p in productsToDelete)
      {
          NWEntities.Products.Remove(p);
          Console.WriteLine("Deleted product {0}", p.ProductID);
      }
      NWEntities.SaveChanges();
  }
```

Note that here we used a variable of the type `IQueryable<Product>`, instead of `IEnumerable<Product>`, to hold the result of the LINQ to Entities query. Since `IQueryable` extends the `IEnumerable` interface, we can use either one of them though with `IQueryable` we can do much more, as we will see in next section.

Running the program

The `Program.cs` file has been used so far. Note that we added one method to contain all of the test cases for table operations. We will add more methods later to test other LINQ to Entities functionalities. The following is the content of this file now:

```
using System;
using System.Collections.Generic;
using System.Linq;
using System.Text;
using System.Threading.Tasks;

namespace TestLINQToEntitiesApp
{
  class Program
  {

    static void Main(string[] args)
    {
      // CRUD operations on tables
      TestTables();

      Console.WriteLine("Press any key to continue ...");
      Console.ReadKey();
    }

    static void TestTables()
    {
      using(NorthwindEntities NWEntities =
        new NorthwindEntities())
      {

        // retrieve all Beverages
        IEnumerable<Product> beverages =
          from p in NWEntities.Products
          where p.Category.CategoryName == "Beverages"
          orderby p.ProductName
```

```
    select p;
  Console.WriteLine("There are {0} Beverages",
    beverages.Count());

  // update one product
  Product bev1 = beverages.ElementAtOrDefault(10);
  if (bev1 != null)
  {
    decimal newPrice = (decimal)bev1.UnitPrice + 10.00m;
    Console.WriteLine("The price of {0} is {1}. Update
    to {2}",
    bev1.ProductName, bev1.UnitPrice, newPrice);
    bev1.UnitPrice = newPrice;
  }

  // submit the change to database
  NWEntities.SaveChanges();

  // insert a product
  Product newProduct = new Product { ProductName =
    "new test product" };
  NWEntities.Products.Add(newProduct);
  NWEntities.SaveChanges();

  Console.WriteLine("Added a new product");

  // delete a product
  IQueryable<Product> productsToDelete =
    from p in NWEntities.Products
  where p.ProductName == "new test product"
    select p;
  if (productsToDelete.Count() > 0)
  {
    foreach (var p in productsToDelete)
    {
      NWEntities.Products.Remove(p);
      Console.WriteLine("Deleted product {0}",
      p.ProductID);
    }
    NWEntities.SaveChanges();
  }
      }
    }
  }
}
```

If you set the `TestLINQToEntitiesApp` project as the startup project and run the program now, the output will be as shown in the following screenshot:

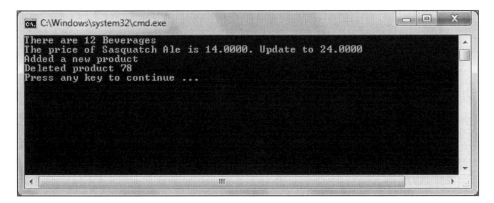

Viewing generated SQL statements

You may wonder which actual SQL statements are used by LINQ to Entities to interact with the databases. In this section, we will use two ways to view the generated SQL statements used by LINQ to Entities queries.

There are two ways to view the generated LINQ to Entities SQL statements. The first one is to use the `ToString` method and the second one is to use SQL Profiler.

Viewing SQL statements using ToString

First let's write a new test method to contain one LINQ to Entities query:

```
static void ViewGeneratedSQL()
{
    using(NorthwindEntities NWEntities =
        new NorthwindEntities())
    {

        IQueryable<Product> beverages =
            from p in NWEntities.Products
            where p.Category.CategoryName == "Beverages"
            orderby p.ProductName
            select p;
    }
}
```

Now with .NET 4.5, we can print out the SQL statement of the LINQ to Entities query using this statement:

```
// view SQL using ToString method
Console.WriteLine("The SQL statement is:" +
    beverages.ToString());
```

In .NET 4.0 or earlier, if you apply `.ToString()` to a LINQ to Entities query variable, you will get the type of the variable, which is `System.Data.Objects.ObjectQuery`.

The `Program.cs` file should now be as follows:

```
using System;
using System.Collections.Generic;
using System.Linq;
using System.Text;
using System.Threading.Tasks;


namespace TestLINQToEntitiesApp
{
    class Program
    {

        static void Main(string[] args)
        {
            // CRUD operations on tables
            //TestTables();

            ViewGeneratedSQL();

            Console.WriteLine("Press any key to continue ...");
            Console.ReadKey();
        }

        static void TestTables()
        {
            // the body of this method is omitted to save space
        }

        static void ViewGeneratedSQL()
        {
            using(NorthwindEntities NWEntities =
                new NorthwindEntities())
```

```
                {
                    IQueryable<Product> beverages =
                        from p in NWEntities.Products
                        where p.Category.CategoryName == "Beverages"
                        orderby p.ProductName
                        select p;

                    // view SQL using ToString method
                    Console.WriteLine("The SQL statement is:\n" +
                        beverages.ToString());
                }
            }
        }
    }
```

Run this program and you will see the output as shown in the following screenshot:

Viewing SQL statements using SQL Profiler

With the `ToString` method we can view generated SQL statements for some LINQ to Entities expressions, but not all of them. For example, when we add a new product to the database or when we execute a stored procedure in the database there is no `IQueryable` object for us to use to view the generated SQL statements. In this case, we can use the SQL Profiler to view the SQL statements.

SQL Server Profiler is a tool from Microsoft that can be used to create and manage traces and analyze and replay trace results. With SQL Profiler, you can capture all and any events that are happening to a database engine in real time, including the SQL statements that are being executed at that moment.

To view the SQL statements for LINQ to Entities queries by using SQL Profiler, we need to run some LINQ to Entities queries. So we will keep this in mind for now and try this in the next section while we are learning about another important feature of LINQ to Entities—deferred execution.

Deferred execution

One important thing to remember when working with LINQ to Entities is the deferred execution of LINQ.

Standard query operators differ in the timing of their execution depending on whether they return a singleton value or a sequence of values. Those methods that return a singleton value (for example `Average` and `Sum`) execute immediately. Methods that return a sequence, defer the query execution and return an enumerable object. These methods do not consume the target data until the query object is enumerated. This is known as **deferred execution**.

In the case of the methods that operate on in-memory collections, that is, those methods that extend `IEnumerable<(Of <(T>)>)`, the returned enumerable object captures all of the arguments that were passed to the method. When that object is enumerated, the logic of the query operator is employed and the query results are returned.

In contrast, methods that extend `IQueryable<(Of <(T>)>)` do not implement any querying behavior, but build an expression tree that represents the query to be performed. The query processing is handled by the source `IQueryable<(Of <(T>)>)` object.

Checking deferred execution with SQL Profiler

To test the deferred execution of LINQ to Entities, let's first add the following method to our `Program.cs` file:

```
static void TestDeferredExecution()
{
    using(NorthwindEntities NWEntities =
        new NorthwindEntities())
    {

        // SQL is not yet executed
```

```
IQueryable<Product> beverages =
    from p in NWEntities.Products
    where p.Category.CategoryName == "Beverages"
    orderby p.ProductName
    select p;

// SQL is executed on this statement
Console.WriteLine("There are {0} Beverages",
    beverages.Count());
    }
}
```

Call this method from the `Main` method of the program and comment out the calls to the two previous test methods (`TestTables` and `ViewGeneratedSQL`). Then perform the following steps:

1. Open the Profiler (`All Programs\Microsoft SQL Server\Performance Tools\SQL Server Profiler`).

2. Start a new trace on the `Northwind` database engine. You can refer to MSDN SQL Server Profiler documentation to learn how to start a new trace on a database engine.

3. Go back to Visual Studio and set a break point on the first line of the `TestDeferredExecution` method.

4. Press *F5* to start debugging the program.

The program is now running and the cursor should be stopped on the first line of the method. Press *F10* to move to the next line of code and press *F10* again to step over this line of code:

```
IQueryable<Product> beverages =
    from p in NWEntities.Products
    where p.Category.CategoryName == "Beverages"
    orderby p.ProductName
        select p;
```

Switch to Profiler and you will find that there is nothing in there.

However, when you press *F10* in Visual Studio and when the following statement is executed, you will see from the Profiler that a query has been executed in the database:

```
Console.WriteLine("There are {0} Beverages", beverages.Count());
```

The query executed in the database is as follows:

```
SELECT
[GroupBy1].[A1] AS [C1]
FROM ( SELECT
  COUNT(1) AS [A1]
  FROM   [dbo].[Products] AS [Extent1]
  INNER JOIN [dbo].[Categories] AS [Extent2] ON
  [Extent1].[CategoryID] = [Extent2].[CategoryID]
  WHERE N'Beverages' = [Extent2].[CategoryName]
)  AS [GroupBy1]
```

The **SQL Server Profiler** window should look as shown in the following screenshot:

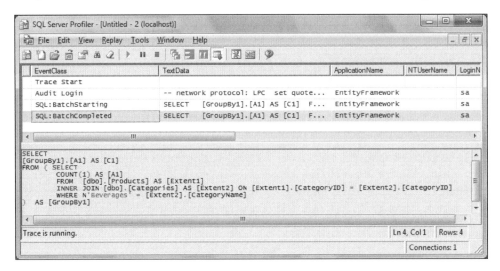

From Profiler we know that, under the hood, LINQ actually first created a sub-query to get the total beverage products count and then got this count from the sub-query result. It also used an inner join to get the categories of products.

Deferred execution for singleton methods

If the query expression returns a singleton value, the query will be executed as soon as it is defined. For example, we can add this statement to our test deferred execution method to get the average price of all products:

```
// SQL is executed on this statement
decimal? averagePrice = (from p in NWEntities.Products
                         select p.UnitPrice).Average();
Console.WriteLine("The average price is {0}", averagePrice);
```

Start SQL Profiler and then press *F5* to start debugging the program. When the cursor is stopped on the line to print out the average price, from the **SQL Server Profiler** window, we see that a query has been executed to get the average price and when the printing statement is being executed, no more query is executed in database.

The **SQL Server Profiler** window is as shown in the following screenshot:

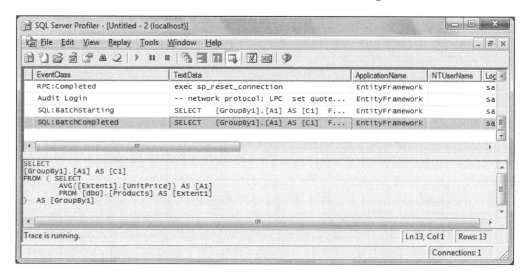

Deferred execution for singleton methods within sequence expressions

However, just because a query is using one of the singleton methods such as sum, average, or count, this doesn't mean that the query will be executed as soon as it is defined. If the query result is a sequence, the execution will still be deferred. The following is an example of this kind of query:

```
// SQL is not executed even though there is a singleton method
var cheapestProductsByCategory =
  from p in NWEntities.Products
  group p by p.CategoryID into g
  select new
  {
    CategoryID = g.Key,
    CheapestProduct =
        (from p2 in g
        where p2.UnitPrice == g.Min(p3 => p3.UnitPrice)
        select p2).FirstOrDefault()
  };
```

```
// SQL is executed on this statement
Console.WriteLine("Cheapest products by category:");
foreach (var p in cheapestProductsByCategory)
{
if (p.CategoryID == null || p.CheapestProduct == null)
  continue;
  Console.WriteLine("categery {0}: product name: {1} price: {2}",
                  p.CategoryID, p.CheapestProduct.ProductName,
                  p.CheapestProduct.UnitPrice);
}
```

Start SQL Profiler and then press *F5* to start debugging the program. When the cursor is stopped at the beginning of the `foreach` line, from Profiler, we don't see the query statement to get the minimum price for any product. When we press *F10* again, the cursor is stopped on the `cheapestProductsByCategory` variable, in the `foreach` line of code, but we still don't see the query statement to get the cheapest products.

Then after we press *F10* again, the cursor is stopped on the `in` keyword in the `foreach` line of code and this time, from Profiler, we see that the query is executed.

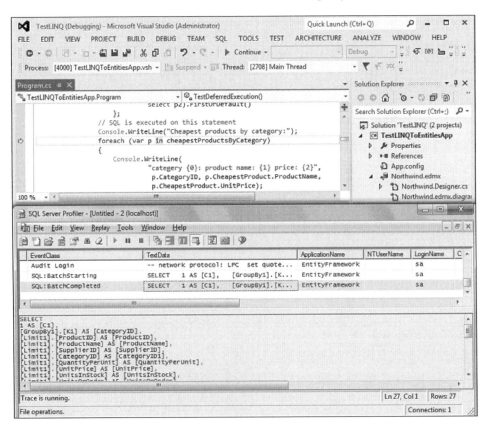

The actual SQL statements for this LINQ to Entities expression are as follows:

```
SELECT
1 AS [C1],
[GroupBy1].[K1] AS [CategoryID],
[Limit1].[ProductID] AS [ProductID],
[Limit1].[ProductName] AS [ProductName],
[Limit1].[SupplierID] AS [SupplierID],
[Limit1].[CategoryID] AS [CategoryID1],
[Limit1].[QuantityPerUnit] AS [QuantityPerUnit],
[Limit1].[UnitPrice] AS [UnitPrice],
[Limit1].[UnitsInStock] AS [UnitsInStock],
[Limit1].[UnitsOnOrder] AS [UnitsOnOrder],
[Limit1].[ReorderLevel] AS [ReorderLevel],
[Limit1].[Discontinued] AS [Discontinued]
FROM    (SELECT
  [Extent1].[CategoryID] AS [K1],
  MIN([Extent1].[UnitPrice]) AS [A1]
  FROM [dbo].[Products] AS [Extent1]
  GROUP BY [Extent1].[CategoryID] ) AS [GroupBy1]
OUTER APPLY  (SELECT TOP (1)
  [Extent2].[ProductID] AS [ProductID],
  [Extent2].[ProductName] AS [ProductName],
  [Extent2].[SupplierID] AS [SupplierID],
  [Extent2].[CategoryID] AS [CategoryID],
  [Extent2].[QuantityPerUnit] AS [QuantityPerUnit],
  [Extent2].[UnitPrice] AS [UnitPrice],
  [Extent2].[UnitsInStock] AS [UnitsInStock],
  [Extent2].[UnitsOnOrder] AS [UnitsOnOrder],
  [Extent2].[ReorderLevel] AS [ReorderLevel],
  [Extent2].[Discontinued] AS [Discontinued]
  FROM [dbo].[Products] AS [Extent2]
  WHERE (([GroupBy1].[K1] = [Extent2].[CategoryID]) OR
  ((([GroupBy1].[K1] IS NULL) AND ([Extent2].[CategoryID] IS
  NULL))) AND ([Extent2].[UnitPrice] = [GroupBy1].[A1]) ) AS
  [Limit1]
```

From this output you can see that when the cheapestProductsByCategory variable is accessed, it first calculates the minimum price for each category. Then, for each category, it returns the first product with that price. In a real application, you probably wouldn't want to write such a complex query in your code. Instead you may want to put it in a stored procedure, which we will discuss in the next chapter.

The test method is as follows:

```
static void TestDeferredExecution()
{
  using(NorthwindEntities NWEntities =
      new NorthwindEntities())
  {

  // SQL is not executed
  IQueryable<Product> beverages =
    from p in NWEntities.Products
    where p.Category.CategoryName == "Beverages"
    orderby p.ProductName
    select p;

  // SQL is executed on this statement
  Console.WriteLine("There are {0} Beverages",
        beverages.Count());

  // SQL is executed on this statement
  decimal? averagePrice = (from p in NWEntities.Products
                           select p.UnitPrice).Average();
  Console.WriteLine("The average price is {0}", averagePrice);

  // SQL is not executed even there is a singleton method
  var cheapestProductsByCategory =
      from p in NWEntities.Products
      group p by p.CategoryID into g
      select new
    {
      CategoryID = g.Key,
      CheapestProduct =
          (from p2 in g
          where p2.UnitPrice == g.Min(p3 => p3.UnitPrice)
          select p2).FirstOrDefault()
    };
    // SQL is executed on this statement
    Console.WriteLine("Cheapest products by category:");
    foreach (var p in cheapestProductsByCategory)
    {
      if (p.CategoryID == null || p.CheapestProduct == null)
        continue;
```

```
Console.WriteLine(
        "categery {0}: product name: {1} price: {2}",
        p.CategoryID, p.CheapestProduct.ProductName,
        p.CheapestProduct.UnitPrice);
    }
  }
}
```

If you comment out all other test methods (`TestTables` and `ViewGeneratedSQL`) and run the program, you should get an output similar to the one shown in the following screenshot:

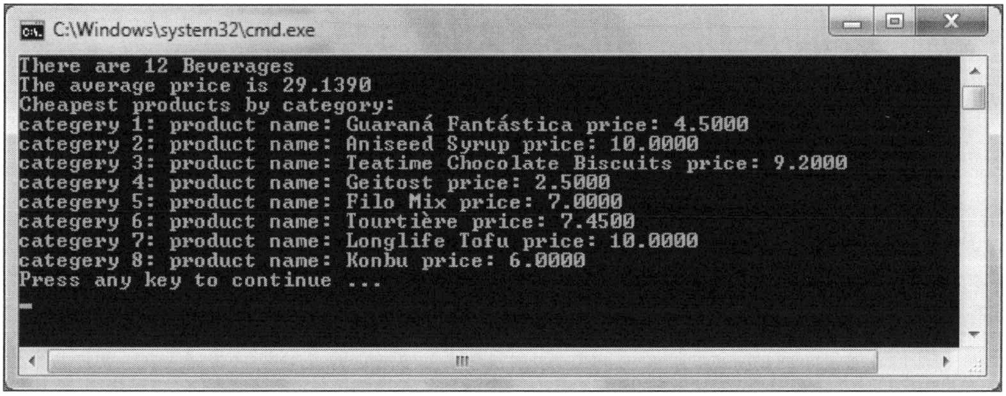

Deferred (lazy) loading versus eager loading

In one of the above examples, we retrieved the category name of a product using the following expression:

```
p.Category.CategoryName == "Beverages"
```

Even though there is no field called `categoryname` in the Products table, we can still get the category name of a product because there is an association between the Products and Category tables. In the **Northwind.edmx** design pane, click on the line that connects the **Products** table and the **Categories** table, and you will see all of the properties of the association. Note that its `Referential Constraint` properties are `Category.CategoryID -> Product.CategoryID`, meaning that `category ID` is the key field to link these two tables.

Because of this association, we can retrieve the category for each product and also retrieve products for each category.

Lazy loading by default

However, even with an association the associated data is not loaded when the query is executed. For example, suppose we use the following test method to retrieve all of the categories, and then access the products for each category:

```
static void TestAssociation()
{
using (NorthwindEntities NWEntities = new NorthwindEntities())
  {
    var categories = from c in NWEntities.Categories select c;
    foreach (var category in categories)
    {
      Console.WriteLine("There are {0} products in category {1}",
      category.Products.Count(), category.CategoryName);
    }
  }
}
```

Start SQL Profiler and then press *F5* to start debugging the program. When the cursor is stopped on the `foreach` line (after you press *F10* twice to move the cursor to the `in` keyword), from Profiler, we see the following SQL statement:

```
SELECT
[Extent1].[CategoryID] AS [CategoryID],
[Extent1].[CategoryName] AS [CategoryName],
[Extent1].[Description] AS [Description],
[Extent1].[Picture] AS [Picture]
FROM [dbo].[Categories] AS [Extent1]
```

When you press *F10* to execute the printout line, from Profiler, we see the following SQL statement:

```
exec sp_executesql N'SELECT
[Extent1].[ProductID] AS [ProductID],
[Extent1].[ProductName] AS [ProductName],
[Extent1].[SupplierID] AS [SupplierID],
[Extent1].[CategoryID] AS [CategoryID],
[Extent1].[QuantityPerUnit] AS [QuantityPerUnit],
[Extent1].[UnitPrice] AS [UnitPrice],
[Extent1].[UnitsInStock] AS [UnitsInStock],
[Extent1].[UnitsOnOrder] AS [UnitsOnOrder],
[Extent1].[ReorderLevel] AS [ReorderLevel],
[Extent1].[Discontinued] AS [Discontinued]
FROM [dbo].[Products] AS [Extent1]
WHERE [Extent1].[CategoryID] = @EntityKeyValue1',N'@EntityKeyValue1
int',@EntityKeyValue1=1
```

From these SQL statements, we know that the Entity Framework first goes to the database to query all of the categories. Then, for each category, when we need to get the total count of products, it goes to the database again to query all of the products for that category. Because there are eight categories in the database, it goes to the database nine times in total (including the first one to retrieve all categories).

This is because, by default, lazy loading is set to `true`, meaning that the loading of all associated data (children) is deferred until the data is needed.

Eager loading with the Include method

To change this behavior, we can use the `Include` method to tell `DbContext` to automatically load the specified children during the initial query:

```
static void TestEagerLoading()
{
    using(NorthwindEntities NWEntities = new NorthwindEntities())
    {
     // eager loading products of categories
     var categories = from c
                       in NWEntities.Categories.Include(c=>c.Products)
                       select c;
     foreach (var category in categories)
     {
         Console.WriteLine("There are {0} products in category {1}",
             category.Products.Count(), category.CategoryName);
     }
    }
}
```

Inside this test method, when constructing the LINQ to Entities query, we added an `Include` clause to tell the framework to load all products when loading the categories.

To use `Include` with a lambda expression, you need to add the following `using` statement to the class:

```
using System.Data.Entity;
```

If you didn't add the previous `using` statement to the class, you will have to use a string to specify the child object to be eager loaded, like in the following code snippet:

```
NWEntities.Categories.Include("Products")
```

To test it, start SQL Profiler and then press *F5* to start debugging the program. When the cursor is stopped on the `foreach` line (at the `in` keyword), from Profiler, you will see the following SQL statement:

```
SELECT
[Project1].[CategoryID] AS [CategoryID],
[Project1].[CategoryName] AS [CategoryName],
[Project1].[Description] AS [Description],
[Project1].[Picture] AS [Picture],
[Project1].[C1] AS [C1],
[Project1].[ProductID] AS [ProductID],
[Project1].[ProductName] AS [ProductName],
[Project1].[SupplierID] AS [SupplierID],
[Project1].[CategoryID1] AS [CategoryID1],
[Project1].[QuantityPerUnit] AS [QuantityPerUnit],
[Project1].[UnitPrice] AS [UnitPrice],
[Project1].[UnitsInStock] AS [UnitsInStock],
[Project1].[UnitsOnOrder] AS [UnitsOnOrder],
[Project1].[ReorderLevel] AS [ReorderLevel],
[Project1].[Discontinued] AS [Discontinued]
FROM ( SELECT
  [Extent1].[CategoryID] AS [CategoryID],
  [Extent1].[CategoryName] AS [CategoryName],
  [Extent1].[Description] AS [Description],
  [Extent1].[Picture] AS [Picture],
  [Extent2].[ProductID] AS [ProductID],
  [Extent2].[ProductName] AS [ProductName],
  [Extent2].[SupplierID] AS [SupplierID],
  [Extent2].[CategoryID] AS [CategoryID1],
  [Extent2].[QuantityPerUnit] AS [QuantityPerUnit],
  [Extent2].[UnitPrice] AS [UnitPrice],
  [Extent2].[UnitsInStock] AS [UnitsInStock],
  [Extent2].[UnitsOnOrder] AS [UnitsOnOrder],
  [Extent2].[ReorderLevel] AS [ReorderLevel],
  [Extent2].[Discontinued] AS [Discontinued],
  CASE WHEN ([Extent2].[ProductID] IS NULL) THEN CAST(NULL AS int)
ELSE 1 END AS [C1]
  FROM  [dbo].[Categories] AS [Extent1]
  LEFT OUTER JOIN [dbo].[Products] AS [Extent2] ON [Extent1].
[CategoryID] = [Extent2].[CategoryID]
)  AS [Project1]
ORDER BY [Project1].[CategoryID] ASC, [Project1].[C1] ASC
```

As you can see from this SQL statement, all products for all categories are loaded during the first query.

Comparing lazy loading and eager loading

As you have learned in the previous sections, lazy loading and eager loading are two very different options for the loading-related objects. With lazy loading, the first query will get back only the main objects, and every time a related object is needed, another query has to be executed. Each query will have a smaller payload, but there will be multiple queries to the database. With eager loading, the first query will bring back all objects, including any related objects. When a related object is needed, it will be retrieved right from the object model, not from the database. There will be only one database trip, but the payload will be larger. You should weigh the pros and cons of each option and choose one appropriately.

Joining two tables

Although an association is a kind of join in LINQ, we can also explicitly join two tables using the `Join` keyword, as shown in the following code snippet:

```
static void TestJoin()
{
    using(NorthwindEntities NWEntities = new NorthwindEntities())
    {
    var categoryProducts =
        from c in NWEntities.Categories
        join p in NWEntities.Products
        on c.CategoryID equals p.CategoryID
        into productsByCategory
        select new {
            c.CategoryName,
            productCount = productsByCategory.Count()
        };

    foreach (var cp in categoryProducts)
    {
      Console.WriteLine("There are {0} products in category
      {1}",
            cp.productCount, cp.CategoryName);
    }
    }
}
```

This is not so useful in the previous example because the `Products` and `Categories` tables are associated with a foreign key relationship. If there is no foreign key association between two tables or if we had not added the associations between these two tables, this will be particularly useful.

From the following SQL statement, we can see that only one query is executed to get the results:

```
SELECT
[Extent1].[CategoryID] AS [CategoryID],
[Extent1].[CategoryName] AS [CategoryName],
(SELECT
  COUNT(1) AS [A1]
  FROM [dbo].[Products] AS [Extent2]
  WHERE [Extent1].[CategoryID] = [Extent2].[CategoryID]) AS [C1]
FROM [dbo].[Categories] AS [Extent1]
```

In addition to joining two tables, you can also:

- Join three or more tables
- Join a table to itself
- Create left, right, and outer joins
- Join using composite keys

Querying a view

Querying a view is the same as querying a table. For example, you can query the view "current product lists" as follows:

```
static void TestView()
{
  using(NorthwindEntities NWEntities = new NorthwindEntities())
  {
   var currentProducts = from p
                    in NWEntities.Current_Product_Lists
                    select p;
   foreach (var p in currentProducts)
     {
        Console.WriteLine("Product ID: {0} Product Name: {1}",
           p.ProductID, p.ProductName);
     }
   }
 }
```

This will get and print all of the current products using the view.

Summary

In this chapter, we learned what an ORM is, why we need an ORM, and what LINQ to Entities is. We also compared LINQ to SQL with LINQ to Entities and explored some basic features of LINQ to Entities.

In the next chapter, we will cover the advanced concepts and features of LINQ to Entities such as stored procedure support, inheritance, simultaneous updating, and transaction processing.

8
LINQ to Entities: Advanced Concepts and Features

In the previous chapter, we learned some basic concepts and features of LINQ to Entities such as querying and updating database tables and views and changing loading behaviors by using the `Include` method.

In this chapter, we will learn some advanced features of LINQ to Entities such as stored procedure support, concurrency control, and transactional processing. After this chapter, we will rewrite the data access layer of our WCF service to utilize LINQ to Entities technology.

In this chapter we will cover:

- Calling a stored procedure
- Inheritance support
- Concurrency control
- Transaction support

Calling a stored procedure

Calling a stored procedure is different from calling a table or a view because a stored procedure can't be called directly. A function import has to be added for the stored procedure and its result set has to be mapped. The modeling of a stored procedure is also different from modeling a table or view. In the following sections, we will learn how to call a simple stored procedure, how to map the returned result of a stored procedure to an entity class, and how to create a new entity for the result set.

We will re-use the same application that we used in the previous chapter and add more methods to the program.

Mapping a stored procedure to a new entity class

First, we will try to call a simple stored procedure. In the sample database, there is a stored procedure called `Ten Most Expensive Products`. We will call this stored procedure to get the top ten most expensive products.

Modeling a stored procedure

Before we can call this stored procedure we need to model it. Perform the following steps:

1. Open the `Northwind.edmx` designer.

2. Right-click on an empty space of the designer surface and select **Update Model from Database...**:

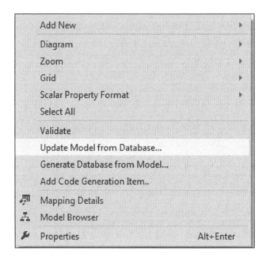

3. From the **Update Wizard** window, on the **Choose Your Database Objects and Settings** page, make sure the **Add** tab is selected, and then expand the **dbo** node under **Stored Procedures and Functions**, and check **Ten Most Expensive Products**.

4. Make sure the **Import selected stored procedures and functions into the entity model** option is checked.

5. Click on the **Finish** button.

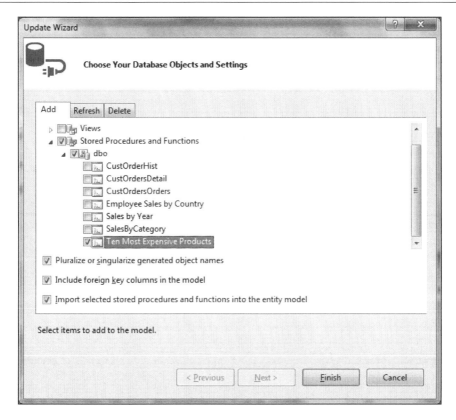

After you save the `Northwind.edmx` diagram, it will add the `Ten_Most_Expensive_Products` method to the `NorthwindEntities` class and add a new class `Ten_Most_Expensive_Products_Result` as the result datatype of the stored procedure.

Querying a stored procedure

Now, from `Program.cs`, we can call this stored procedure as follows:

```
var tenProducts = from p in
    NWEntities.Ten_Most_Expensive_Products()
    select p;
foreach (var p in tenProducts)
{
    Console.WriteLine("Product Name: {0}, Price: {1}",
    p.TenMostExpensiveProducts, p.UnitPrice);
}
```

As we know the return result of the stored procedure, we can also replace the `var` datatype with the specific return type, as shown in the following code snippet:

```
IEnumerable<Ten_Most_Expensive_Products_Result> tenProducts =
    from p
    in NWEntities.Ten_Most_Expensive_Products()
    select p;
foreach (Ten_Most_Expensive_Products_Result p in tenProducts)
{
    Console.WriteLine("Product Name: {0}, Price; {1}",
    p.TenMostExpensiveProducts, p.UnitPrice);
}
```

In this way, we can clearly see the datatype of the `tenProducts` variable, so later on we can compare this query with the one that maps to an existing entity class.

The SQL statement is pretty straightforward, as follows:

```
exec [dbo].[Ten Most Expensive Products]
```

The output will look like the one shown in the following screenshot:

Mapping a stored procedure to an existing entity class

In the above example, LINQ to Entities created a new type for the return result of the stored procedure. It actually just added the word `Result` after the stored procedure name to create the name of the return datatype. If we know that the return result is a kind of entity, we can tell LINQ to Entities to use that specific entity as the return type instead of creating a new type.

For example, let's create a stored procedure as follows:

```
Create PROCEDURE [dbo].[GetProduct]
    (
    @ProductID int
    )
AS
    SET NOCOUNT ON
    Select * from Products where ProductID = @ProductID
```

You can create this stored procedure in Microsoft SQL Server Management Studio or by right-clicking on the **Stored Procedures** node in Server Explorer of Visual Studio and selecting **Data Connections | Northwind.dbo | Add New Stored Procedure** from the context menu.

After the stored procedure has been created, follow these steps to add it to the entity data model and add a function import:

1. Open the `Northwind.edmx` designer.
2. Right-click on an empty space of the designer surface and select **Update Model from Database…**.
3. From the **Update Wizard** window, on the **Choose Your Database Objects and Settings** page, make sure the **Add** tab is selected, and then expand the **dbo** node under **Stored Procedures and Functions**, and check **GetProduct**.
4. This time make sure the **Import selected stored procedures and functions into the entity model** option is not checked.
5. Click on the **Finish** button.
6. As we didn't check the option **Import selected stored procedures and functions into the entity model**, the stored procedure has not been imported to the entity model for us. The reason is we don't want to create a new result type for this stored procedure; instead, we will map this stored procedure to an existing entity as described in the following steps.
7. On the designer surface, right-click on an empty space and **select Add New** from the context menu, and then select **Function Import…**.

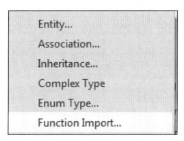

8. In the **Add Function Import** window, type `GetProduct` in the **Function Import Name** field and select **GetProduct** as the stored procedure name from the drop-down list.

9. Select **Entities** as **Returns a Collection Of** and choose **Product** as the entity from the drop-down list.

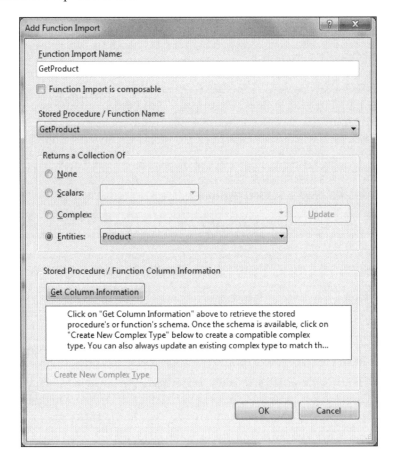

10. Click on the **OK** button.

11. Click on the **Save** button to save the model so the new function for the new stored procedure can be created in the context class.

12. Now LINQ to Entities will use the `Product` class as the return type of this stored procedure.

To call this method you can write a statement as follows:

```
Product getProduct = NWEntities.GetProduct(1).FirstOrDefault();
```

The complete method for the stored procedure should be as follows:

```
static void TestStoredProcedure()
{
using(NorthwindEntities NWEntities = new NorthwindEntities())
  {
    IEnumerable<Ten_Most_Expensive_Products_Result> tenProducts =
            from p
            in NWEntities.Ten_Most_Expensive_Products()
            select p;
    Console.WriteLine("Ten Most Expensive Products:");
    foreach (Ten_Most_Expensive_Products_Result p in tenProducts)
    {
      Console.WriteLine("Product Name: {0}, Price; {1}",
            p.TenMostExpensiveProducts, p.UnitPrice);
    }

    // map a stored procedure to an entity class
  Product getProduct = NWEntities.GetProduct(1).FirstOrDefault();
  Console.WriteLine("\nProduct name for product 1:{0}",
    getProduct.ProductName);
  }
}
```

And if you run the program, you should have an output as shown in the following screenshot:

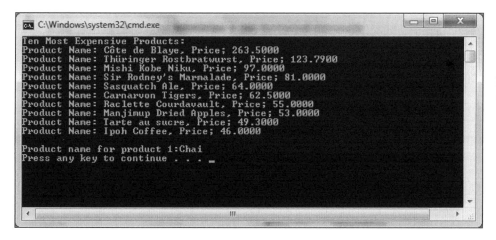

Interestingly, you can add another function for the same stored procedure but with a different function name (GetProduct1), and for the new function, you can check the **Complex** radio button to create a new type (GetProduct1_Result) for the result of the stored procedure instead of using the Product class. LINQ to Entities will automatically create a new class for the return type.

The generated return type class `GetProduct1_Result` is almost identical to the `Product` class.

A big difference between the `GetProduct` and `GetProduct1` methods is that the product you retrieved using `GetProduct` is managed by the `DbContext` entity. Any changes you made to it will be committed back to the database if you call `SaveChanges()` later. However, the product you retrieved using `GetProduct1` is not managed by the `DbContext` entity, and thus won't be committed back to the database if you call `SaveChanges()` later.

Inheritance

LINQ to Entities supports three types of inheritance:

- **Table per Hierarchy (TPH)** inheritance
- **Table per Type (TPT)** inheritance
- **Table per Concrete (TPC)** inheritance

As Table per Concrete inheritance is not used as often as Table per Hierarchy and Table per Type inheritances, in this book we will only cover the first two inheritance types.

LINQ to Entities Table per Hierarchy inheritance

In **Table per Hierarchy** inheritance, there is a single database table that contains fields for both parent information and child information. With relational data, a discriminator column contains the value that determines which class any given record belongs to.

For example, consider a `Persons` table that contains everyone employed by a company. Some people are employees and some are managers. The `Persons` table contains a column named `EmployeeType` that has a value of 1 for managers and a value of 2 for employees; this is the discriminator column.

In this scenario, you can create a child entity of employees and populate the class only with records that have an `EmployeeType` value of 2. You can also remove columns that do not apply from each of the classes.

In our `Northwind` database, the `Customers` table contains all of the customers in different countries. Suppose that all customers share some common properties and customers from each country also have some unique properties of their own. We can then define a `BaseCustomer` entity class for all of the common properties of the customers and define a unique child entity class for each country.

We assume that all customers have the following properties:

- `CustomerID`
- `CompanyName`
- `ContactName`
- `ContactTitle`
- `Address`
- `City`
- `Region`
- `PostalCode`

To simplify the example, we will define only two child entity classes in this example—one for customers in USA (called `USACustomers`) and another for customers in UK (`UKCustomers`). We assume that a `USACustomer` has one more property of `Phone` and a UKCustomer has one more property of `Fax`.

Modeling the BaseCustomer and USACustomer entities

We will first model these entities with the LINQ to Entities designer:

1. Open the entities conceptual model `Northwind.edmx` and right-click on an empty space on the designer surface. Then, from the context menu, choose **Update Model from Database...** and add the **Customers** table to the model, in the same way as we did for the **Products** table in the previous chapter. Save the model and then from the **Properties** window of the **Customers** entity, change the entity class name from **Customer** to **BaseCustomer** (**Entity Set Name** should be changed to **BaseCustomer** automatically).

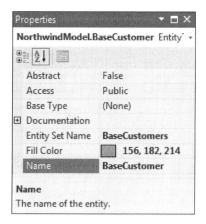

2. Right-click on an empty space on the designer surface, then choose **Add New | Entity...** from the context menu.

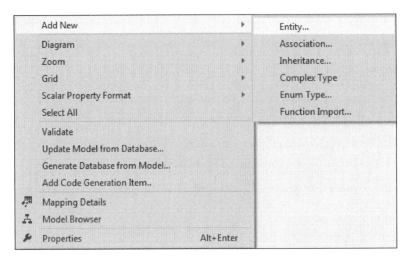

3. In the **Add Entity** window, enter USACustomer as **Entity Name**, and select **BaseCustomer** as **Base type**. Click on **OK** to close this window.

4. On the entity model designer surface, right-click on the **Phone** property of the **BaseCustomer** entity, and select **Cut** from the context menu.

5. Still on the entity model designer surface, right-click on the **Properties** node of the **USACustomer** entity and select **Paste** from the context menu.

6. Right-click on the **Country** property of the **BaseCustomer** entity and select **Delete from Model** from the context menu. We need to delete this property because we will use it as our discriminator.

7. Now select the **USACustomer** entity on the model designer and go to the **Mapping Details** window (it should be next to your **Output** window or you can open it by navigating to **View | Other Windows | Entity Data Model Mapping Details**).

8. On the **Mapping Details** window, click on **<Add a Table or View>** and select **Customers** from the drop-down list. Make sure **Phone** is mapped to **Phone** and **Country** is not mapped.

9. Again in the **Mapping Details** window, click on **<Add a Condition>** and select **Country** from the drop-down list. Select **=** as the operator, and enter USA as **Value/Property**.

10. Now save the model and we have finished modeling the base customer and USA customer entities. If you build the solution now you should see no errors.

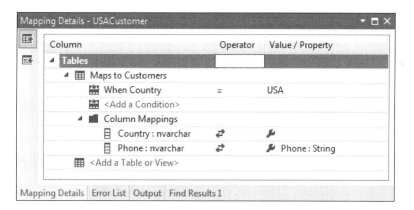

Modeling the UKCustomer entity

Next we need to model the UKCustomer entity. This entity will inherit from the BaseCustomer entity, but will have an extra property of Fax.

1. On the Northwind.edmx entity designer surface, right-click on an empty space, then choose **Add New | Entity...** from the context menu.

2. On the **Add Entity** window, enter UKCustomer as **Entity Name** and select **BaseCustomer** as **Base type**. Click on **OK** to close this window.

3. On the entity model designer surface, right-click on the **Fax** property of the **BaseCustomer** entity and select **Cut** from the context menu.

4. Still on the entity model designer surface, right-click on the **Properties** node of the **UKCustomer** entity and select **Paste** from the context menu.

5. Now select the **UKCustomer** entity on the model designer and go to the **Mapping Details** window (it should be next to your **Output** window or you can open it by navigating to **View | Other Windows | Entity Data Model Mapping Details**).

6. In the **Mapping Details** window, click on **<Add a Table or View>** and select **Customers** from the drop-down list. Make sure **Fax** is mapped to **Fax**, and **Phone** and **Country** are not mapped.

7. On the same window, click on **<Add a Condition>** and select **Country** from the drop-down list. Select **=** as the operator and enter UK as **Value/Property**.

8. Now the TPH inheritance model is finished. The model for the customer part should be as shown in the following screenshot:

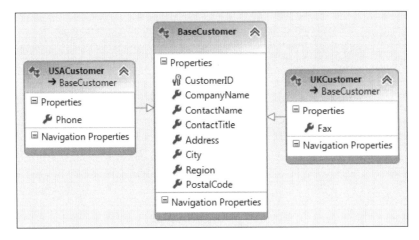

Generated classes with TPH inheritance

Save the model by clicking on the **Save** button. Now you will find that three classes have been added to the model. The first class is the `BaseCustomer` class, which is a pure POCO class.

Note that its class body neither contains the properties, `Phone` and `Fax`, nor `Country`. This is because `Phone` is now contained by the `USACustomer` entity and `Fax` by `UKCustomer`, and `Country` is used as the discriminator for the inheritance.

The other two classes are for the derived classes; each has only one property:

```
public partial class USACustomer : BaseCustomer
public partial class UKCustomer : BaseCustomer
```

Testing the TPH inheritance

Now we can write a query to show the inheritance between `BaseCustomer` and the two derived classes.

First we can retrieve all of the USA customers by using the `is` operator as follows:

```
var USACustomers1 = from c
        in NWEntities.BaseCustomers
        where c is USACustomer
        select c;
```

We can also use the `OfType` operator to retrieve the same products, as follows:

```
var USACustomers2 = from c
        in NWEntities.BaseCustomers.OfType<USACustomer>()
        select c;

Console.WriteLine("Total number of USA customers: {0}",
        USACustomers1.Count());
Console.WriteLine("Total number of USA customers: {0}",
        USACustomers2.Count());
```

Run the program and you will see both queries return 13.

We can also use the `as` operator to search for all the customers that are USA customers:

```
var USACustomers3 = from c
            in NWEntities.BaseCustomers
            select c as USACustomer;
```

In all of the above three queries, `Phone` is a property of the returning item, which means it is of the `USACustomer` type. Also, all of the `BaseCustomer` properties are available because the returning item's datatype is a child of the `BaseCustomer` type.

> If you trace the SQL statements for the previous three queries, you will find that the first two queries are identical and very simple, but the third query is huge and very complex (it actually returns all customers and for non-USA customers, it returns `null`). Between the first two queries, the first one returns a variable of type `BaseCustomer`, but holds a list of objects of type `USACustomer`. You have to cast them to type `USACustomer` if you need to get the child properties. The second one is the best, if you need to retrieve all USA customers.

Similarly we can retrieve all `UKCustomers` and use its `Fax` property, as follows:

```
var UKCustomers = from c
              in NWEntities.BaseCustomers.OfType<UKCustomer>()
              select c;
```

The method should be as follows:

```
static void TestTPHInheritance()
{
    using(NorthwindEntities NWEntities = new
    NorthwindEntities())
    {
    var USACustomers1 = from c
                  in NWEntities.BaseCustomers
                  where c is USACustomer
                  select c;

    var USACustomers2 = from c
                  in NWEntities.BaseCustomers.OfType<USACustomer>()
                  select c;

    Console.WriteLine("Total number of USA customers: {0}",
                  USACustomers1.Count());
    Console.WriteLine("Total number of USA customers: {0}",
                  USACustomers2.Count());

    var USACustomers3 = from c
                  in NWEntities.BaseCustomers
                  select c as USACustomer;
```

```
foreach (var c in USACustomers3)
{
    if (c != null)
    {
        Console.WriteLine("USA customer: {0}, Phone: {1}",
            c.CompanyName, c.Phone);
    }
}

var UKCustomers = from c
        in NWEntities.BaseCustomers.OfType<UKCustomer>()
        select c;

foreach (var c in UKCustomers)
    Console.WriteLine("UK customer: {0}, Fax: {1}",
        c.CompanyName, c.Fax);
    }
}
```

The output of this is shown in the following screenshot:

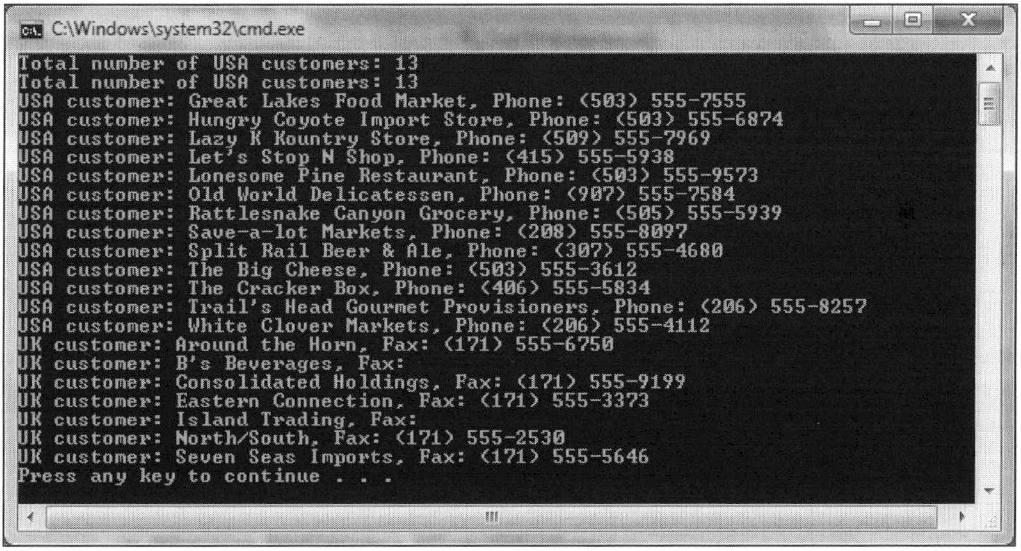

LINQ to Entities Table per Type inheritance

In **Table per Type** inheritance, there is a parent database table that contains fields for parent information and a separate database table that contains additional fields for child information. With relational data, a foreign key constraint links those tables together to provide the detailed information for each entity.

For example, let's consider the same `Persons` table that contains common properties for everyone employed by a company. Some people are employees and some are managers. All employee-specific information is saved in a separate table `Employees`, while all manager-specific information is saved in the `Managers` table.

In this scenario, you can create a parent entity for people and two child entities —one for employees and another for managers.

Again in our `Northwind` database, the `Customers` table contains all of the customers in different countries. Suppose that all customers share some common properties and customers from each country also have some unique properties of their own. We can then define a `BaseCustomer` entity class for all of the common properties of the customers and define a unique child entity class for each country.

We assume that all customers have the following properties:

- `CustomerID`
- `CompanyName`
- `ContactName`
- `ContactTitle`
- `Address`
- `City`
- `Region`
- `PostalCode`

To simplify the example, we will define only two child entity classes in this example —one for customers in USA (called `USACustomers`) and another for customers in UK (`UKCustomers`). We assume that `USACustomer` has one more property of `Phone` and `UKCustomer` has one more property of `Fax`.

However, this time we will create those two child entities from two new database tables, not from the same `Customers` table as we did in the last section.

Preparing database tables

We first need to create those two new database tables so that later on we can add them to our model.

1. Open SQL Management Studio and execute the following SQL statements to create two new tables. These two statements also fill in these two new tables with some initial data from the `Customers` table:

```
select CustomerID,Phone
into USACustomers
from Customers
where Country = 'USA'

select CustomerID,Fax
into UKCustomers
from Customers
where Country = 'UK'
```

2. Set `CustomerID` as the primary keys for both tables.

3. Add a foreign key relationship between the `USACustomers` table and the `Customers` table. The `CustomerID` column should be used for the foreign key. Do the same for the `UKCustomers` table. The foreign key mappings for `USACustomers` should be as shown in the following screenshot:

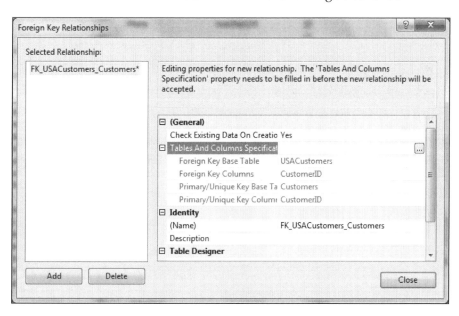

Modeling USACustomer1 and UKCustomer1 entities

Now that we have the database tables ready, we need to go to the entity designer to add them to our model.

1. From Visual Studio, open the `Northwind.edmx` entity designer, right-click on an empty space and select **Update Model from Database...**. Add the two new tables `USACustomers` and `UKCustomers` to the model. Note that the entity names for these two tables are `USACustomer1` and `UKCustomer1` as there are already two entities with the name of `USACustomer` and `UKCustomer`.

2. Because of the foreign keys between those two tables and the `Customers` table, there is an association between `USACustomer1` and `BaseCustomer` as well as between `UKCustomer1` and `BaseCustomer`. Right-click on each of these two associations and delete them. This is because we don't want these two child tables to be associated with the base table; instead, we want them to be inherited from the base table.

> With association, you can access all base customers' properties from the child entity through the navigation property `Customer` and vice versa. Once you delete the associations, those navigation properties will also be deleted. For learning purpose, we are deleting these associations, but in your real project, you may want to keep them.

3. Then right-click on an empty space and select **Add New | Inheritance...** from the context menu. Specify **BaseCustomer** as the base entity and **USACustomer1** as the derived entity. Click on **OK** to close this window. Also add an inheritance between `UKCustomer1` and `BaseCustomer`.

4. Select **CustomerID** from the **USACustomer1** entity and delete it. Also delete **CustomerID** from the **UKCustomer1** entity.

5. Select the **USACustomer1** entity, go to the **Mapping Details** window, and make sure **CustomerID : nchar** is maped to **CustomerID : String**. Verify the same mapping for the **CustomerID** property in the **UKCustomer1** entity.

The finished model should now contain eight entities. The part of the model that contains the two new customer entities should look like the following screenshot:

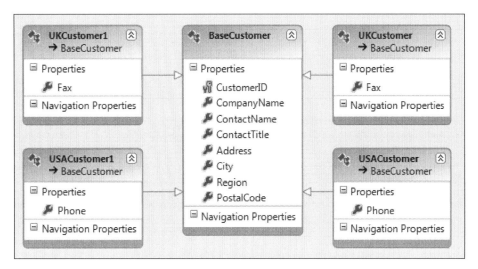

Generated classes with TPT inheritance

Save the model and you will find that two classes have been added to the model, each having only one property:

```
public partial class USACustomer1 : BaseCustomer
public partial class UKCustomer1 : BaseCustomer
```

Testing the TPT inheritance

Now we can write a query to show the inheritance between `BaseCustomer` and the two new derived classes.

For example, the following code will retrieve the first USA customer from the `USACustomers` table and print out its phone:

```
var usaCustomer1 = (from c
        in NWEntities.BaseCustomers.OfType<USACustomer1>()
        select c).FirstOrDefault();
if (usaCustomer1 != null)
```

```
    {
        var phone1 = usaCustomer1.Phone;
        Console.WriteLine("Phone for USA customer1:{0}",
            phone1);
    }
```

The following code will retrieve and print out the first UK customer's fax:

```
var ukCustomer1 = (from c
    in NWEntities.BaseCustomers.OfType<UKCustomer1>()
    select c).FirstOrDefault();
if (ukCustomer1 != null)
{
    var fax1 = ukCustomer1.Fax;
    Console.WriteLine("Fax for UK customer1:{0}",
        fax1);
}
```

In the same way, as with the test result in previous sections, when we used TPH inheritance in the previous query to the USACustomer1 entity, Phone was a property of the returning item and all of the BaseCustomer properties were also available because the returning item's datatype is a child of the BaseCustomer type. To the UKCustomer1 entity, it has all of the properties from the BaseCustomer entity plus the Fax property.

Then, what about the Phone column in the BaseCustomer entity? We know that there is a Phone column in the database table Customers and now USACustomer1 inherits BaseCustomer. Does this mean the Phone property in the child entity overrides the Phone property in the parent entity? The answer is no. Actually, there is no Phone property in the parent entity BaseCustomer, because we have moved it to another child entity USACustomer.

We can get the Phone value in the database table Customers through the USACustomer entity, like in the following code snippet:

```
var usaCustomer = (from c
    in NWEntities.BaseCustomers.OfType<USACustomer>()
    where c.CustomerID == usaCustomer1.CustomerID
    select c
    ).SingleOrDefault();
```

There is no compiling error for this code snippet, but if you run the program now, you will get an error as shown in the following screenshot:

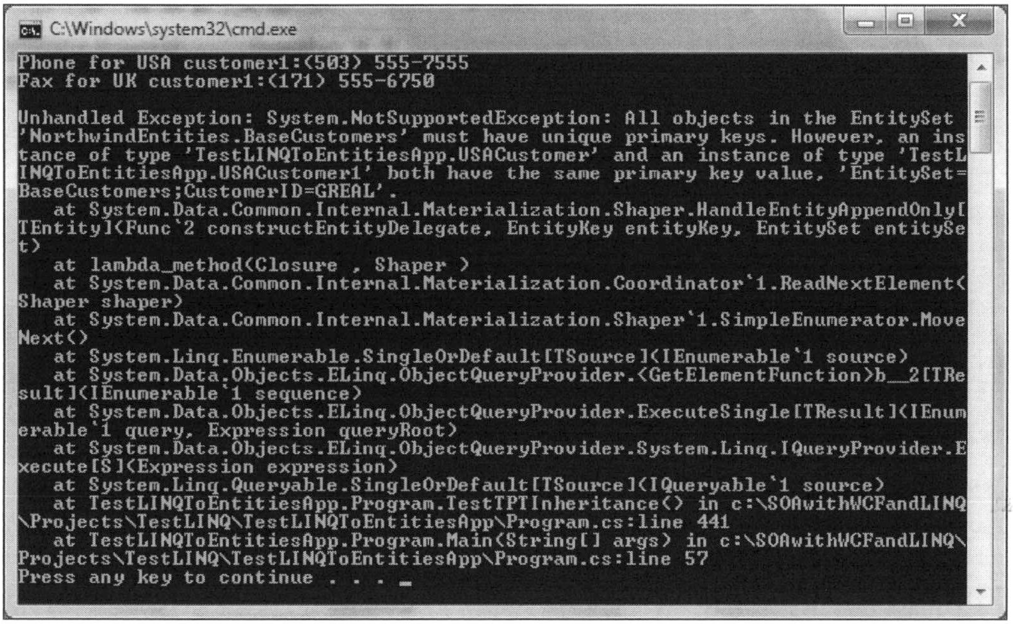

This is because within the same object context, there should be only one entity for a primary key. In our model, both USACustomer and USACustomer1 share the same primary key customerID. So if two entity objects are pointing to the same record in the database, we have a problem.

To solve this problem, we can change the preceding code to construct a new objet, which will not be managed by the object context:

```
var usaCustomer = (from c
    in NWEntities.BaseCustomers.OfType<USACustomer>()
    where c.CustomerID == usaCustomer1.CustomerID
    select new { c.CustomerID, c.Phone }
    ).SingleOrDefault();
```

If you run the program, you will see that both phones from the usaCustomer1 and usaCustomer for the first USA customer are (503) 555-7555, though we know they are from two different database tables. If you are not sure if they are all retrieved from the right tables, you can go to the database, change one of the phones to a different value, run it again, and verify that each entity is from the correct database table.

The method should be as follows:

```
static void TestTPTInheritance()
{
    using(NorthwindEntities NWEntities = new
    NorthwindEntities())
    {
      var usaCustomer1 = (from c
        in NWEntities.BaseCustomers.OfType<USACustomer1>()
        select c).FirstOrDefault();
      if (usaCustomer1 != null)
      {
          var phone1 = usaCustomer1.Phone;
          Console.WriteLine("Phone for USA customer1:{0}",
              phone1);
      }

      var ukCustomer1 = (from c
          in NWEntities.BaseCustomers.OfType<UKCustomer1>()
          select c).FirstOrDefault();
        if (ukCustomer1 != null)
      {
          var fax1 = ukCustomer1.Fax;
          Console.WriteLine("Fax for UK customer1:{0}",
              fax1);
      }

      /*
      var usaCustomer = (from c
          in NWEntities.BaseCustomers.OfType<USACustomer>()
          where c.CustomerID == usaCustomer1.CustomerID
          select c
          ).SingleOrDefault();
      */

      var usaCustomer = (from c
        in NWEntities.BaseCustomers.OfType<USACustomer>()
        where c.CustomerID == usaCustomer1.CustomerID
        select new { CustomerID = "new PK", c.Phone }
        ).SingleOrDefault();
```

```
        if (usaCustomer != null)
        {
            var phone = usaCustomer.Phone;
            Console.WriteLine(
              "Phone for USA customer from Customers table:{0}",
                  phone);
        }
    }
}
```

The output of this is shown in the following screenshot (note the phone number for the first customer has been changed to (503) 555-7000 in the USACustomers table, to distinguish it from the phone in the Customers table):

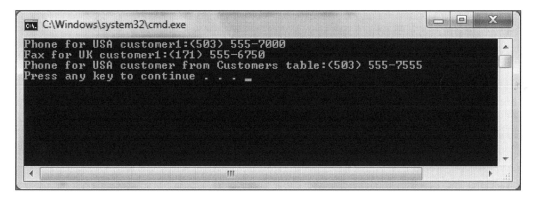

Handling simultaneous (concurrent) updates

If two users are updating the same record at the same time, a conflict will occur. There are normally three different ways to handle this conflict. The first method is to let the last update win so no controlling mechanism is needed. The second one is to use a pessimistic lock, in which case, before updating a record, a user will first lock the record and then process and update the record. At the same time, all other users will have to wait for the lock to be released in order to start the updating process.

The third and most common mechanism in an enterprise product is the optimistic locking. A user does not lock a record for update when the data is retrieved, but when the application is ready to commit the changes it will first check to see if any other user has updated the same record since that data was retrieved. If nobody else has changed the same record, the update will be committed. If any other user has changed the same record, the update will fail and the user has to decide what to do with the conflict. Some possible options include overwriting the previous changes, discarding their own changes, or refreshing the record, and then reapplying (merging) the changes.

LINQ to Entities supports optimistic concurrency control in two ways. Next, we will learn both of them.

Detecting conflicts using a data column

The first way is to use a regular data column to detect the conflicts. We can use the Concurrency Mode property for this purpose.

The Concurrency Mode property

At design time, the **Concurrency Mode** property can be set for a column to be one of the following two values:

- **Fixed**
- **None**

For a column, there are three values to remember:

- The original value before update
- The current value to be updated to
- The database value when the change is submitted

For example, consider the case where you fetch a product record from the database with a UnitPrice of 25.00 and update it to 26.00. After you fetch this product, but before you submit your changes back to the database, somebody else may have updated this product's price to 27.00. In this example, the original value of the price is 25.00, the current value to be updated to is 26.00, and the database value when the change is submitted is 27.00.

When the change is submitted to the database, the original value and the database value are compared. If they are different, a conflict is detected.

Now let us look at these two settings. The first setting of the `Concurrency Mode` property is `Fixed`, which means that the column will be used for conflict detecting. Whenever this column is being changed, its current value and database value will be checked to see if it has been updated by other users. If it has been, a conflict will be raised.

The second setting `None` means that the column will not be used for conflict checking. When a change is submitted to the database, the application will not check the status of this column. Therefore, even if this column has been updated by other users, it won't raise an error. This is the default setting of this property. So, by default, no column will be used for conflict detecting.

Adding another entity data model

To test the concurrency of Entity Framework we need to add a second entity data model to the project for the same database. The reason is that, with Entity Framework, each database record has a unique entity key within the entity data model. All entity instances of the same database record will share the same entity key in the data model—even the entities are created within different object contexts.

To understand why this will stop us from testing the concurrency support of Entity Framework, let's first list the steps that we will perform to test the concurrency control.

By performing the following steps, we will test the concurrency control of Entity Framework:

1. Retrieve a product from the database.
2. Update its price in memory.
3. Retrieve the same product from the database.
4. Update its price in memory again.
5. Submit the changes made in step 4 to the database.
6. Submit the changes made in step 2 to the database.

Theoretically, with the concurrency control, the commit in step 6 should fail because the product price has been changed by another user/process. However, if we use the same entity data model, the product that is retrieved in step 1 will be cached. So, in step 3, the product object from the cache will be returned, thus the update in step 4 will be based on the update in step 2. The commit to the database in step 5 will actually contain both changes in step 2 and step 4, therefore the commit to the database in step 6 will not fail because it really doesn't change anything in the database.

That's why we need to add another entity data model to the project, so we can have two independent entity objects pointing to the same record in the database. The following are the steps to add this new entity data model:

1. From Visual Studio Solution Explorer, right-click on the **TestLINQToEntitiesApp** project and select **Add | New Item**.

2. Select **Visual C# Items | ADO.NET Entity Data Model** as the template and change the item name to **Northwind1.edmx**.

3. Select **Generate from database** as **Model Contents**.

4. Select the existing **Northwind** connection as **Data Connection** and keep the default entities name as **NorthwindEntities1**.

5. Choose the **Products** table as **Database Objects** and keep the default model namespace as **NorthwindModel1**.

6. Click on the **Finish** button to add the model to the project.

7. Open Northwind1.edmx and select the **Product** entity.

8. Change its **Entity Set Name** to **Product1s**.

9. Change its (entity) **Name** to **Product1** and then save the model.

Steps 8 and 9 are essential because there is already a public class with the name of Product in our project. If you leave it unchanged and try to build/run the solution, you will find that your Northwind1.designer.cs file is empty because the designer can't generate it due to the name conflicts. In this case, you need to delete the new entity data model and re-add it to generate the new entity model designer file.

After you save this new model, your original Product class may disappear because Visual Studio thinks you are going to move the Product entity from the old model to this new model, even though we have renamed it to Product1. In this case, you can open the original model and re-save it to re-generate the Product class.

Writing the test code

Now that we have a new entity data model added to the project, we can write the following code to test the concurrency control of Entity Framework:

```
// first user
Console.WriteLine("First User ...");
Product product = (from p in NWEntities.Products
                   where p.ProductID == 2
                   select p).First();
Console.WriteLine("Original price: {0}", product.UnitPrice);
product.UnitPrice += 1.0m;
Console.WriteLine("Current price to update: {0}",
                  product.UnitPrice);
// process more products

// second user
Console.WriteLine("\nSecond User ...");
using(NorthwindEntities1 NWEntities1 = new NorthwindEntities1())
{
      Product1 product1 = (from p in NWEntities1.Product1s
                           where p.ProductID == 2
                           select p).First();
      Console.WriteLine("Original price: {0}", product1.UnitPrice);
      product1.UnitPrice += 2.0m;
      Console.WriteLine("Current price to update: {0}",
                        product1.UnitPrice);
      NWEntities1.SaveChanges();
   Console.WriteLine("Price update submitted to database");
}
   // first user is ready to submit changes
   Console.WriteLine("\nFirst User ...");
   NWEntities.SaveChanges();
   Console.WriteLine("Price update submitted to database");
```

In this example, we will first retrieve product 2 and increase its price by 1.0. Then we will simulate another user to retrieve the same product and increase its price by 2.0. The second user will submit the changes first with no error. When the first user tries to submit the changes and the price has already been changed by the second user, the update will still be saved to the database without any problem. This is because, by default, the concurrency control is not turned on so the later change will always overwrite the previous change.

Testing the conflicts

Now run the program. You will get an output as shown in the following screenshot:

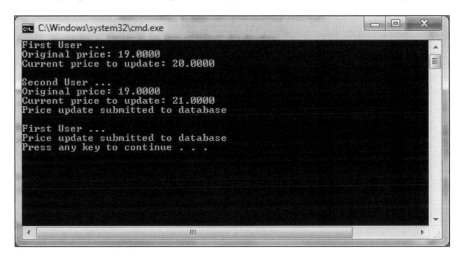

From this image we know both updates have been submitted to the database without any problem. If you query the database, you will find the price of product 2 is now 20, not 21, because the first user's update overwrote the second user's update.

Turning on concurrency control

Now open `Northwind.edmx`, click on the **UnitPrice** member of the **Product** entity, and change its **Concurrency Mode** to **Fixed**, as shown in following screenshot:

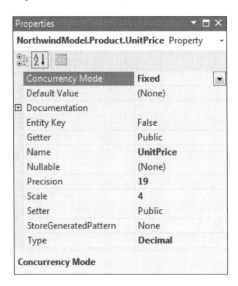

Make sure you open the `Northwind.edmx` model, not the new `Northwind1.edmx` model, because the second user within the new `Northwind1.edmx` model will submit to the database first, meaning that there will be no conflict for this update.

Run the program again. You will see an exception this time because the `price` column is now used for conflict detecting. If you query the database, you will find the price for product 2 is now 22 because it hasn't been overwritten by the first user's update, which would have updated its price to 21 if it hadn't failed due to the concurrent conflict.

The output is as shown in the following screenshot:

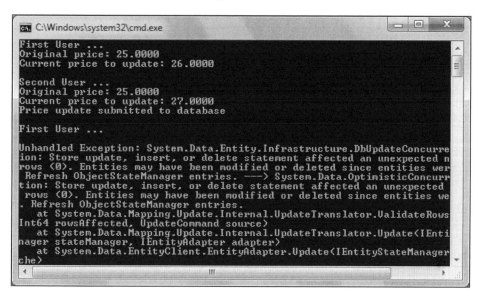

To resolve this conflict, we can add an exception handling block around the first user's update, as shown in the following code snippet:

```
// first user is ready to submit changes
Console.WriteLine("\nFirst User ...");
try
{
    NWEntities.SaveChanges();
    Console.WriteLine("Price update submitted to database");
}
catch (DbUpdateConcurrencyException e)
{
    Console.WriteLine("Conflicts detected. Refreshing ...");
```

```
        var entry = e.Entries.Single();
        entry.OriginalValues.SetValues(entry.GetDatabaseValues());

        NWEntities.SaveChanges();
        Console.WriteLine("Price update submitted to database after
refresh");
    }
```

You need to add a `using` block to the `Program.cs` file for the concurrency exception type:

```
using System.Data.Entity.Infrastructure;
```

The complete method should be as follows:

```
static void TestSimultaneousChanges()
{
using(NorthwindEntities NWEntities = new NorthwindEntities())
   {

    // first user
    Console.WriteLine("First User ...");
    Product product = (from p in NWEntities.Products
                       where p.ProductID == 2
                       select p).First();
    Console.WriteLine("Original price: {0}", product.UnitPrice);
    product.UnitPrice += 1.0m;
    Console.WriteLine("Current price to update: {0}",
                      product.UnitPrice);
    // process more products

    // second user
    Console.WriteLine("\nSecond User ...");
using(NorthwindEntities1 NWEntities1 = new NorthwindEntities1())
    {
        Product1 product1 = (from p in NWEntities1.Product1s
                             where p.ProductID == 2
                             select p).First();
        Console.WriteLine("Original price: {0}",
        product1.UnitPrice);
        product1.UnitPrice += 2.0m;
        Console.WriteLine("Current price to update: {0}",
                          product1.UnitPrice);
        NWEntities1.SaveChanges();
        Console.WriteLine("Price update submitted to database");
    }
```

```
        // first user is ready to submit changes
        Console.WriteLine("\nFirst User ...");
        try
        {
            NWEntities.SaveChanges();
            Console.WriteLine("Price update submitted to database");
        }
        catch (DbUpdateConcurrencyException e)
        {
            Console.WriteLine("Conflicts detected. Refreshing ...");

            var entry = e.Entries.Single();
            entry.OriginalValues.SetValues(entry.GetDatabaseValues());
            NWEntities.SaveChanges();
            Console.WriteLine("Price update submitted to database
            after refresh");
        }
    }
}
```

Run the program now and you will get an output as shown in the
following screenshot:

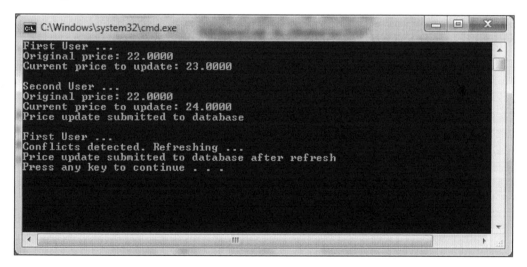

From this output we know that the first user's update failed due to the
concurrency conflict, but after the refresh, it won the conflict so the final
price in the database should be 23 — the second user's update has been
overwritten by the first user's update.

With this mechanism, only the involved column is protected for concurrent updates. All other columns can still be updated by multiple users or processes without causing conflicts. For example, if you change the previous code to update the `UnitsInStock` property, you won't get a concurrency exception because the concurrency mode of `UnitsInStock` is not set to Fixed and the concurrency setting of `UnitPrice` doesn't check the `UnitsInStock` column in the database.

Detecting conflicts using a version column

The second and more efficient way to provide conflict control is to use a version column. If you add a column of type `Timestamp` or `ROWVERSION`, when you add this table to the entity model, this column will be marked as a concurrency control version property.

Version numbers are incremented and timestamp columns are updated every time the associated row is updated. Before the update, if there is a column of this type, LINQ to Entities will first check this column to make sure that this record has not been updated by any of the other users. This column will also be synchronized immediately after the data row is updated. The new values are visible after `SaveChanges` finishes.

Adding a version column

Now let us try this in the `Products` table. First we need to add a new column called **RowVersion**, which is of the **timestamp** type. You can add it within SQL Server Management Studio, as shown in the following screenshot:

MYLAPTOP.Northwind - dbo.Products*		
Column Name	Data Type	Allow Nulls
ProductID	int	☐
ProductName	nvarchar(40)	☐
SupplierID	int	☑
CategoryID	int	☑
QuantityPerUnit	nvarchar(20)	☑
UnitPrice	money	☑
UnitsInStock	smallint	☑
UnitsOnOrder	smallint	☑
ReorderLevel	smallint	☑
Discontinued	bit	☐
RowVersion	timestamp	☑
		☐

Modeling the Products table with a version column

After saving the changes, we need to refresh our data model to take this change to the data model. Follow these steps to refresh the model:

1. From Visual Studio, open the `Northwind.edmx` entity designer, right-click on an empty space, and select **Update Model from Database...**. Click on the **Refresh** tab and you will see **Products** in the refresh list.

2. Click on the **Finish** button and save the model.

Now a new property `RowVersion` has been added to the `Northwind.edmx` data model. However, its **Concurrency Mode** is set to **None** now, so you need to change it to **Fixed**. Note that its **StoreGeneratedPattern** is set to **Computed**, which is to make sure this property will be refreshed every time after an update. The following screenshot displays the **Concurrency Mode** and **StoreGeneratedPattern** properties of the new `RowVersion` entity property:

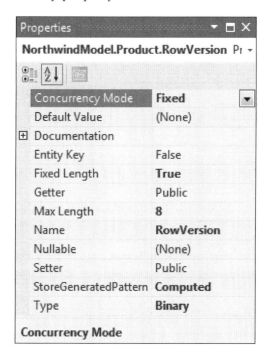

Writing the test code

We can write similar code to test this new version controlling mechanism:

```
static void TestVersionControl()
{
using(NorthwindEntities NWEntities = new NorthwindEntities())
{

  // first user
  Console.WriteLine("First User ...");
  Product product = (from p in NWEntities.Products
                     where p.ProductID == 3
                     select p).First();
  Console.WriteLine("Original unit in stock: {0}",
  product.UnitsInStock);
  product.UnitsInStock += 1;
  Console.WriteLine("Current unit in stock to update: {0}",
    product.UnitsInStock);
  // process more products

  // second user
  Console.WriteLine("\nSecond User ...");
  using(NorthwindEntities1 NWEntities1 = new NorthwindEntities1())
  {
    Product1 product1 = (from p in NWEntities1.Product1s
                         where p.ProductID == 3
                         select p).First();
    Console.WriteLine("Original unit in stock: {0}",
        product1.UnitsInStock);
    product1.UnitsInStock += 2;
    Console.WriteLine("Current unit in stock to update: {0}",
        product1.UnitsInStock);
    NWEntities1.SaveChanges();
    Console.WriteLine("update submitted to database");
  }

  // first user is ready to submit changes
  Console.WriteLine("\nFirst User ...");
  try
  {
    NWEntities.SaveChanges();
  }
    catch (DbUpdateConcurrencyException e)
    {
      Console.WriteLine("Conflicts detected. Refreshing ...");
```

```
var entry = e.Entries.Single();
entry.OriginalValues.SetValues(entry.GetDatabaseValues());
NWEntities.SaveChanges();
Console.WriteLine("update submitted to database after
refresh");
        }
    }
}
```

Testing the conflicts

This time we tried to update UnitInStock for product 3. From the output, we can see a conflict was detected again when the first user submitted changes to the database, but this time the versioning is controlled by a version column, not by the unit in stock column itself.

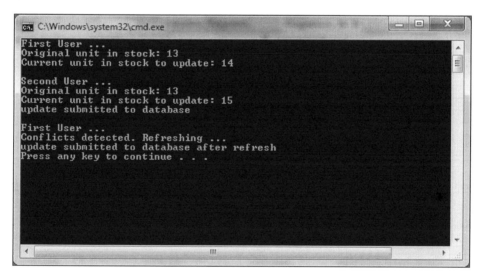

Transaction support

In the previous section, we learned that simultaneous changes by different users can be controlled by using a version column or the **Concurrency Mode** property. Sometimes the same user may have made several changes and some of the changes might not succeed. In this case, we need a way to control the behavior of the overall update result. This is handled by transaction support.

LINQ to Entities uses the same transaction mechanism as ADO.NET, that is, it uses implicit or explicit transactions.

Implicit transactions

By default, LINQ to Entities uses an implicit transaction for each SaveChanges call. All updates between two SaveChanges calls are wrapped within one transaction.

For example, in the following code, we are trying to update two products. The second update will fail due to a constraint. However, as the first update is in a separate transaction, the update has been saved to the database and the first update will stay in the database:

```
static void TestImplicitTransaction()
{
  using(NorthwindEntities NWEntities = new NorthwindEntities())
  {
    Product prod1 = (from p in NWEntities.Products
                     where p.ProductID == 4
                     select p).First();
    Product prod2 = (from p in NWEntities.Products
                     where p.ProductID == 5
                     select p).First();
    prod1.UnitPrice += 1;
    // update will be saved to database
    NWEntities.SaveChanges();
    Console.WriteLine("First update saved to database");

    prod2.UnitPrice = -5;
    // update will fail because UnitPrice can't be < 0
    // but previous update stays in database
    try
    {
        NWEntities.SaveChanges();
        Console.WriteLine("Second update saved to database");
    }
    catch (Exception)
    {
        Console.WriteLine("Second update not saved to database");
    }
  }
}
```

The output will look as shown in the following screenshot:

Explicit transactions

In addition to implicit transactions, you can also define a transaction scope to explicitly control the update behavior. All updates within a transaction scope will be within a single transaction. Thus, they will all either succeed or fail.

For example, in the following code snippet, we first start a transaction scope. Then, within this transaction scope, we update one product and submit the change to the database. However, at this point, the update has not really been committed because the transaction scope is still not closed. We then try to update another product, which fails due to the same constraint as in the previous example. The final result is that neither of these two products has been updated in the database.

```
static void TestExplicitTransaction()
{
  using(NorthwindEntities NWEntities = new NorthwindEntities())
  {

    using (TransactionScope ts = new TransactionScope())
    {
      try
      {
        Product prod1 = (from p in NWEntities.Products
                         where p.ProductID == 4
                         select p).First();
        prod1.UnitPrice += 1;
        NWEntities.SaveChanges();
        Console.WriteLine("First update saved to database, but not
        commited.");
```

```
            // now let's try to update another product
            Product prod2 = (from p in NWEntities.Products
                             where p.ProductID == 5
                             select p).First();
            // update will fail because UnitPrice can't be < 0
            prod2.UnitPrice = -5;
            NWEntities.SaveChanges();
            ts.Complete();
        }
        catch (Exception e)
        {
            // both updates will fail because they are within one
            // transaction
            Console.WriteLine("Exception caught. Rollback the first
            update.");
        }
    }
  }
}
```

Note that `TransactionScope` is in .NET Assembly `System.Transactions`. Therefore, first you need to add a reference to `System.Transactions` and then add the following using statement to the `Program.cs` file:

```
using System.Transactions;
```

> In the **Reference Manager** window, if you cannot find the assembly `System.Transactions` under the **Framework** tab in **Assemblies**, you can browse to the `System.Transactions.dll` file and add it as a reference. In Windows 7, this `.dll` file is under the folder `C:\Windows\Microsoft.NET\Framework\v4.0.30319`.

The output of the program is shown in the following screenshot:

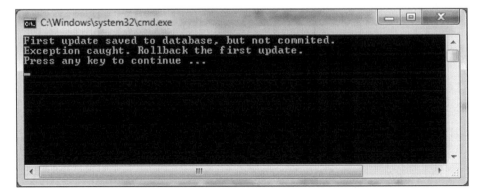

To use `TransactionScope`, you need to have **Microsoft Distributed Transaction Coordinator (MSDTC)** configured properly. We will cover distributed transaction in detail in a subsequent chapter, so if you encounter any problem related to MSDTC here, you can refer to that chapter to set up your MSDTC environment or you can just skip this section for now and come back later after reading that chapter.

If you start the program in debugging mode, after the first `SaveChanges` is called, you can go to SQL Server Management Studio and query the price of product 4 by using the following statement:

```
select UnitPrice from products (nolock) where productID = 4
```

The `nolock` hint is equivalent to `READUNCOMMITTED` and it is used to retrieve dirty data that has not been committed. With this hint, you can see that its price has been increased by the first change. Then, after the second `SaveChanges` is called, an exception is thrown, and the transaction scope is closed. At this point if you run the query again, you will see that the price of product 4 is rolled back to its original value.

After the first call to the `SaveChanges` method, you shouldn't use the following statement to query the price value of the product:

```
select UnitPrice from products where productID = 4
```

If you do so, you will not get back a result. Instead, you will be waiting forever as it is waiting for the transaction to be committed.

This also brings up a big tradeoff of using explicit/distributed transactions—deadlocks. We will cover more about distributed transactions in *Chapter 10, Distributed Transaction Support of WCF*.

Summary

In this chapter, we learned advanced features of LINQ to Entities. We learned how to use stored procedures. We also learned how to use transaction support and how to use concurrency control for LINQ to Entities. At this point, you should have a good understanding of LINQ to Entities.

In the next chapter, we will apply these skills to the data access layer of our WCF service to connect to databases securely and reliably with LINQ to Entities.

9
Applying LINQ to Entities to a WCF Service

Now that we have learned all of the features related to LINQ and LINQ to Entities, we will use them in the data access layer of a WCF service. We will create a new WCF service very similar to the one we created in the previous chapters, but in this service, we will use LINQ to Entities to connect to the Northwind database to retrieve and update a product.

In the data access layer, we will use LINQ to Entities to retrieve product information from the database and return it to the business logic layer. You will see that with LINQ to Entities, we will need only one LINQ statement to retrieve the product details from the database in the GetProduct method and we will no longer need to worry about the database connection or the actual query statement.

In this chapter, we will also learn how to update a product with LINQ to Entities in the data access layer. We will see how to apply changes of a client object to LINQ to Entities and leave all of the update work to LINQ to Entities, and will also see how to control the concurrency of updates with LINQ to Entities.

In this chapter we will cover the following:

- Creating the solution
- Modeling the Northwind database in the LINQ to Entities designer
- Adding the business domain object project
- Implementing the data access layer using LINQ to Entities
- Adding the business logic layer
- Adding the service interface layer

- Implementing the test client
- Testing the get and update operations of the WCF service
- Testing concurrent updates with LINQ to Entities

Creating the LINQNorthwind solution

The first thing we need to do is create a test solution. In this chapter, we will start from the data access layer. Perform the following steps:

1. Start Visual Studio.
2. Create a new class library project `LINQNorthwindDAL` with solution name `LINQNorthwind` (make sure the `Create` directory for the solution is checked to specify the solution name).
3. Delete the `Class1.cs` file.
4. Add a new class `ProductDAO` to the project.
5. Change the new class `ProductDAO` to be public.

Now you should have a new solution with the empty data access layer class. Next, we will add a model to this layer and create the business logic layer and the service interface layer.

Modeling the Northwind database

In the previous section, we created the `LINQNorthwind` solution. Next, we will apply LINQ to Entities to this new solution.

For the data access layer, we will use LINQ to Entities instead of the raw ADO.NET data adapters. As you will see in the next section, we will use one LINQ statement to retrieve product information from the database and the update LINQ statements will handle the concurrency control for us easily and reliably.

As you may recall, to use LINQ to Entities in the data access layer of our WCF service, we first need to add an entity data model to the project. The following steps are very similar to those described in the *Chapter 8*, *LINQ to Entities: Advanced Concepts and Features*. You can refer back to that chapter for more information and screenshots if necessary.

1. In the Solution Explorer, right-click on the project item **LINQNorthwindDAL**, select menu options **Add | New Item...**, and then choose **Visual C# Items | ADO.NET Entity Data Model** as **Template** and enter `Northwind.edmx` as the name.

2. Select **Generate from database**, choose the existing **Northwind** connection, and add the **Products** table to the model.

3. Click on the **Finish** button to add the model to the project.

4. The new column **RowVersion** should be in the **Product** entity as we added it in the previous chapter. If it is not there, add it to the database table with a type of **Timestamp** and refresh the entity data model from the database (you can look at the *Modeling the Products table with a version column* section in *Chapter 8, LINQ to Entities: Advanced Concepts and Features* for more details about how to refresh an entity model from a database).

5. In the EMD designer, select the **RowVersion** property of the **Product** entity and change its **Concurrency Mode** from **None** to **Fixed**. Note that its **StoreGeneratedPattern** should remain as **Computed**. You can refer to the *Turning on concurrency control* section in *Chapter 8, LINQ to Entities: Advanced Concepts and Features* for a screenshot.

Just as in the previous chapter, this will generate a file called `Northwind.Context.cs`, which contains the Db context for the `Northwind` database. Another file called `Product.cs` is also generated, which contains the `Product` entity class. You need to save the data model in order to see these two files in the Solution Explorer.

> In Visual Studio Solution Explorer, the `Northwind.Context.cs` file is under the template file `Northwind.Context.tt` and `Product.cs` is under `Northwind.tt`. However, in Windows Explorer, they are two separate files from the template files.

Creating the business domain object project

In *Chapter 4, Implementing a WCF Service in the Real World*, we created a **business domain object (BDO)** project to hold the intermediate data between the data access objects and the service interface objects. In this section, we will also add such a project to the solution for the same purpose.

1. In the Solution Explorer, right-click on the **LINQNorthwind** solution.

2. Select **Add | New Project...** to add a new class library project named `LINQNorthwindBDO`.

3. Delete the `Class1.cs` file.

4. Add a new class file `ProductBDO.cs`.

5. Change the new class `ProductBDO` to be public.

6. Add the following properties to this class:
   - `ProductID`
   - `ProductName`
   - `QuantityPerUnit`
   - `UnitPrice`
   - `Discontinued`
   - `UnitsInStock`
   - `UnitsOnOrder`
   - `ReorderLevel`
   - `RowVersion`

The following is the code list of the `ProductBDO` class:

```
using System;
using System.Collections.Generic;
using System.Linq;
using System.Text;
using System.Threading.Tasks;

namespace LINQNorthwindBDO
{
    public class ProductBDO
    {
        public int ProductID { get; set; }
        public string ProductName { get; set; }
        public string QuantityPerUnit { get; set; }
        public decimal UnitPrice { get; set; }
        public int UnitsInStock { get; set; }
        public int ReorderLevel { get; set; }
        public int UnitsOnOrder { get; set; }
        public bool Discontinued { get; set; }
        public byte[] RowVersion { get; set; }
    }
}
```

As noted earlier, in this chapter we will use BDO to hold the intermediate data between the data access objects and the data contract objects. Besides this approach, there are some other ways to pass data back and forth between the data access layer and the service interface layer, and two of them are listed as follows:

- The first one is to expose the Entity Framework context objects from the data access layer up to the service interface layer. In this way, both the service interface layer and the business logic layer—we will implement them soon in following sections—can interact directly with the Entity Framework. This approach is not recommended as it goes against the best practice of service layering, as we have discussed in *Chapter 4, Implementing a WCF Service in the Real World.*

- Another approach is to use self-tracking entities. **Self-tracking entities** are entities that know how to do their own change tracking regardless of which tier those changes are made on. You can expose self-tracking entities from the data access layer to the business logic layer, then to the service interface layer, and even share the entities with the clients. Because self-tracking entities are independent of entity context, you don't need to expose the entity context objects. The problem of this approach is, you have to share the binary files with all the clients, thus it is the least interoperable approach for a WCF service. Now this approach is not recommended by Microsoft, so in this book we will not discuss it.

Using LINQ to Entities in the data access layer

Next we will modify the data access layer to use LINQ to Entities to retrieve and update products. We will first create `GetProduct` to retrieve a product from the database and then create `UpdateProduct` to update a product in the database.

Adding a reference to the BDO project

Now we have the BDO project in the solution, we need to modify the data access layer project to reference it.

1. In the Solution Explorer, right-click on the **LINQNorthwindDAL** project.
2. Select **Add Reference...**.
3. Select the **LINQNorthwindBDO** project from the **Projects** tab under **Solution**.
4. Click on the **OK** button to add the reference to the project.

Creating GetProduct in the data access layer

We can now create the GetProduct method in the data access layer class ProductDAO, to use LINQ to Entities to retrieve a product from the database. Just as we did in the previous chapter, we will first create an entity DbContext object and then use LINQ to Entities to get the product from the DbContext object. The product we get from DbContext will be a conceptual entity model object. However, we don't want to pass this product object back to the upper-level layer because we don't want to tightly couple the business logic layer with the data access layer. Therefore, we will convert this entity model product object to a ProductBDO object and then pass this ProductBDO object back to the upper-level layers.

To create the new method, first add the following using statement to the ProductBDO class:

```
using LINQNorthwindBDO;
```

Then add the following method to the ProductBDO class:

```
public ProductBDO GetProduct(int id)
{
    ProductBDO productBDO = null;
    using (var NWEntities = new NorthwindEntities())
    {
        Product product = (from p in NWEntities.Products
                            where p.ProductID == id
                            select p).FirstOrDefault();
        if (product != null)
            productBDO = new ProductBDO()
            {
                ProductID = product.ProductID,
                ProductName = product.ProductName,
                QuantityPerUnit = product.QuantityPerUnit,
                UnitPrice = (decimal)product.UnitPrice,
                UnitsInStock = (int)product.UnitsInStock,
                ReorderLevel = (int)product.ReorderLevel,
                UnitsOnOrder = (int)product.UnitsOnOrder,
                Discontinued = product.Discontinued,
                RowVersion = product.RowVersion
            };
    }
    return productBDO;
}
```

You will recall that from *Chapter 4, Implementing a WCF Service in the Real World*, within the `GetProduct` method, we had to create an ADO.NET connection, create an ADO.NET command object with that connection, specify the command text, connect to the `Northwind` database, and send the SQL statement to the database for execution. After the result was returned from the database, we had to loop through the `DataReader` and cast the columns to our entity object one by one.

With LINQ to Entities, we only construct one LINQ to Entities statement and everything else is handled by LINQ to Entities. Not only do we need to write less code, but now the statement is also strongly typed. We won't have a runtime error such as `invalid query syntax` or `invalid column name`. Also, a SQL Injection attack is no longer an issue, as LINQ to Entities will also take care of this when translating LINQ expressions to the underlying SQL statements.

Creating UpdateProduct in the data access layer

In the previous section, we created the `GetProduct` method in the data access layer, using LINQ to Entities instead of ADO.NET. Now in this section, we will create the `UpdateProduct` method, using LINQ to Entities instead of ADO.NET.

Let's create the `UpdateProduct` method in the data access layer class `ProductBDO`, as follows:

```
public bool UpdateProduct(
    ref ProductBDO productBDO,
    ref string message)
{
    message = "product updated successfully";
    bool ret = true;

    using (var NWEntities = new NorthwindEntities())
    {
        var productID = productBDO.ProductID;
        Product productInDB =
                (from p
                in NWEntities.Products
                where p.ProductID == productID
                select p).FirstOrDefault();
```

```
        // check product
        if (productInDB == null)
        {
            throw new Exception("No product with ID " +
                                productBDO.ProductID);
        }

        NWEntities.Products.Remove(productInDB);

        // update product
        productInDB.ProductName = productBDO.ProductName;
        productInDB.QuantityPerUnit = productBDO.QuantityPerUnit;
        productInDB.UnitPrice = productBDO.UnitPrice;
        productInDB.Discontinued = productBDO.Discontinued;
        productInDB.RowVersion = productBDO.RowVersion;

        NWEntities.Products.Attach(productInDB);
        NWEntities.Entry(productInDB).State =
            System.Data.EntityState.Modified;
        int num = NWEntities.SaveChanges();

        productBDO.RowVersion = productInDB.RowVersion;

        if (num != 1)
        {
            ret = false;
            message = "no product is updated";
        }
    }
    return ret;
}
```

Within this method, we first get the product from database, making sure the product ID is a valid value in the database. Then, we apply the changes from the passed-in object to the object we have just retrieved from the database, and submit the changes back to the database. Let's go through a few notes about this method:

1. You have to save `productID` in a new variable and then use it in the LINQ query. Otherwise, you will get an error saying **Cannot use ref or out parameter 'productBDO' inside an anonymous method, lambda expression, or query expression**.

2. If `Remove` and `Attach` are not called, `RowVersion` from database (not from the client) will be used when submitting to database, even though you have updated its value before submitting to the database. An update will always succeed, but without concurrency control.

3. If `Remove` is not called and you call the `Attach` method, you will get an error saying **The object cannot be attached because it is already in the object context**.

4. If the object state is not set to be `Modified`, Entity Framework will not honor your changes to the entity object and you will not be able to save any change to the database.

Creating the business logic layer

Now let's create the business logic layer. The steps here are very similar to the steps in *Chapter 4, Implementing a WCF Service in the Real World*, so you can refer to that chapter for more details.

1. Right click on the solution item and select **Add | New Project...**. Add a class library project with the name `LINQNorthwindLogic`.

2. Add a project reference to `LINQNorthwindDAL` and `LINQNorthwindBDO` to this new project.

3. Delete the `Class1.cs` file.

4. Add a new class file `ProductLogic.cs`.

5. Change the new class `ProductLogic` to be public.

6. Add the following two `using` statements to the `ProductLogic.cs` class file:
   ```
   using LINQNorthwindDAL;
   using LINQNorthwindBDO;
   ```

7. Add the following class member variable to the `ProductLogic` class:
   ```
   ProductDAO productDAO = new ProductDAO();
   ```

8. Add the following new method `GetProduct` to the `ProductLogic` class:
   ```
   public ProductBDO GetProduct(int id)
   {
       return productDAO.GetProduct(id);
   }
   ```

9. Add the following new method `UpdateProduct` to the `ProductLogic` class:
   ```
   public bool UpdateProduct(
     ref ProductBDO productBDO,
     ref string message)
   ```

```
        {
            var productInDB =
                GetProduct(productBDO.ProductID);
            // invalid product to update
            if (productInDB == null)
            {
                message = "cannot get product for this ID";
                return false;
            }
            // a product cannot be discontinued
            // if there are non-fulfilled orders
            if (productBDO.Discontinued == true
                && productInDB.UnitsOnOrder > 0)
            {
                message = "cannot discontinue this product";
                return false;
            }
            else
            {
                return productDAO.UpdateProduct(ref productBDO,
                    ref message);
            }
        }
    }
```

Build the solution. We now have only one more step to go, that is, adding the service interface layer.

Creating the service interface layer

The last step is to create the service interface layer. Again, the steps here are very similar to the steps in *Chapter 4, Implementing a WCF Service in the Real World*, so you can refer to that chapter for more details.

1. Right-click on the solution item and select **Add | New Project...**. Add a WCF service library project with the name of LINQNorthwindService.

2. Add a project reference to LINQNorthwindLogic and LINQNorthwindBDO to this new service interface project.

3. Change the service interface file IService1.cs, as follows:

    a. Change its filename from IService1.cs to IProductService.cs.

    b. Change the interface name from IService1 to IProductService, if it is not done for you.

c. Remove the original two service operations and add the following two new operations:

```
[OperationContract]
[FaultContract(typeof(ProductFault))]
Product GetProduct(int id);

[OperationContract]
[FaultContract(typeof(ProductFault))]
bool UpdateProduct(ref Product product, ref string
message);
```

d. Remove the original CompositeType and add the following data contract classes:

```
[DataContract]
public class Product
{
    [DataMember]
    public int ProductID { get; set; }
    [DataMember]
    public string ProductName { get; set; }
    [DataMember]
    public string QuantityPerUnit { get; set; }
    [DataMember]
    public decimal UnitPrice { get; set; }
    [DataMember]
    public bool Discontinued { get; set; }
    [DataMember]
    public byte[] RowVersion { get; set; }
}

[DataContract]
public class ProductFault
{
    public ProductFault(string msg)
    {
        FaultMessage = msg;
    }

    [DataMember]
    public string FaultMessage;
}
```

e. The following is the content of the `IProductService.cs` file:

```csharp
using System;
using System.Collections.Generic;
using System.Linq;
using System.Runtime.Serialization;
using System.ServiceModel;
using System.Text;

namespace LINQNorthwindService
{
    [ServiceContract]
    public interface IProductService
    {
        [OperationContract]
        [FaultContract(typeof(ProductFault))]
        Product GetProduct(int id);

        [OperationContract]
        [FaultContract(typeof(ProductFault))]
        bool UpdateProduct(ref Product product,
            ref string message);
    }

    [DataContract]
    public class Product
    {
        [DataMember]
        public int ProductID { get; set; }
        [DataMember]
        public string ProductName { get; set; }
        [DataMember]
        public string QuantityPerUnit { get; set; }
        [DataMember]
        public decimal UnitPrice { get; set; }
        [DataMember]
        public bool Discontinued { get; set; }
        [DataMember]
        public byte[] RowVersion { get; set; }
    }
    [DataContract]
    public class ProductFault
    {
        public ProductFault(string msg)
```

```
    {
        FaultMessage = msg;
    }

    [DataMember]
    public string FaultMessage;
    }
}
```

4. Change the service implementation file `Service1.cs`, as follows:

   a. Change its filename from `Service1.cs` to `ProductService.cs`.

   b. Change its class name from `Service1` to `ProductService`, if it is not done for you.

   c. Add the following two `using` statements to the `ProductService.cs` file:

      ```
      using LINQNorthwindLogic;
      using LINQNorthwindBDO;
      ```

   d. Add the following class member variable:

      ```
      ProductLogic productLogic = new ProductLogic();
      ```

   e. Remove the original two methods and add following two methods:

      ```
      public Product GetProduct(int id)
      {
          ProductBDO productBDO = null;
          try
          {
              productBDO = productLogic.GetProduct(id);
          }
          catch (Exception e)
          {
              string msg = e.Message;
              string reason = "GetProduct Exception";
              throw new FaultException<ProductFault>
                  (new ProductFault(msg), reason);
          }

          if (productBDO == null)
          {
              string msg =
                  string.Format("No product found for id {0}",
                  id);
      ```

```
            string reason = "GetProduct Empty Product";
            throw new FaultException<ProductFault>
                (new ProductFault(msg), reason);
        }
        Product product = new Product();
        TranslateProductBDOToProductDTO(productBDO,
product);
        return product;
    }

    public bool UpdateProduct(ref Product product,
        ref string message)
    {
        bool result = true;

        // first check to see if it is a valid price
        if (product.UnitPrice <= 0)
        {
            message = "Price cannot be <= 0";
            result = false;
        }
        // ProductName can't be empty
        else if (string.IsNullOrEmpty(product.ProductName))
        {
            message = "Product name cannot be empty";
            result = false;
        }
        // QuantityPerUnit can't be empty
        else if
        (string.IsNullOrEmpty(product.QuantityPerUnit))
        {
            message = "Quantity cannot be empty";
            result = false;
        }
        else
        {
            try
            {
                var productBDO = new ProductBDO();
                TranslateProductDTOToProductBDO(product,
                productBDO);
                result = productLogic.UpdateProduct(
                    ref productBDO, ref message);
                product.RowVersion = productBDO.RowVersion;
            }
```

```
                    catch (Exception e)
                    {
                        string msg = e.Message;
                        throw new FaultException<ProductFault>
                            (new ProductFault(msg), msg);
                    }
                }
                return result;
            }
```

5. Because we have to convert between the data contract objects and the business domain objects, we need to add the following two methods:

```
private void TranslateProductBDOToProductDTO(
    ProductBDO productBDO,
    Product product)
{
    product.ProductID = productBDO.ProductID;
    product.ProductName = productBDO.ProductName;
    product.QuantityPerUnit = productBDO.QuantityPerUnit;
    product.UnitPrice = productBDO.UnitPrice;
    product.Discontinued = productBDO.Discontinued;
    product.RowVersion = productBDO.RowVersion;
}

private void TranslateProductDTOToProductBDO(
    Product product,
    ProductBDO productBDO)
{
    productBDO.ProductID = product.ProductID;
    productBDO.ProductName = product.ProductName;
    productBDO.QuantityPerUnit = product.QuantityPerUnit;
    productBDO.UnitPrice = product.UnitPrice;
    productBDO.Discontinued = product.Discontinued;
    productBDO.RowVersion = product.RowVersion;
}
```

6. Change the config file `App.config`, as follows:

    a. Change `Service1` to `ProductService`.

    b. Remove the word `Design_Time_Addresses`.

    c. Change the port to `8080`.

    d. Now, `BaseAddress` should be as follows:

       ```
       http://localhost:8080/LINQNorthwindService/
       ProductService/
       ```

e. Copy the connection string from the `App.config` file in the `LINQNorthwindDAL` project to the following `App.config` file:

```
<connectionStrings>
  <add name="NorthwindEntities"
connectionString="metadata=res://*/Northwind.
csdl|res://*/Northwind.ssdl|res://*/Northwind.
msl;provider=System.Data.SqlClient;provider
connection string=&quot;data source=localhost;initial
catalog=Northwind;integrated security=True;Multipl
eActiveResultSets=True;App=EntityFramework&quot;"
providerName="System.Data.EntityClient" />
</connectionStrings>
```

You should leave the original connection string untouched in the `App.config` file in the data access layer project. This connection string is used by the Entity Model Designer at design time. It is not used at all during runtime, but if you remove it, whenever you open the entity model designer in Visual Studio, you will be prompted to specify a connection to your database.

Now build the solution and there should be no errors.

Testing the service with the WCF Test Client

Now we can run the program to test the `GetProduct` and `UpdateProduct` operations with the WCF Test Client.

You may need to run Visual Studio as administrator to start the WCF Test Client. You can refer to *Chapter 3, Hosting and Debugging the HelloWorld WCF Service,* for more details on how to set up your WCF development environment.

First set `LINQNorthwindService` as the startup project and then press *Ctrl + F5* to start the WCF Test Client. Double-click on the **GetProduct** operation, enter a valid product ID, and click on the **Invoke** button. The detailed product information should be retrieved and displayed on the screen, as shown in the following screenshot:

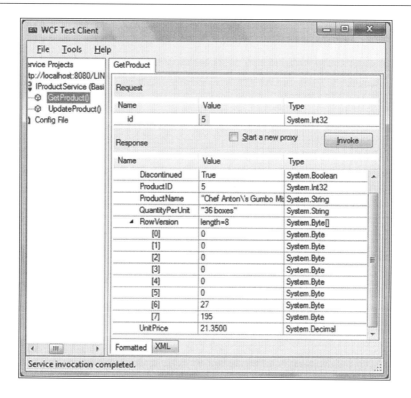

Now double-click on the **UpdateProduct** operation, enter a valid product ID, and specify a name, price, quantity per unit, and then click on **Invoke**.

This time you will get an exception as shown in the following screenshot:

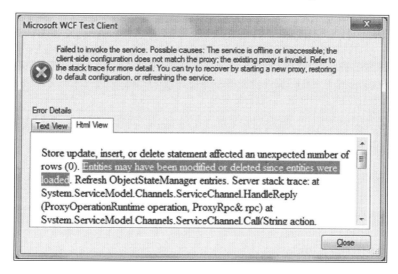

From this image we can see that the update failed. The error details, which are in HTML View in the preceding screenshot, actually tell us it is a concurrency error. This is because, from WCF Test Client, we can't enter a row version as it is not a simple datatype parameter, thus we didn't pass in the original RowVersion for the object to be updated, and when updating the object in the database, the Entity Framework thinks this product has been updated by some other users.

Testing concurrency with our own client

From an earlier section, we know that with WCF Test Client we cannot test the UpdateProduct method, nor can we test the concurrency support of the WCF service, because with WCF Test Client, we cannot update products. To test the concurrency support of the Entity Framework, we have to use our own test client.

Creating the test client

In this section, we will create a WinForm client to get the product details and update price for a product.

Follow these steps to create the test client:

1. In the Solution Explorer, right-click on the solution item, and select **Add | New Project...**.

2. Select **Visual C# | Windows Forms Application** as the template and change the name to LINQNorthwindClient. Click on the **OK** button to add the new project.

3. On the form designer, add the following five controls:

   ◦ A label named **lblProductID** with the text **Product ID**

   ◦ A textbox named **txtProductID**

   ◦ A button named **btnGetProductDetails** with the text **&Get Product Details**

   ◦ A label named **lblProductDetails** with the text **Product Details**

   ◦ A textbox named **txtProductDetails** with the **Multiline** property set to **True**

The layout of the form is as shown in the following screenshot:

4. In the Solution Explorer, right-click on the **LINQNorthwindClient** project and select **Add Service Reference...**.

5. On the **Add Service Reference** window, click on the **Discover** button, wait a minute until the service is displayed, then change **Namespace** from **ServiceReference1** to **ProductServiceRef**, and click on the **OK** button.

The **Add Service Reference** window should be as shown in the following screenshot:

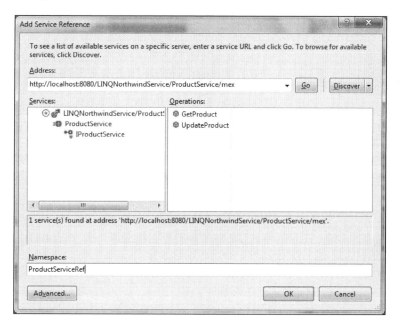

Implementing the GetProduct functionality

Now that we have the test client created, we will customize the client application to test the new WCF service.

First, we need to customize the test client to call the WCF service to get a product from the database so that we can test the `GetProduct` operation with LINQ to Entities.

We will call a WCF service through the proxy, so let's add the following `using` statements to the `form` class in the `Form1.cs` file:

```
using LINQNorthwindClient.ProductServiceRef;
using System.ServiceModel;
```

Then on the Forms Designer, double-click on the **btnGetProductDetails** button and add an event handler for this button, as follows:

```
private void btnGetProductDetail_Click(object sender, EventArgs e)
{
    var client = new ProductServiceClient();
    string result = "";

    try
    {
        int productID = Int32.Parse(txtProductID.Text);
        var product = client.GetProduct(productID);

        var sb = new StringBuilder();
        sb.Append("ProductID:" +
            product.ProductID.ToString() + "\r\n");
        sb.Append("ProductName:" +
            product.ProductName + "\r\n");
        sb.Append("QuantityPerUnit:" +
            product.QuantityPerUnit + "\r\n");
        sb.Append("UnitPrice:" +
            product.UnitPrice.ToString() + "\r\n");
        sb.Append("Discontinued:" +
            product.Discontinued.ToString() + "\r\n");
        sb.Append("RowVersion:");
        foreach (var x in product.RowVersion.AsEnumerable())
        {
            sb.Append(x.ToString());
            sb.Append(" ");
        }
```

```
        result = sb.ToString();
    }
    catch (TimeoutException ex)
    {
        result = "The service operation timed out. " +
            ex.Message;
    }
    catch (FaultException<ProductFault> ex)
    {
        result = "ProductFault returned: " +
            ex.Detail.FaultMessage;
    }
    catch (FaultException ex)
    {
        result = "Unknown Fault: " +
            ex.ToString();
    }
    catch (CommunicationException ex)
    {
        result = "There was a communication problem. " +
            ex.Message + ex.StackTrace;
    }
    catch (Exception ex)
    {
        result = "Other exception: " +
            ex.Message + ex.StackTrace;
    }

    txtProductDetails.Text = result;
}
```

Implementing the UpdateProduct functionality

Next, we need to modify the client program to call the UpdateProduct operation of the web service. This method is particularly important to us because we will use it to test the concurrent update control of LINQ to Entities.

First, we need to add some more controls to the form. We will modify the form UI as follows:

1. Open the Form1.cs file from the LINQNorthwindClient project.
2. Add a label named **lblNewPrice** with the text **New Price**.

3. Add a textbox named **txtNewPrice**.

4. Add a button named **btnUpdatePrice** with the text **&Update Price**.

5. Add a label named **lblUpdateResult** with the text **Update Result**.

6. Add a textbox control named **txtUpdateResult** with the **Multiline** property set to **True** and **Scrollbars** set to **Both**.

The form should now appear as shown in the following screenshot:

Now double-click on the **Update Price** button and add the following event handler method for this button:

```
private void btnUpdatePrice_Click(object sender, EventArgs e)
{
    string result = "";

    if (product != null)
    {
        try
        {
            // update its price
            product.UnitPrice =
                Decimal.Parse(txtNewPrice.Text);
```

```
            var client = new ProductServiceClient();
            var sb = new StringBuilder();
            string message = "";
            sb.Append("Price updated to ");
            sb.Append(txtNewPrice.Text);
            sb.Append("\r\n");
            sb.Append("Update result:");
            sb.Append(client.UpdateProduct(ref product,
                    ref message).ToString());
            sb.Append("\r\n");
            sb.Append("Update message: ");
            sb.Append(message);
            sb.Append("\r\n");
            sb.Append("New RowVersion:");
            foreach (var x in product.RowVersion.AsEnumerable())
            {
                sb.Append(x.ToString());
                sb.Append(" ");
            }
            result = sb.ToString();          }
    catch (TimeoutException ex)
    {
        result = "The service operation timed out. " +
                ex.Message;
    }
    catch (FaultException<ProductFault> ex)
    {
        result = "ProductFault returned: " +
                ex.Detail.FaultMessage;
    }
    catch (FaultException ex)
    {
        result = "Unknown Fault: " +
                ex.ToString();
    }
    catch (CommunicationException ex)
    {
        result = "There was a communication problem. " +
                ex.Message + ex.StackTrace;
    }
```

```
        catch (Exception ex)
        {
            result = "Other exception: " +
                      ex.Message + ex.StackTrace;
        }
    }
    else
    {
        result = "Get product details first";
    }

    txtUpdateResult.Text = result;
}
```

Note that inside the **Update Price** button's event handler listed previously, we don't get the product from the database first. Instead, we re-use the same product object from the btnGetProductDetails_Click method, which means we will update whatever product we get when we click on the **Get Product Details** button. In order to do this, we need to move the product variable outside of the private method btnGetProductDetail_Click, to be a class variable, as follows:

```
Product product;
```

Inside the btnGetProductDetail_Click method, we need not define another variable product, but use the class member product now. Now, the first few lines of code for the Form1 class should be as follows:

```
public partial class Form1 : Form
{
    Product product;

    public Form1()
    {
        InitializeComponent();
    }

    private void btnGetProductDetail_Click(object sender,
    EventArgs e)
    {
        var client = new ProductServiceClient();
        string result = "";
```

```
try
{
    int productID =
            Int32.Parse(txtProductID.Text);
    product = client.GetProduct(productID);
    // More code to follow
```

As you can see, we didn't do anything specific with the concurrent update control of the update, but later in the *Testing concurrent update manually* section within this chapter, we will learn how LINQ to Entities inside the WCF service handles this for us. As done in the previous chapters, we will also capture all kinds of exceptions and display appropriate messages for them.

Testing the GetProduct and UpdateProduct operations

We can build and run the program to test the GetProduct and UpdateProduct operations now. Because we are still using the WCF Service Host to host our service, we need to start it first.

1. Make the LINQNorthwindClient project the startup project and press *F5* to start it.

> The service application (WcfSvcHost) should be started automatically (controlled by the settings at **LINQNorthwindService Project | Properties | WCF Options | Start WCF Service Host** when debugging another project in the same solution).
>
> You can also first start the Service Host in non-debugging mode and then start this test client application. Or set the solution to start with multiple projects, with the service as the first project to start and the client application the second.

2. On the Client form (UI), enter 10 as the product ID in the **Product ID** textbox and click on the **Get Product Details** button to get the product details. Note that **Unit Price** is now **31.0000** and **RowVersion** is **0 0 0 0 0 0 74 159**, as shown in following screenshot (the price and row version may be different in your database):

3. Now enter 32 as the product price in the **New Price** textbox and click on the **Update Price** button to update its price. **Update result** should be **True**. Note that **RowVersion** has been changed to **0 0 0 0 0 0 74 160**:

4. To verify the new price, click on the **Get Product Details** button again to get the product details for this product and you will see that **UnitPrice** has been updated to **32.0000**.

Testing concurrent update manually

We can also test concurrent updates by using the client application `LINQNorthwindClient`.

In this section, we will start two clients (let's call them Client A and Client B) and update the same product from these two clients at the same time. We will create a conflict between the updates from these two clients so that we can test if this conflict is properly handled by LINQ to Entities.

The test sequence will be as follows:

1. Client A starts.
2. Client B starts.
3. Client A reads the product information.
4. Client B reads the same product information.
5. Client B updates the product successfully.
6. Client A tries to update the product but fails.

The last step is where the conflict occurs as the product has been updated in between the read and the update by Client A.

The steps are as follows:

1. Stop the debugging process if it hasn't already been stopped.
2. Start the WCF Service Host application in non-debugging mode, if you have stopped it (you have to set `LINQNorthwindService` as the startup project first). Remember that you have to leave the WCF Test Client running while we are performing the following tests.
3. Start the client application in non-debugging mode by pressing *Ctrl + F5* (you have to make `LINQNorthwindClient` the startup project). We will refer to this client as Client A. As we mentioned in the previous section, you have options such as starting the WCF service and the client applications at the same time.

4. In the Client A application, enter 10 in the **Product ID** textbox and click on the **Get Product Details** button to get the product's details. Note that **UnitPrice** is **35.0000** and **RowVersion** is **0 0 0 0 0 0 98 14**.

5. Start another client application in non-debugging mode by pressing *Ctrl + F5*. We will refer to this client as Client B.

6. In the Client B application, enter 10 in the **Product ID** textbox and click on the **Get Product Details** button to get the product's details. Note that the **UnitPrice** is still **35.0000** and **RowVersion** is **0 0 0 0 0 0 98 14**. Client B's form window should be identical to Client A's form window.

7. On Client B's form, enter 36 as the product price in the **New Price** textbox and click on the **Update Price** button to update its price.

8. Client B's update is committed to the database and the **Update result** value is **True**. The price of this product has now been updated to **36** and **RowVersion** has been updated to a new value of **0 0 0 0 0 0 98 15**.

9. In the Client B application, click on the **Get Product Details** button to get the product details to verify the update. Note that **UnitPrice** is now **36.0000** and **RowVersion** is now **0 0 0 0 0 0 98 15**.

10. On Client A's form, enter 37 as the product price in the **New Price** textbox and click on the **Update Price** button to update its price.

11. Client A's update fails with an error message, **Entities may have been modified or deleted since entities were loaded**.

12. In the Client B application, click on the **Get Product Details** button again to get the product's details. You will see that the **UnitPrice** is still **36.0000** and **RowVersion** is still **0 0 0 0 0 0 98 15**, which means that Client A's update didn't get committed to the database.

The following screenshot is for Client B. You can see **Update result** is **True** and the price after the update is **36**:

The following screenshot is for Client A. You can see that the price before the update is **35.0000** and the update fails with an error message. This error message is caught as an unknown fault from the client side, because we didn't handle the concurrency exception in our service.

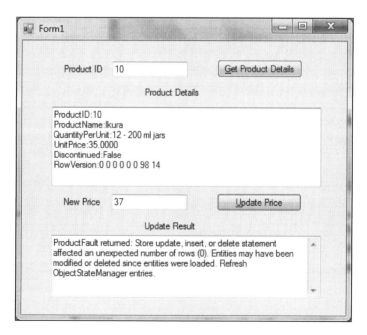

From the preceding test, we know that the concurrent update is controlled by LINQ to Entities. An optimistic locking mechanism is enforced and one client's update won't overwrite another client's update. The client that has a conflict will be notified by a fault message.

 Concurrent update locking is applied at the record level in the database. If two clients try to update different records in the database, they will not interfere with each other. For example, if you repeat the previous steps to update product 10 in one client and product 11 in another client, there will be no problem at all.

Testing concurrent updates automatically

In the previous section, we tested the concurrent update control of LINQ to Entities, but as you can see, the timing of the update is fully controlled by our input. We know exactly when the conflict will happen. In a real production, a conflict may happen at any time, with no indication as to when and how it will happen. In this section, we will simulate a situation such that a conflict happens randomly. We will add a new functionality to update one product 100 times and let two clients compete with each other until one of the updates fails.

For this test, we will put the actual updates in a background worker thread so that the main UI thread won't be blocked.

1. Open the `Form1.cs` file from the `LINQNorthwindClient` project.

2. Add a new class member to the `form` class for the worker thread, as follows:

   ```
   BackgroundWorker bw;
   ```

3. Go to the `Form1.cs` design mode.

4. Add another button called **btnAutoUpdate** with the text **&Auto Update**.

5. Add the following click event handler for this new button:

   ```
   private void btnAutoUpdate_Click(object sender, EventArgs e)
   {
       if (product != null)
       {
           btnAutoUpdate.Text = "Updating Price ...";
           btnAutoUpdate.Enabled = false;

           bw = new BackgroundWorker();
           bw.WorkerReportsProgress = true;
   ```

```
        bw.DoWork += AutoUpdatePrice;
        bw.ProgressChanged += PriceChanged;
        bw.RunWorkerCompleted += AutoUpdateEnd;
        bw.RunWorkerAsync();
    }
    else
    {
      txtUpdateResult.Text = "Get product details first";
    }
}
```

6. Add the following methods to track the status of the updates, as the updates may take a while:

```
private void AutoUpdateEnd(object sender,
RunWorkerCompletedEventArgs e)
{
    btnAutoUpdate.Text = "&Auto Update";
    btnAutoUpdate.Enabled = true;
}


private void PriceChanged(object sender,
ProgressChangedEventArgs e)
{
    txtUpdateResult.Text = e.UserState.ToString();
    // Scroll to end of textbox
    txtUpdateResult.SelectionStart =
    txtUpdateResult.TextLength-4;
    txtUpdateResult.ScrollToCaret();
}
```

7. And finally add the following method to do the actual update:

```
private void AutoUpdatePrice(object sender, DoWorkEventArgs e)
{
    var client = new ProductServiceClient();
    string result = "";
    try
    {
      // update its price
      for (int i = 0; i < 100; i++)
      {
          // refresh the product first
          product = client.GetProduct(product.ProductID);
```

```
// update its price
product.UnitPrice += 1.0m;

var sb = new StringBuilder();
String message = "";
sb.Append("Price updated to ");
sb.Append(product.UnitPrice.ToString());
sb.Append("\r\n");
sb.Append("Update result:");
bool updateResult = client.UpdateProduct(ref
product,
ref message);
sb.Append(updateResult.ToString());
sb.Append("\r\n");
sb.Append("Update message: ");
sb.Append(message);
sb.Append("\r\n");
sb.Append("New RowVersion:");
foreach (var x in
product.RowVersion.AsEnumerable())
{
    sb.Append(x.ToString());
    sb.Append(" ");
}
sb.Append("\r\n");

sb.Append("Price updated ");
sb.Append((i + 1).ToString());
sb.Append(" times\r\n\r\n");

result += sb.ToString();

// report progress
bw.ReportProgress(i+1, result);

// sleep a while
var random = new Random();
int randomNumber = random.Next(0, 1000);
System.Threading.Thread.Sleep(randomNumber);
    }
}
catch (TimeoutException ex)
{
```

```
        result += "The service operation timed out. " +
                ex.Message;
    }
    catch (FaultException<ProductFault> ex)
    {
        result += "ProductFault returned: " +
                ex.Detail.FaultMessage;
    }
    catch (FaultException ex)
    {
        result += "Unknown Fault: " +
                ex.ToString();
    }
    catch (CommunicationException ex)
    {
        result += "There was a communication problem. " +
                ex.Message + ex.StackTrace;
    }
    catch (Exception ex)
    {
        result += "Other exception: " +
                ex.Message + ex.StackTrace;
    }

    // report progress
    bw.ReportProgress(100, result);
}
```

The concept here is that once this button is clicked, it will keep updating the price of the selected product 100 times, with a price increase of 1.00 in each iteration. If two clients—again let's call them Client A and Client B—are running and this button is clicked for both the clients, one of the updates will fail as the other client will also be updating the same record.

The sequence of the updates will be as follows:

1. Client A reads the product's details, updates the product, and commits the changes back to the database.
2. Client A sleeps for a while, then repeats the preceding step.
3. Client B reads the product's details, updates the same product, and commits the changes back to the database.

4. Client B sleeps for a while, then repeats the preceding step.

5. At some point, these two sets of processes will cross; so the following events will happen:

    a. Client A reads the product's details.

    b. Client A processes the product in memory.

    c. Client B reads the product's details.

    d. Client A finishes processing and commits the changes back to the database.

    e. Client B finishes processing and tries to commit the changes back to the database.

    f. Client B update fails, because it finds that the product has been updated while it was still processing the product.

    g. Client B stops.

    h. Client A keeps updating the product until it has done so 100 times.

Now follow these steps to finish this test:

1. Start the WCF Service Host application in non-debugging mode, if you had stopped it (you have to set LINQNorthwindService as the startup project first).

2. Make LINQNorthwindClient the startup project and then run it twice in non-debugging mode by pressing *Ctrl + F5*. Two clients should be up and running.

3. From each client, enter 3 in the **Product ID** textbox and click on **Get Product Details** to get the product details. Both clients should display the price as **10.0000**.

4. Click on the **Auto Update** button on each client.

You will see that one of the clients fails while the other one is keeping the updates to the end of 100 times.

The following screenshot shows the results in the successful client. As you can see, the initial price of the product was **10.0000**, but after the updates, it has been changed to **207.0000**. From the source code, we know that this client only updates the price 100 times with an increase of 1.00 each time, so we know that another client has updated this product 97 times.

The following screenshot shows the results in the failed client. As you can see, the initial price of the product was **10.000**. After updating the price 97 times, when this client tries to update the price again, it fails with the error message **Entities may have been modified or deleted since entities were loaded**. From the results of the other client, we also know that this client has updated the product 97 times.

However, if you enter two different product IDs in each client, both client updates will be successful until all 100 updates have been made. This again proves that locking is applied on a record level of the database.

Summary

In this chapter, we used LINQ to Entities to communicate with the database in the data access layer rather than using the raw ADO.NET APIs. We have used only one LINQ statement to retrieve product information from the database and as you have seen, the updates with LINQ to Entities prove to be much easier than with the raw ADO.NET data adapters. Now, WCF and LINQ are combined together for our services, so we can take advantage of both technologies.

In the next chapter, we will explore transaction support of WCF with LINQ to Entities, so that we can write transactional WCF services.

10
Distributed Transaction Support of WCF

In previous chapters, we created a WCF service by using LINQ to Entities in the data access layer. Next, we will apply settings so that this WCF service will be a distributed service, which means that it can participate in distributed client transactions, if there are any. Client applications will control the transaction scope and decide whether a service should commit or rollback its transaction.

In this chapter, we will first verify that the `LINQNorthwind` WCF service, which we built in the previous chapter, does not support distributed transaction processing. We will then learn how to enhance this WCF service to support the distributed transaction processing and how to configure all related computers to enable the distributed transaction support. To demonstrate this, we will propagate a transaction from the client to the WCF service and verify that all sequential calls to the WCF service are within one single distributed transaction. We will also explore the multiple database support of the WCF service and discuss how to configure **Microsoft Distributed Transaction Coordinator (MSDTC)** and the firewall for the distributed WCF service.

We will cover the following topics in this chapter:

- Creating the solution files
- Testing the transaction behavior of the `DistNorthwind` WCF service
- Enabling transaction flow in the service bindings
- Modifying the service operation contract to allow transaction flow
- Modifying the service operation implementation to require a transaction scope
- Configuring Distributed Transaction Coordinator for the distributed WCF service

- Configuring the firewall for the distributed WCF service
- Propagating a transaction from the client to the WCF service
- Testing the multiple database support of the distributed WCF service

Creating the DistNorthwind solution

In this chapter, we will create a new solution based on the `LINQNorthwind` solution. We will copy all of the source code from the `LINQNorthwind` directory to a new directory and then customize it to suit our needs.

Follow these steps to create the new solution:

1. Create a new directory named `DistNorthwind` under the existing `C:\SOAwithWCFandLINQ\Projects\` directory.

2. Copy all of the files under the `C:\SOAwithWCFandLINQ\Projects\ LINQNorthwind` directory to the `C:\SOAwithWCFandLINQ\Projects\ DistNorthwind` directory.

3. Remove the `LINQNorthwindClient` folder. We will create a new client for this solution.

4. Change the solution file's name from `LINQNorthwind.sln` to `DistNorthwind.sln` and also from `LINQNorthwind.v11.suo` to `DistNorthwind.v11.suo`.

Now, we have the file structures ready for the new solution. Here we will re-use the old service to demonstrate how to plug in transaction support to an existing WCF service.

First, we need to make sure this old service in the new solution still works and we also need to make a small change to the service implementation so that we can test transaction support with it. Once we have the service up and running, we will create a new client to test this new service by using the following steps:

1. Start Visual Studio and open the `C:\SOAWithWCFandLINQ\Projects\ DistNorthwind\DistNorthwind.sln` solution.

2. Click on the **OK** button to close the **projects were not loaded correctly** warning dialog.

3. From the Solution Explorer, remove the `LINQNorthwindClient` project.

4. Open the `ProductService.cs` file in the `LINQNorthwindService` project in this new solution and remove the condition check for negative price check in the `UpdateProduct` method. Later we will try to update a product's price to be negative to test the distributed transaction support of WCF.

> If this check is not removed, when we try to update a price to be negative later in this chapter, the operation will stop right at this validation check. It won't be able to reach the DAL where LINQ to Entities will be used, and the remote database will get involved, which is the key part for a distributed transaction support test.

The following screenshot shows the final structure of the new solution `DistNorthwind`:

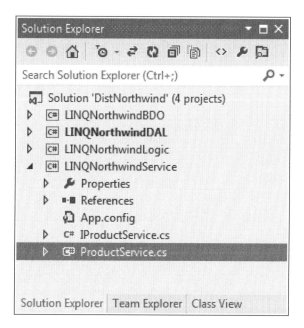

Now, we have finished creating the solution. If you build the solution now, you should see no errors. You can set the service project as the startup project, run the program, and the output should be the same as seen in the *Testing the service with the WCF Test Client* section in *Chapter 9, Applying LINQ to Entities to a WCF Service*.

Hosting the WCF service in IIS

The WCF service is now hosted within a WCF Service Host. You may remember in the last chapter we had to start the WCF Service Host before we ran our test client. Not only do you have to start the WCF Service Host, but you also have to start the WCF Test Client and leave it running while you are doing your test with your own client. In addition, we will add another service later in this chapter to test the distributed transaction support with two databases and it is not that easy to host two services with one WCF Service Host. So, in this section, we will first decouple our WCF service from Visual Studio. We will host it in IIS.

You can follow these steps to host this WCF service in IIS (refer to the *Hosting the service in the Internet Information Services server using the HTTP protocol* section in *Chapter 3, Hosting and Debugging the HelloWorld WCF Service*).

1. In the Solution Explorer, under the **LINQNorthwindService** project, copy the App.config file to Web.config.

2. Within the web.config file, add the following node as a child node of the service model node system.serviceModel:

```
<serviceHostingEnvironment >
  <serviceActivations>
    <add factory="System.ServiceModel.
    Activation.ServiceHostFactory"
      relativeAddress="./ProductService.svc"
      service="LINQNorthwindService.ProductService"/>
  </serviceActivations>
</serviceHostingEnvironment>
```

3. Change the endpoint binding from basicHttpBinding to wsHttpBinding.

4. Remove the following lines from the Web.config file:

```
<host>
  <baseAddresses>
    <add baseAddress="http://localhost:8080/
          LINQNorthwindService/ProductService/" />
  </baseAddresses>
</host>
```

5. Now open IIS Manager, add a new application DistNorthwindService, and set its physical path to C:\SOAWithWCFandLINQ\Projects\DistNorthwind\ LINQNorthwindService. If you choose to use the default application pool DefaultAppPool, make sure it is a .NET 4.0 application pool.

6. Within Visual Studio, in the Solution Explorer, right-click on the **LINQNorthwindService** project item, select **Properties**, then click on the **Build Events** tab, and enter the following code to the **Post-build event command line** box:

```
copy .\*.* ..\
```

With this **Post-build event command line**, whenever LINQNorthwindService is rebuilt, the service binary files will be copied to the C:\SOAWithWCFandLINQ\ Projects\DistNorthwind\LINQNorthwindService\bin directory so that the service hosted in IIS will always be up-to-date.

7. Within Visual Studio, in the Solution Explorer, right-click on the **LINQNorthwindService** project item and select **Rebuild**.

The steps here are very similar to the steps in *Chapter 3, Hosting and Debugging the HelloWorld WCF Service*. You can refer to that chapter for more details, such as how to install IIS and how to enable WCF support within IIS.

Now, you have finished setting up the service to be hosted in IIS. Open Internet Explorer, go to the following address, and you should see the ProductService description in the browser:

```
http://localhost/DistNorthwindService/ProductService.svc
```

Testing the transaction behavior of the WCF service

Before learning how to enhance this WCF service to support distributed transactions, we will first confirm that the existing WCF service doesn't support distributed transactions. In this section, we will test the following scenarios:

1. Create a WPF client to call the service twice in one method.

2. The first service call should succeed and the second service call should fail.

3. Verify that the update in the first service call has been committed to the database, which means that the WCF service does not support distributed transactions.

4. Wrap the two service calls in one TransactionScope and redo the test.

5. Verify that the update in the first service call has still been committed to the database, which means the WCF service does not support distributed transactions even if both service calls are within one transaction scope.

6. Add a second database support to the WCF service.

7. Modify the client to update both databases in one method.

8. The first update should succeed and the second update should fail.

9. Verify that the first update has been committed to the database, which means the WCF service does not support distributed transactions with multiple databases.

Creating a client to call the WCF service sequentially

The first scenario to test is that within one method of the client application, two service calls will be made and one of them will fail. We then verify whether the update in the successful service call has been committed to the database. If it has been, this will mean that the two service calls are not within a single atomic transaction and will indicate that the WCF service does not support distributed transactions.

You can follow these steps to create a WPF client for this test case:

1. In Solution Explorer, right-click on the solution item and select **Add | New Project...** from the context menu.

2. Select **Visual C# | WPF Application** as the template.

3. Enter DistNorthwindWPF as **Name**.

4. Click on the **OK** button to create the new client project.

Now the new test client should have been created and added to the solution. Let's follow these steps to customize this client so that we can call ProductService twice within one method and test the distributed transaction support of this WCF service:

1. On the WPF MainWindow designer surface, add the following controls (you can double-click on the **MainWindow.xaml** item to open this window and make sure you are on the design mode, not the XAML mode):

    ◦ A label with **Content Product ID**

    ◦ Two textboxes named **txtProductID1** and **txtProductID2**

- ○ A button named **btnGetProduct** with the content **Get Product Details**
- ○ A separator to separate the preceding controls from the following controls
- ○ Two labels with content **Product1 Details** and **Product2 Details**
- ○ Two textboxes named **txtProduct1Details** and **txtProduct2Details**, with the following properties:
    - ○ **AcceptsReturn**: checked
    - ○ **HorizontalScrollbarVisibility**: Auto
    - ○ **VerticalScrollbarVisibility**: Auto
    - ○ **IsReadOnly**: checked
- ○ A separator to separate the preceding controls from the following controls
- ○ A label with content **New Price**
- ○ Two textboxes named **txtNewPrice1** and **txtNewPrice2**
- ○ A button named **btnUpdatePrice** with the content **Update Price**
- ○ A separator to separate the preceding controls from the following controls
- ○ Two labels with content **Update1 Results** and **Update2 Results**
- ○ Two textboxes named **txtUpdate1Results** and **txtUpdate2Results** with the following properties:
    - ○ **AcceptsReturn**: checked
    - ○ **HorizontalScrollbarVisibility**: Auto
    - ○ **VerticalScrollbarVisibility**: Auto
    - ○ **IsReadOnly**: checked

Your **MainWindow** design surface should be as shown in the following screenshot:

2. In the Solution Explorer, right-click on the **DistNorthwindWPF** project item, select **Add Service Reference…**, and add a service reference of the product service to the project. The namespace of this service reference should be ProductServiceProxy and the URL of the product service should be http://localhost/DistNorthwindService/ProductService.svc.

> If you get an error saying **An error (Details) occurred while attempting to find service and the error details are Metadata contains a reference that cannot be resolved**, you may need to give your IIS identity proper access rights to your windows\temp directory.

3. On the MainWindow.xaml designer surface, double-click on the **Get Product Details** button to create an event handler for this button.

4. In the MainWindow.xaml.cs file, add the following using statement:

    ```
    using DistNorthwindWPF.ProductServiceProxy;
    ```

5. Again in the MainWindow.xaml.cs file, add the following two class members:

    ```
    Product product1, product2;
    ```

6. Now add the following method to the `MainWindow.xaml.cs` file:

```
private string GetProduct(TextBox txtProductID,
                              ref Product product)
{
    string result = "";

    try
    {
        int productID = Int32.Parse(txtProductID.Text);
        var client = new ProductServiceClient();
        product = client.GetProduct(productID);

        var sb = new StringBuilder();
        sb.Append("ProductID:" +
            product.ProductID.ToString() + "\n");
        sb.Append("ProductName:" +
            product.ProductName + "\n");
        sb.Append("UnitPrice:" +
            product.UnitPrice.ToString() + "\n");
        sb.Append("RowVersion:");
        foreach (var x in
        product.RowVersion.AsEnumerable())
        {
            sb.Append(x.ToString());
            sb.Append(" ");
        }
        result = sb.ToString();

    }
    catch (Exception ex)
    {
        result = "Exception: " + ex.Message.ToString();
    }

    return result;
}
```

This method will call the product service to retrieve a product from the database, format the product details to a string and return the string. This string will be displayed on the screen. The product object will also be returned so that later on we can re-use this object to update the price of the product.

7. Inside the event handler of the **Get Product Details** button, add the following two lines of code to get and display the product details:

```
txtProduct1Details.Text = GetProduct(txtProductID1, ref product1);
txtProduct2Details.Text = GetProduct(txtProductID2, ref product2);
```

Now, we have finished adding code to retrieve products from the database through the Product WCF service. Set `DistNorthwindWPF` as the startup project, press *Ctrl + F5* to start the WPF Test Client, enter `30` and `31` as the product IDs, and then click on the **Get Product Details** button. You should get a window as shown in the following screenshot:

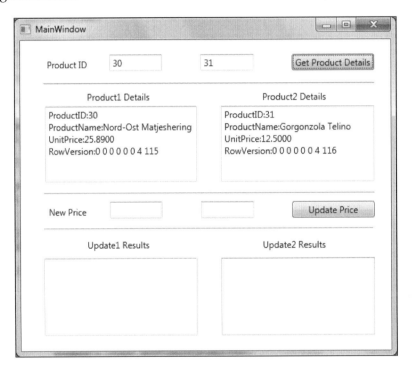

From the preceding screenshot, we see price of the product `30` is now **25.8900** and price of the product `31` is now **12.5000**. Next, we will write code to update the prices of these two products to test the distributed transaction support of the WCF service.

To update the prices of these two products, follow these steps to add the code to the project:

1. On the `MainWindow.xaml` design surface, double-click on the **Update Price** button to add an event handler for this button.

2. Add the following method to the `MainWindow.xaml.cs` file:

```
private string UpdatePrice(
  TextBox txtNewPrice,
  ref Product product,
  ref bool updateResult)
{
  string result = "";
  string message = "";

  try
  {
    product.UnitPrice =
        Decimal.Parse(txtNewPrice.Text);

    var client =
      new ProductServiceClient();
    updateResult =
      client.UpdateProduct(ref product, ref message);
    var sb = new StringBuilder();

    if (updateResult == true)
    {
      sb.Append("Price updated to ");
      sb.Append(txtNewPrice.Text.ToString());
      sb.Append("\n");
      sb.Append("Update result:");
      sb.Append(updateResult.ToString());
      sb.Append("\n");
      sb.Append("Update message:");
      sb.Append(message);
      sb.Append("\n");
      sb.Append("New RowVersion:");
    }
    else
    {
      sb.Append("Price not updated to ");
      sb.Append(txtNewPrice.Text.ToString());
      sb.Append("\n");
      sb.Append("Update result:");
      sb.Append(updateResult.ToString());
      sb.Append("\n");
      sb.Append("Update message:");
      sb.Append(message);
```

```
        sb.Append("\n");
        sb.Append("Old RowVersion:");
      }
      foreach (var x in product.RowVersion.AsEnumerable())
      {
        sb.Append(x.ToString());
        sb.Append(" ");
      }

      result = sb.ToString();
    }
    catch (Exception ex)
    {
      result = "Exception: " + ex.Message;
    }

    return result;
}
```

This method will call the product service to update the price of a product in the database. The update result will be formatted and returned so that later on we can display it. The updated product object with the new RowVersion will also be returned so that later on we can update the price of the same product repeatedly.

3. Inside the event handler of the **Update Price** button, add the following code to update the product prices:

```
if (product1 == null)
{
    txtUpdate1Results.Text = "Get product details first";
}
else if (product2 == null)
{
    txtUpdate2Results.Text = "Get product details first";
}
else
{
    bool update1Result = false, update2Result = false;

    txtUpdate1Results.Text = UpdatePrice(
        txtNewPrice1, ref product1, ref update1Result);
    txtUpdate2Results.Text = UpdatePrice(
        txtNewPrice2, ref product2, ref update2Result);
}
```

Testing the sequential calls to the WCF service

Now, let's run the program to test the distributed transaction support of the WCF service. We will first update two products with two valid prices to make sure our code works with normal use cases. Then, we will update one product with a valid price and another with an invalid price. We will verify that the update with the valid price has been committed to the database, regardless of the failure of the other update.

Let's follow these steps for this test:

1. Press *Ctrl + F5* to start the program.

2. Enter 30 and 31 as product IDs in the top two textboxes and click on the **Get Product Details** button to retrieve the two products. Note that the prices for these two products are **25.89** and **12.5** respectively.

3. Enter 26.89 and 13.5 as new prices in the **New Price** textboxes and click on the **Update Price** button to update these two products. The update results are **True** for both updates, as shown in the following screenshot:

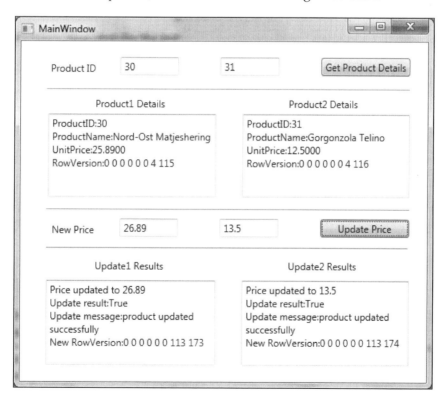

4. Now enter 27.89 and -14.5 as new prices in the **New Price** textboxes and click on the **Update Price** button to update these two products. This time, the update result for product 30 is still **True**, but for the second update, the result is **False**. Click on the **Get Product Details** button again to refresh the product prices so that we can verify the update results.

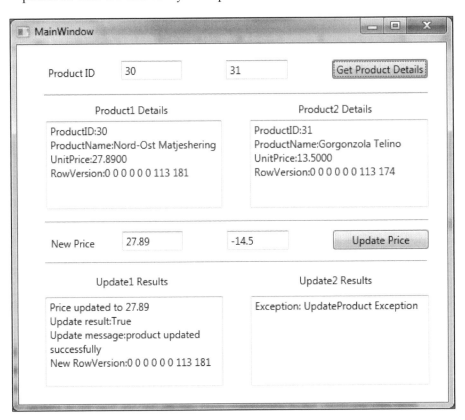

We know that the second service call should fail, so the second update should not be committed to the database. From the test result, we know this is true (the second product price did not change). However, from the test result we also know that the first update in the first service call has been committed to the database (the first product price has been changed). This means that the first call to the service is not rolled back even when a subsequent service call has failed. Therefore, each service call is in a separate standalone transaction. In other words, the two sequential service calls are not within one distributed transaction.

Wrapping the WCF service calls in one transaction scope

This test is not a complete distributed transaction test. On the client side, we didn't explicitly wrap the two updates in one transaction scope. We should test to see what will happen if we put the two updates within one transaction scope.

Follow these steps to wrap the two service calls in one transaction scope:

1. Add a reference to `System.Transactions` in the client project.

    `System.Transactions` may not be in your .NET reference list. In this case, you can browse to the file and add it. The file should be in the `C:\Windows\Microsoft.NET\Framework` folder (or Framework64). On my machine, this file is in the `C:\Windows\Microsoft.NET\Framework\v4.0.30319` folder.

2. Add a `using` statement to the `MainWindow.xaml.cs` file, as follows:

   ```
   using System.Transactions;
   ```

3. Add a `using` statement to put both updates within one transaction scope. Now, the click event handler for the **Update Price** button should be as follows:

   ```
   if (product1 == null)
   {
     txtUpdate1Results.Text = "Get product details first";
   }
   else if (product2 == null)
   {
     txtUpdate2Results.Text = "Get product details first";
   }
   else
   {
     bool update1Result = false, update2Result = false;

     using (var ts = new TransactionScope())
     {
       txtUpdate1Results.Text = UpdatePrice(
       txtNewPrice1, ref product1, ref update1Result);
   ```

```
        txtUpdate2Results.Text = UpdatePrice(
        txtNewPrice2, ref product2, ref update2Result);
        if (update1Result == true && update2Result == true)
            ts.Complete();
    }
}
```

Run the client program again, still using 30 and 31 as product IDs, and enter 28.89 and -14.5 as new prices. You will find that even though we have wrapped both updates within one transaction scope, the first update is still committed to the database—it is not rolled back even though the outer transaction on the client side is not complete, and requests all participating parties to roll back. After the updates, price of the product 30 will be changed to 28.89 and price of the product 31 will remain as 13.5.

At this point, we have proved that the WCF service does not support distributed transactions with multiple sequential service calls. Irrespective of whether the two sequential calls to the service have been wrapped in one transaction scope or not, each service call is treated as a standalone separate transaction and they do not participate in any distributed transaction.

Testing multiple database support of the WCF service

In the previous sections, we tried to call the WCF service sequentially to update records in the same database. We have proved that this WCF service does not support distributed transactions. In this section, we will do one more test, to add a new WCF service—DistNorthwindRemoteService—to update records in another database on another computer. We will call the UpdateProduct operation in this new service together with the original UpdateProduct operation in the old service and then verify whether the two updates to the two databases will be within one distributed transaction or not.

This new service is very important for our distributed transaction support test because the distributed transaction coordinator will only be activated if more than two servers are involved in the same transaction. For test purposes, we cannot just update two databases on the same SQL server even though a transaction within a single SQL server that spans two or more databases is actually a distributed transaction. This is because the SQL server manages the distributed transaction internally—to the user it operates as a local transaction.

Creating a new WCF service

First, we will add a new WCF service to update a product in a remote database. We will re-use the same WCF service that we created for this solution, but just change the connection string to point to a remote database in a remote machine.

Follow these steps to add this new service:

1. Discover another machine with the SQL server installed (you can use a virtual machine, if you don't have a physical one). We will refer to this machine as the remote machine from now on.

2. Install a `Northwind` database to this SQL server on the remote machine. Make sure you add a new column `RowVersion`, to the `Products` table in this remote `Northwind` database. This is all we need to do on the remote machine in this section.

3. On the local server, in Windows Explorer, create a new folder `LINQNorthwindRemoteService`, under the `DistNorthwind` solution folder `C:\SOAWithWCFandLINQ\Projects\DistNorthwind`.

4. Copy the following items from the `LINQNorthwindService` folder to the new `LINQNorthwindRemoteService` folder:

    ○ `Web.config`

    ○ `bin`

5. Open the `Web.config` file in the new service folder, change the **Data Source** part within the `connectionString` node from **localhost** to the remote machine name.

> You may also need to adjust your login credentials to the remote database in the connection string, according to the security settings of the remote database on the remote machine.
>
> If your computers are not within a domain, you may need to change the connection string to use SQL Server login, since connecting to the remote machine with integrated Windows authentication might not work in a work group environment.

6. In IIS Manager, add a new application `DistNorthwindRemoteService` and set its physical path to the new `LINQNorthwindRemoteService` folder. You can open the following address in Internet Explorer to verify that the new service is up and running:

    `http://localhost/DistNorthwindRemoteService/ProductService.svc`

7. To make it easier to maintain this new service, from Visual Studio in Solution Explorer, add a new solution folder `LINQNorthwindRemoteService` to the solution and add the `Web.config` file and the `bin` folder of this new service to be under the new solution folder.

8. Also from Visual Studio, in the Solution Explorer, right-click on the project item **LINQNorthwindService**, select **Properties**, then click on the **Build Events** tab, and add the following to the **Post-build event command line** box, below the original line of the `copy` command:

    `copy .\*.* ..\..\..\LINQNorthwindRemoteService\bin`

Again, this **Post-build event command line** will make sure the remote service folder will always contain the latest service binary files.

Calling the new WCF service in the client application

The new service is now up and running. Next, we will add a checkbox to the WPF client. If this checkbox is checked, when the **Get Product Details** button is clicked, we will get the second product from the remote database, using the new WCF service. When the **Update Price** button is clicked, we will also update its price in the remote database, using the new WCF service.

Now follow these steps to modify the WPF Client application to call the new service:

1. Within Visual Studio, in the Solution Explorer, right-click on the **DistNorthwindWPF** project item and add a service reference to the new WCF service `DistNorthwindRemoteService`. The namespace of this service reference should be `RemoteProductServiceProxy` and the URL of the product service should be `http://localhost/DistNorthwindRemoteService/ProductService.svc`.

2. Open the `MainWindow.xaml` file, go to design mode, and add a checkbox to indicate we are going to get and update a product in the remote database by using the remote service. Set this checkbox's properties as follows:

    ○ **Content: Get and Update 2nd Product in Remote Database**

    ○ **Name: chkRemote**

3. Open the `MainWindow.xaml.cs` file and add a new class member:

```
RemoteProductServiceProxy.Product remoteProduct;
```

4. Still in the `MainWindow.xaml.cs` file, copy the `GetProduct` method and paste it as a new method, `GetRemoteProduct`. Change the `Product` type within this new method to be `RemoteProductServiceProxy.Product` and change the `client` type to `RemoteProductServiceProxy.ProductServiceClient`. The new method should be as follows:

```
private string GetRemoteProduct(TextBox txtProductID,
  ref RemoteProductServiceProxy.Product product)
{
  string result = "";

  try
  {
    int productID = Int32.Parse(txtProductID.Text);
    var client =
    new RemoteProductServiceProxy.ProductServiceClient();
    product = client.GetProduct(productID);

    var sb = new StringBuilder();
    sb.Append("ProductID:" +
        product.ProductID.ToString() + "\n");
    sb.Append("ProductName:" +
        product.ProductName + "\n");
    sb.Append("UnitPrice:" +
        product.UnitPrice.ToString() + "\n");
    sb.Append("RowVersion:");
    foreach (var x in product.RowVersion.AsEnumerable())
    {
      sb.Append(x.ToString());
      sb.Append(" ");
    }
    result = sb.ToString();

  }
  catch (Exception ex)
  {
    result = "Exception: " + ex.Message.ToString();
  }

  return result;
}
```

5. Change the `btnGetProduct_Click` method to call the new service if the checkbox is checked, as follows:

```
private void btnGetProduct_Click(object sender, RoutedEventArgs e)
{
    txtProduct1Details.Text = GetProduct(
        txtProductID1, ref product1);
    if(chkRemote.IsChecked == true)
        txtProduct2Details.Text = GetRemoteProduct(
            txtProductID2, ref remoteProduct);
    else
        txtProduct2Details.Text = GetProduct(
            txtProductID2, ref product2);
}
```

6. Copy the `UpdatePrice` method and paste it as a new method `UpdateRemotePrice`. Change the `Product` type within this new method to `RemoteProductServiceProxy.Product` and change the `client` type to `RemoteProductServiceProxy.ProductServiceClient`.

The new method should be as follows:

```
private string UpdateRemotePrice(
  TextBox txtNewPrice,
  ref RemoteProductServiceProxy.Product product,
  ref bool updateResult)
{
  string result = "";
  string message = "";

  try
  {
    product.UnitPrice =
    Decimal.Parse(txtNewPrice.Text);

    var client =
    new RemoteProductServiceProxy.ProductServiceClient();
    updateResult =
    client.UpdateProduct(ref product, ref message);
    var sb = new StringBuilder();

    if (updateResult == true)
```

```
        {
          sb.Append("Price updated to ");
          sb.Append(txtNewPrice.Text.ToString());
          sb.Append("\n");
          sb.Append("Update result:");
          sb.Append(updateResult.ToString());
          sb.Append("\n");
          sb.Append("Update message:");
          sb.Append(message);
          sb.Append("\n");
          sb.Append("New RowVersion:");
        }
        else
        {
          sb.Append("Price not updated to ");
          sb.Append(txtNewPrice.Text.ToString());
          sb.Append("\n");
          sb.Append("Update result:");
          sb.Append(updateResult.ToString());
          sb.Append("\n");
          sb.Append("Update message:");
          sb.Append(message);
          sb.Append("\n");
          sb.Append("Old RowVersion:");
        }
        foreach (var x in product.RowVersion.AsEnumerable())
        {
          sb.Append(x.ToString());
          sb.Append(" ");
        }

        result = sb.ToString();
    }
    catch (Exception ex)
    {
      result = "Exception: " + ex.Message;
    }

    return result;
}
```

7. Change the `btnUpdatePrice_Click` method to call the new service if the checkbox is checked.

    The new method should be as follows:

```
private void btnUpdatePrice_Click(object sender,
        RoutedEventArgs e)
{
  if (product1 == null)
  {
    txtUpdate1Results.Text = "Get product details first";
  }
  else if (chkRemote.IsChecked == false && product2 ==
  null ||
  chkRemote.IsChecked == true && remoteProduct == null)
  {
    txtUpdate2Results.Text = "Get product details first";
  }
  else
  {
    bool update1Result = false, update2Result = false;

    using (var ts = new TransactionScope())
    {
      txtUpdate1Results.Text = UpdatePrice(
        txtNewPrice1,
        ref product1,
        ref update1Result);
      if(chkRemote.IsChecked == true)
        txtUpdate2Results.Text = UpdateRemotePrice(
        txtNewPrice2,
        ref remoteProduct,
        ref update2Result);
      else
        txtUpdate2Results.Text = UpdatePrice(
        txtNewPrice2,
        ref product2,
        ref update2Result);
      if (update1Result == true && update2Result == true)
        ts.Complete();
    }
  }
}
```

Testing the WCF service with two databases

Now let's run the program to test the distributed transaction support of the WCF service with two databases.

Follow these steps for this test:

1. Press *Ctrl + F5* to start the client application.

2. Check the **Get and Update 2nd Product in Remote Database** checkbox.

3. Enter 30 and 31 as product IDs in the top two textboxes.

4. If there is a firewall on the remote machine, make sure you have the SQL Server port open before you go to next step.

    To enable SQL Server port in firewall, go to **Allow a program through Windows Firewall** (type this command text in your **Search programs and files** box under **Start**), find **SQL Server Port** and make sure it is enabled (if it is not in the list, just add one):

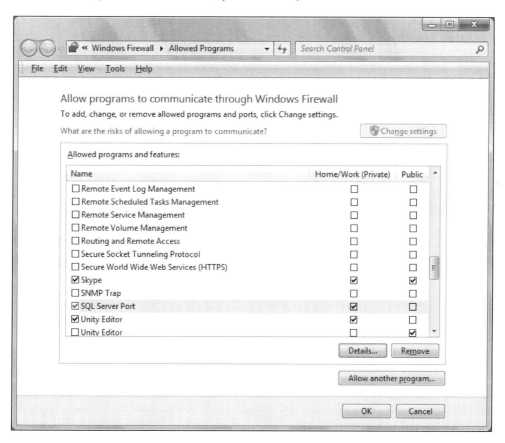

5. Verify the port properties are as shown in the following screenshot (click on the **Details** button in the dialog window shown in the preceding screenshot):

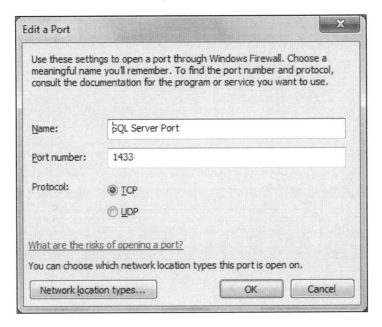

6. You also need to enable TCP on the remote SQL database server (SQL Server Configuration Manager) and make sure it allows remote connections (**SQL Server Management Studio | Database properties | Connections**). You should first try to connect to the remote database server, using SQL Server Management Studio from another machine to make sure this remote SQL Server is set up properly.

7. Once the remote database server is ready, click on the **Get Product Details** button to get product details for product ID 30 and 31. Note that details of the product 31 are now retrieved from the remote database. Price of the product 30 should be **28.89** and price of the product 31 should be still **12.5** in the remote database.

   If you get an exception in the second product's details textbox, make sure you have specified the correct connection string in the Web.config file of the new WCF service and make sure you have added the RowVersion column in the Products table of the remote Northwind database.

8. If you see the price for product 31 is not **12.5** but **13.5**, it is likely that you did not check the remote database checkbox. For this test, we need to involve the remote database, so you need to check the remote database checkbox and again click on the **Get Product Details** button before you continue the test.

9. Now enter 29.89 and -14.5 as the new prices in the **New Price** textboxes and click on the **Update Price** button.

10. The update result for the first product should be **True** and for the second product should be **False**. This means the second product in the remote database has not been updated.

11. Click on the **Get Product Details** button to refresh the product details so that we can verify the update results.

Just as in the previous test, we know that the second service call fails due to the invalid price, so the second update is not committed to the database. From the refreshed product details, we know this is true (price of the product 31 did not change). However, from the refreshed product details we also know that the first update of the first service call has been committed to the remote database (price of the product 30 has been changed). This means that the first call to the service is not rolled back even when a subsequent service call has failed. Each service call is in a separate standalone transaction. In other words, the two sequential service calls are not within one distributed transaction.

If you debug the code and examine inner exception of the product service update product exception, you will see the error message is **The UPDATE statement conflicted with the CHECK constraint**. This is very important to us, as this proves the update was made to the remote database, then failed due to a constraint. In a following test, we need the remote database to get involved so that we can test the settings of MSDTC.

Enabling distributed transaction support

In the previous sections, we verified that the WCF service currently does not support the distributed transactions irrespective of whether these are two sequential calls to the same service or two sequential calls to two different services, with one database or with two databases.

In the following sections, we will learn how to allow this WCF service to support distributed transactions. We will allow the WCF service to participate in the client transaction. From another point of view, we will learn how to flow or propagate a client transaction across the service boundaries so that the client can include service operation calls on multiple services in the same distributed transaction.

Enabling transaction flow in service binding

The first thing that we need to pay attention to is the bindings. As we learned in the previous chapters, the three elements of a WCF service end point are the address, the binding, and the contract (WCF ABC). Although the address has nothing to do with the distributed transaction support, the other two elements do.

We know that WCF supports several different bindings. All of them support transactions except the following three:

- `BasicHttpBinding`
- `BasicHttpContextBinding`
- `NetPeerTcpBinding`

In this chapter, we will use `WSHttpBinding` as our example.

However, using a transaction-aware binding doesn't mean that a transaction will be propagated to the service. The transaction propagation is disabled by default and we have to enable it manually. Unsurprisingly, the attribute to enable the transaction flow in the bindings is called `transactionFlow`.

In the following section, we will do the following to enable the transaction propagation:

- Use `wsHttpBinding` on the host application as binding
- Set the value of the `transactionFlow` attribute to `true` on the host application binding configuration

Enabling transaction flow on the service hosting application

In this section, we will enable transaction flow in bindings for both `ProductService` and `RemoteProductService`.

1. In the Solution Explorer, open the **web.config** file under the `C:\SOAWithWCFandLINQ\Projects\DistNorthwind\LINQNorthwindService` folder.

2. Change the following line:

   ```
   <endpoint address="" binding="wsHttpBinding"
       contract="LINQNorthwindService.IProductService">
   ```

   To this line:

   ```
   <endpoint address="" binding="wsHttpBinding"
       contract="LINQNorthwindService.IProductService"
           bindingConfiguration="transactionalWsHttpBinding">
   ```

3. Add the following node to the `web.config` file inside the `system.serviceModel` node and in parallel with node services:

   ```
   <bindings>
     <wsHttpBinding>
       <binding name="transactionalWsHttpBinding"
           transactionFlow="true" receiveTimeout="00:10:00"
           sendTimeout="00:10:00" openTimeout="00:10:00"
           closeTimeout="00:10:00" />
     </wsHttpBinding>
   </bindings>
   ```

4. In this configuration section, we have set the `transactionFlow` attribute to `true` for the binding, so a transaction is allowed to flow from the client to the service.

5. Make the same changes to the **web.config** file under the `C:\SOAWithWCFandLINQ\Projects\DistNorthwind\LINQNorthwindRemoteService` folder.

In the preceding configuration file, we have verified and left the bindings for both `ProductService` and `RemoteProductService` to `wsHttpBinding` and set the `transactionFlow` attribute of the binding to `true`. This will enable distributed transaction support from the WCF service binding side.

Modifying the service operation contract to allow a transaction flow

Now the service is able to participate in a propagated transaction from the client application, but the client is still not able to propagate a distributed transaction into the service. Before we enable the distributed transaction support from the client side, we need to make some more changes to the service side code, that is, modify the service operation to opt in to participate in a distributed transaction. By default, it is opted out.

Two things need to be done in order to allow an operation to participate in a propagated transaction. The first thing is to enable the transaction flow in operation contracts. Follow these steps to enable this option:

1. Open the `IProductServiceContract.cs` file under the `LINQNorthwindService` project.

2. Add the following line before the `UpdateProduct` method:

   `[TransactionFlow(TransactionFlowOption.Allowed)]`

In the preceding code line, we set `TransactionFlowOption` in the `UpdateProduct` operation to be `Allowed`. This means a transaction is allowed to be propagated from the client to this operation.

The three transaction flow options for a WCF service operation are `Allowed`, `NotAllowed`, and `Mandatory`, as shown in the following table:

Option	Description
NotAllowed	A transaction should not be flowed; this is the default value
Allowed	Transaction may be flowed
Mandatory	Transaction must be flowed

Modifying the service operation implementation to require a transaction scope

The second thing we need to do is specify the TransactionScopeRequired behavior for the service operation. This has to be done on the service implementation project.

1. Open the ProductService.cs file under the LINQNorthwindService project.

2. Add the following line before the UpdateProduct method:

   ```
   [OperationBehavior(TransactionScopeRequired = true)]
   ```

The TransactionScopeRequired attribute means that for the UpdateProduct method, the whole service operation will always be executed inside one transaction. If a transaction is propagated from the client application, this operation will participate in this existing distributed transaction. If no transaction is propagated, a new transaction will be created and this operation will be run within this new transaction.

> At end of this chapter, after you have finished setting up everything for transaction support and run the program, you can examine the ambient transaction inside the WCF service (Transaction.Current) and compare it with the ambient transaction of the client to see if they are the same. You can also examine the TransactionInformation property of the ambient transaction object to see if it is a local transaction (TransactionInformation.LocalIdentifier) or a distributed transaction (TransactionInformation.DistributedIdentifier).

We now need to regenerate the service proxy and the configuration files on the client project because we have changed the service interfaces. Remember that in your real project, you should avoid making any non-backward compatible service interface changes. Once the service goes live, if you have to make changes to the service interface, you should version your service and allow the client applications to migrate to the new versions of the service when they are ready to do so. To simplify our example, we will just update the proxy and configuration files and recompile our client application.

These are the steps to regenerate the configuration and proxy files:

1. Rebuild the solution. As we have set up the post-build event for the LINQNorthwindService project to copy all assembly files to two IIS directories, both ProductService and RemoteProductService should now contain the latest assemblies with distributed transaction support enabled.

2. In the Solution Explorer, right-click on **RemoteProductServiceProxy** under the **Service References** directory of the DistNorthwindWPF project.

3. Select **Update Service Reference** from the context menu.

4. Right-click on **ProductServiceProxy** under the **Service References** directory of the DistNorthwindWPF project.

5. Select **Update Service Reference** from the context menu.

Open the App.config file under the DistNorthwindWPF project. You will find that the transactionFlow attribute is now populated as true because the code generator finds that some operations in the service now allow transaction propagation.

Understanding the distributed transaction support of a WCF service

As we have seen, distributed transaction support of a WCF service depends on the binding of the service, the operation contract attribute, the operation implementation behavior, and the client applications.

The following table shows some possible combinations of the WCF-distributed transaction support:

Binding permits transaction flow	Client flows transaction	Service contract opts in transaction	Service operation requires transaction scope	Possible result
True	Yes	Allowed or Mandatory	True	Service executes under the flowed-in transaction
True or False	No	Allowed	True	Service creates and executes within a new transaction
True	Yes or No	Allowed	False	Service executes without a transaction
True or False	No	Mandatory	True or False	SOAP exception
True	Yes	NotAllowed	True or False	SOAP exception

Testing the distributed transaction support of the WCF service

Now that we have changed the service to support distributed transaction and let the client propagate the transaction to the service, we will test this. We will first change the Distributed Transaction Coordinator and Firewall settings for the distributed transaction support of the WCF service, then propagate a transaction from the client to the service, and test the multiple database support of the WCF service.

Configuring the Microsoft Distributed Transaction Coordinator

In a subsequent section, we will call two services to update two databases on two different computers. As these two updates are wrapped within one distributed transaction, **Microsoft Distributed Transaction Coordinator (MSDTC)** will be activated to manage this distributed transaction. If MSDTC is not started or not configured properly, the distributed transaction will not be successful. In this section, we will learn how to configure MSDTC on both machines.

You can follow these steps to configure MSDTC on your local and remote machines:

1. Open **Component Services from Control Panel | Administrative Tools** (or start `dcomcnfg.exe`).

2. In the **Component Services** window, expand **Component Services**, then **Computers**, and then right-click on **My Computer**.

3. Select **Properties** from the context menu.

4. On the **My Computer Properties** window, click on the **MSDTC** tab.

5. Verify that **Use local coordinator** is checked and then close the **My Computer Properties** window. Expand **Distributed Transaction Coordinator** under the **My Computer** node, right-click on **Local DTC**, select **Properties** from the context menu, and then from the **Local DTC Properties** window, click on the **Security** tab.

6. You should now see the Security Configuration for DTC on this machine. Set it as shown in the following screenshot:

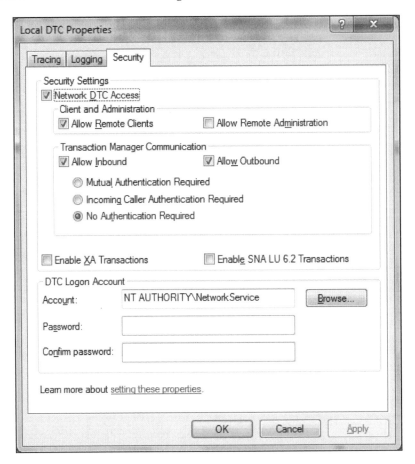

 You have to restart the MSDTC service after you have changed your MSDTC settings, for the changes to take effect.

Also, to simplify our example, we have chosen the **No Authentication Required** option. You should be aware that not needing authentication is a serious security issue in production.

Remember you have to make these changes for both your local and remote machines.

Configuring the firewall

Even though Distributed Transaction Coordinator has been enabled, the distributed transaction may still fail if the firewall is turned on and hasn't been set up properly for MSDTC.

To set up the firewall for MSTC, follow these steps:

1. Open the **Windows Firewall** window from the **Control Panel**.

2. If the firewall is not turned on, you can skip this section.

3. Go to the **Allow a program or feature through Windows Firewall** window.

4. Add **Distributed Transaction Coordinator** to the program list (`windows\system32\msdtc.exe`), if it is not already on the list. Make sure the checkbox before this item is checked.

5. Again, you need to change your firewall settings for both your local and remote machines.

6. You can also configure this through Windows Firewall with Advanced Security.

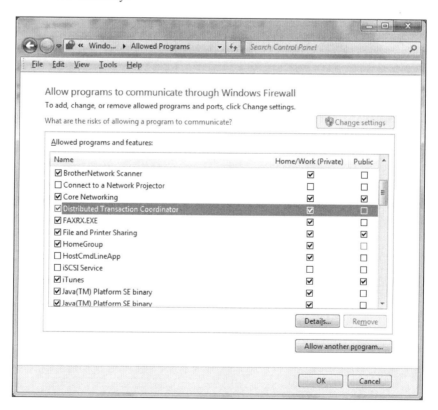

Now the firewall will allow `msdtc.exe` to go through so our next test won't fail due to the firewall restrictions.

 You may have to restart IIS after you have changed your firewall settings. In some cases, you may also have to stop and then restart your firewall for the changes to take effect.

Propagating a transaction from the client to the WCF service

Now we have the services and MSDTC ready. In this section, we will rerun the distributed test client and verify the distributed transaction support of the enhanced WCF service.

Testing distributed transaction support with one database

First we will test the distributed transaction support of the WCF service within one database. We will try to update two products (30 and 31). The first update will succeed but the second update will fail. Both updates are wrapped in one client transaction, which will be propagated into the service, and the service will participate in this distributed transaction. Due to the failure of the second update, the client application will roll back this distributed transaction at the end and the service should also roll back every update that is within this distributed transaction. So, in the end, the first update should not be committed to the database.

Now follow these steps to do this test:

1. Press *Ctrl + F5* to start the client application.
2. Enter 30 and 31 as product IDs in the top two textboxes.
3. Make sure **Get and Update 2nd Product in Remote Database** is not checked.
4. Click on the **Get Product Details** button. The prices for these two products should be **29.89** and **13.5** respectively.
5. Enter 30.89 and -14.5 as new prices in the **New Price** textboxes.
6. Click on the **Update Price** button.
7. Click on the **Get Product Details** button to refresh the product details so that we can verify the results.

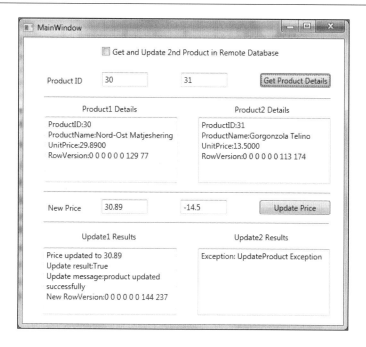

From the output window, we can see that the prices of both products remain unchanged which proves that the first update has been rolled back. From this output, we know that both service calls are within a distributed transaction and the WCF service now fully supports the distributed transaction within one database.

Testing the distributed transaction support with two databases

Next we will test the distributed transaction support of the WCF service with two databases or machines involved. As mentioned before, this is a true distributed transaction test as MSDTC will be activated only when the machine boundary is crossed.

In this test, we will try to update two products (product 30 and 31). However, this time the second product (product 31) is in a remote database on another machine. As in the previous test, the first update will succeed, but the second update will fail. Both updates are wrapped in one client transaction, which will be propagated into the service and the service will participate in this distributed transaction. Due to the failure of the second update, the client application will roll back this distributed transaction at the end and the service should also roll back every update that is within this distributed transaction. The first update should finally not be committed to the database.

Now follow these steps to carry out this test:

1. Press *Ctrl + F5* to start the client application.

2. Enter 30 and 31 as product IDs in the top two textboxes.

3. Make sure **Get and Update 2nd Product in Remote Database** is checked.

4. Click on the **Get Product Details** button. The prices for these two products should be **29.89** and **12.5** respectively.

5. Enter 30.89 and -14.5 as new prices in the **New Price** textboxes.

6. Click on **Update Price**.

7. Then click on the **Get Product Details** button to refresh the product details so that we can verify the results.

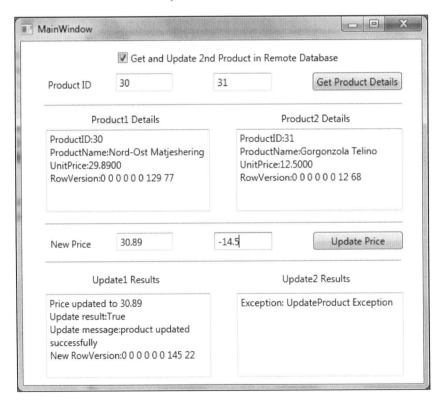

From the output window we can see that the prices of both products remain unchanged, which proves that the first update has been rolled back. From this output, we know that both service calls are within a distributed transaction and the WCF service now fully supports the distributed transaction with multiple databases involved.

Now to prove that the distributed transaction support works, click on the **Get Product Details** button to refresh `product1` (make sure **Get and Update 2nd Product in Remote Database** is still checked), enter two valid prices, such as `30.89` and `14.5`, then click on the **Update Price** button. This time you should see that both products' prices are updated successfully.

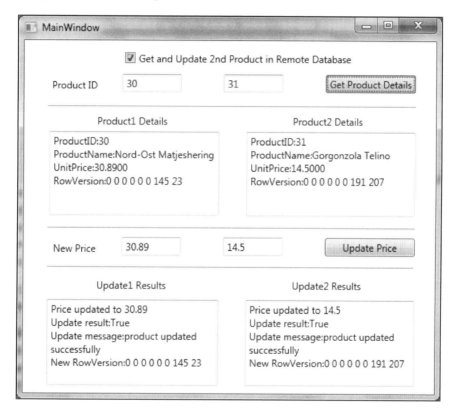

To see the status of all your distributed transactions, you can go to **Component Services**, and select **Transaction Statistics**, as shown in the following screenshot:

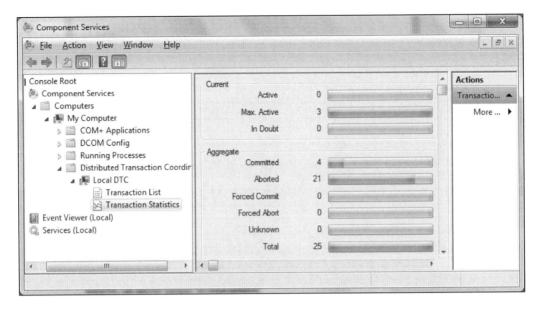

For the last successful test, you might not get an output as shown in the preceding screenshot, but instead still get an exception. If you debug your code, inside the UpdatePrice operation of your product service (note you need to step in to your service code from the client UpdateRemotePrice method), when you examine the update product exception, you may see one of the following error messages:

- **MSDTC on server 'xxxxxx' is unavailable**
- **Network access for Distributed Transaction Manager (MSDTC) has been disabled**
- **The transaction has already been implicitly or explicitly committed or aborted**
- **The MSDTC transaction manager was unable to push the transaction to the destination transaction manager**

This might be because you have not set your Distributed Transaction Coordinator or firewall correctly. In this case, you need to follow the instructions in the previous sections to configure these settings, then come back and redo these tests.

If you get an exception of the `OptimisticConcurrencyException` type inside the `UpdateRemotePrice` method, double-check your client proxy object within the `UpdateRemotePrice` method. You may have forgotten to change the client proxy from `ProductServiceProxy.ProductServiceClient` to `RemoteProductServiceProxy. ProductServiceClient`. Once you have corrected it, you should be able to perform this test successfully.

If you get a timeout exception while you are debugging, increase your client application's service binding settings of `sendTimeout` and `receiveTimeout` to a larger value such as 5 minutes and try again.

Tradeoffs of distributed transactions

Now you have learned how to turn on distributed transaction support for a WCF service. Before you dive into the distributed transaction world in your real work environment, you need to be aware that distributed transaction support will impact your applications in a few areas, sometimes maybe significantly.

The following is a list of some of the impacts for distributed transactions:

- Distributed transactions may introduce more complexity to your applications
- Distributed transactions may decrease the performance of your applications
- Distributed transactions may increase the deadlock probability of your processes

You should analyze your requirements, consider all pros and cons of turning the distributed transaction support on, and then make your own judgment for your applications.

Summary

In this chapter, we have discussed how to enable distributed transaction support for a WCF service. Now we can wrap the sequential WCF service calls within one transaction scope and flow the distributed transaction into the WCF services. We can also update multiple databases on different computers all within one single distributed transaction.

In the next chapter, we will learn how to secure our WCF services.

11
WCF Security

At this point, we have learned how to develop a three-layer WCF service with LINQ to Entities. To further enhance our WCF service, in this chapter we will explore the security settings of a WCF service. As big a topic as WCF security is, in this chapter we will only cover the basic concepts, and we will host our `HelloWorld` WCF service using Basic and Windows Authentication with the HTTPS protocol.

We will cover the following topics in this chapter:

- WCF security components
- WCF transfer security
- WCF Authentication
- Hosting a WCF service with Basic Authentication
- Hosting a WCF service with HTTPS protocol
- Testing the WCF service with Basic Authentication
- Hosting the WCF service with Windows Authentication
- Testing the WCF service with Windows Authentication
- WCF Security Guidance

WCF security components

WCF security spans multiple components in the WCF architecture. The main goal of security in WCF is to provide integrity, confidentiality, authentication, authorization, and auditing for the applications that are built on top of the WCF framework. A good WCF architecture splits these functions into the following pieces:

- **Transfer security**: Responsible for providing message confidentiality, data integrity, and authentication of communicating parties

- **Authorization**: Responsible for providing a framework for making authorization decisions
- **Auditing**: Responsible for logging the security-related events to the audit log

In this section, we will cover WCF authorization and auditing briefly and in the next section, we will discuss WCF transfer security in details.

WCF authorization

Authorization is the process of controlling access and rights to resources, such as services or files. Unlike the WCF service authentication, which is usually handled automatically by the communication framework, for WCF service authorization, you will have to come up with your own strategy and infrastructure. You can choose one of the following to implement authorization for your WCF service:

- **Role-based**: User is authorized based on his/her role membership. Users belonging to the same role will share the same security privileges within the application.

- **Identity-based**: Identity Model is an extension of the role-based authorization. Identity Model enables you to manage claims and policies in order to authorize clients. You can verify claims contained within the users' credentials and compare the claims with a set of authorization policies to determine if the user is authorized for an operation.

- **Resource-based**: Windows **access control lists (ACLs)** are used for securing individual resources. The caller will be impersonated and the operating system will perform standard access checks, using the original caller's security context when a resource is accessed.

In this book, we will not discuss WCF service authorization any further, as it is fundamentally the same as authorizations of any other types' applications.

WCF auditing

WCF applications can log security events (either success, failure, or both), using the auditing feature. The events are written to the Windows system event log and can be examined by using the Event Viewer.

The benefits of WCF auditing include the following:

- Audit security events such as authentication and authorization failures
- Detect attacks which have occurred or which are in progress
- Help debug security-related problems

You can configure the WCF service security logging through the `ServiceSecurityAudit` behavior in the service configuration file. You can specify security audit levels for both message authentication and service authorization events.

For example, the following behavior configuration will enable a security audit for all events for both authorization and authentication of a WCF service:

```
<behavior name = "MySecurityAudit">
    <serviceSecurityAudit auditLogLocation = "Default"
      serviceAuthorizationAuditLevel = "SuccessOrFailure"
      messageAuthenticationAuditLevel = "SuccessOrFailure" />
</behavior>
```

WCF transfer security

In the rest of this chapter, we will focus on the transfer security part of WCF services. We will discuss WCF transport-level and message-level security, transfer security modes supported by various bindings, and WCF authentications.

WCF security modes

WCF transfer security is also referred to as security mode. There are two transfer security levels for WCF services — transport level and message level. You can also mix these two levels to create a mixed-level security mode.

The WCF security modes that are available are as follows:

- None
- Transport
- Message
- Both
- TransportWithMessageCredential
- TransportCredentialOnly

Not every WCF binding supports every security mode. For example, `basicHttpBinding` supports transport, message, or mixed security modes, but not both, while `netNamedPipeBinding` only supports transport-level security (or none). The following table lists the most common bindings and their supported security modes:

Binding name	None	Transport	Message	Mixed	Both
`basicHttpBinding`	√(Default)	√	√	√	X
`netTCPBinding`	√	√(Default)	√	√	X
`netPeerTCPBinding`	√	√(Default)	√	√	X
`netNamedPipeBinding`	√	√(Default)	X	X	X
`wsHttpBinding` or `ws2007HttpBinding`	√	√	√(Default)	√	X
`wsFederationHttpBinding` or `wsfederationHttpBinding`	√	X	√(Default)	X	X
`wsDualHttpBinding`	√	X	√(Default)	X	X
`netMsmqBinding`	√	√(Default)	√	X	√

WCF transport security

WCF transport security is applied at the transport level on the byte stream below the message layer. In this case, a message does not have a security header and it does not carry any user authentication data. Transport security mode only provides point-to-point security between the two endpoints and it is the least flexible in terms of WS-Security usage because it is highly dependent on the transport layer. However, the transport security mode is the fastest in terms of performance, and it gives the best interoperability with client applications.

The most common approach for transport security mode is to combine it with **Secure Sockets Layer** (**SSL**) or HTTPS to encrypt and sign the contents of all packets. We will secure a WCF service with transport security and SSL in later sections of this chapter.

WCF message security

WCF message security is applied on the message level. With message security, the user credentials and claims are encapsulated in every message. The message security mode provides end-to-end security and it provides a high flexibility from an authentication perspective. Since messages are directly encrypted and signed, having intermediaries does not break the security. You can use any type of authentication credential you want, largely independent of the transport layer as long as both client and server agree.

WCF mixed security

WCF mixed security gives you the best of both transport security and message security. In this case, WCF transport security ensures the integrity and confidentiality of the messages, while WCF message security encapsulates the user credentials and claims in every message. The WCF mixed security mode allows you to use a variety of user credentials that are not possible when using strict transport security mechanisms, while leveraging transport security's performance.

WCF transport and message (both) security

When WCF transport security and WCF message security are combined, the user credentials and claims are transferred at both the transport layer and the message level. Similarly, message protection is provided at both the transport layer and the message level. Note that this is not a common scenario, and the **Microsoft Message Queuing (MSMQ)** binding is the only binding that supports this mode.

Authentication options for transport security

The WCF authentication options depend on the transfer security mode being used. For this reason, the authentication choices are partly determined by the transfer security mode. The following are the available authentication options for transport security mode:

- **None**: When using the None option, the callers are not authenticated at all.
- **Basic**: The Basic option is available with the HTTP protocol only. The client is authenticated by using the username and password against the Microsoft Active Directory service. Note the username and password are transported by using a Base64 encoded string, which is very similar to a clear string and therefore not the most secure option.

- **NTLM**: The NTLM option is also available with the HTTP protocol only. The client is authenticated by using a challenge-response scheme against Windows accounts. NTLM Authentication is well suited for a workgroup environment and is more secure than Basic Authentication.

- **Windows**: When using the Windows option, the WCF service uses Kerberos Authentication when in a domain, or NTLM Authentication when deployed in a workgroup environment. This option uses a Windows token presented by the caller to authenticate against the Active Directory. This is the most secure option compared to Basic or NTLM Authentication.

- **Certificate**: When using the Certificate option, the caller presents an X.509 client certificate that the WCF service validates by trusting the certificate (peer trust) or trusting the issuer of the certificate (chain trust). This option should be considered only when Windows Authentication is not possible, as in the case of **business-to-business** (**B2B**) scenarios.

Authentication options for message security

For WCF services using the message security mode, authentication choices are different from the services using the transport security mode. The following are the available authentication options for the message security mode:

- **None**: When using the None option, the callers are not authenticated at all.

- **Windows**: When using the Windows option, the WCF service uses Kerberos Authentication when in a domain or NTLM Authentication when deployed in a workgroup environment. The Windows option uses the Windows token presented by the caller to authenticate against the Active Directory.

- **Username**: When using the Username option, the caller provides a username and password to the service. The service can then authenticate the caller against Windows credentials or use a membership provider. This option should be considered only when Windows Authentication is not possible.

- **Certificate**: When using the Certificate option, the caller presents an X.509 client certificate. The WCF service looks up the certificate information on the host side and validates it (peer trust), or trusts the issuer of the client certificate (chain trust). This option should be considered only when Windows Authentication is not possible.

- **Issue Token**: When using the Issue Token option, the client and service depend on **Secure Token Service** (**STS**) to issue tokens that the client and service trust.

Hosting a WCF service using Basic Authentication

In previous sections, we learned the basic concepts and theories about WCF security. Now, we will do some practical work. We will host a WCF service with Basic Authentication and then consume this service in a client application.

Since with Basic Authentication, username and password are transmitted in Base64 encoded text, SSL will be configured with this authentication mode to enhance the security of the service.

To keep the code simple and focus only on the security side of the WCF service, `HelloWorldService` and `HelloWorldClient` will be used for this practice.

Setting up the service

First, we will set up a copy of `HelloWorldService` with no authentication. We will enhance this service in the following sections to enable Basic Authentication and host it with HTTPS protocol.

To set up the service, follow these steps:

1. You can refer *Chapter 2, Implementing a Basic HelloWorld WCF Service* and *Chapter 3, Hosting and Debugging the HelloWorld WCF Service* in this book to get the `HelloWorld` solution ready.

2. Create a new folder `HostIISSecure` under the folder `C:\SOAwithWCFandLINQ\Projects\HelloWorld`.

3. Copy all files from `HostIIS` to this new folder.

4. Start IIS manager, and add a new application `HelloWorldServiceSecure`, pointing to this new folder.

5. Test it with this URL in a browser:

   `http://localhost/HelloWorldServiceSecure/HelloWorldService.svc`

You should see the WSDL description page of the `HelloWorldService` service. Click on the link to make sure you can get the WSDL of this new service.

Enabling the Basic Authentication feature

Basic Authentication is a feature of Internet Information Service. By default, the module is not installed. In this section, we will install and enable this feature.

1. Open **Control Panel**.

2. Open **Programs | Turn Windows features on or off**.

3. Now the **Windows Features** dialog window should pop up.

4. Expand the nodes **Internet Information Services | World Wide Web Service | Security**.

5. Check **Basic Authentication**.

6. Note **Windows Authentication** is unchecked for now. Later in this chapter, we will learn how to host this same WCF service with Windows Authentication, in which case you need to come back to this same place and check the **Windows Authentication** option.

Configuring Basic Authentication on IIS

Now the Basic Authentication feature is enabled for the computer, but the IIS application is still not using it. We need to configure the `HelloWorldServiceSecure` application to be authenticated with this feature.

1. Start IIS manager.

2. Select the **HelloWorldServiceSecure** application.

3. In the **Features View** panel, double-click on **Authentication**:

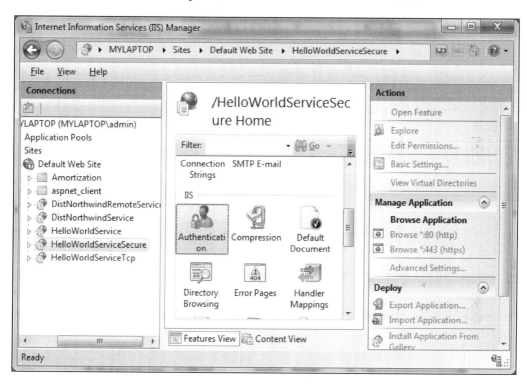

4. In the **Authentication** panel, disable **Anonymous Authentication** and enable **Basic Authentication**:

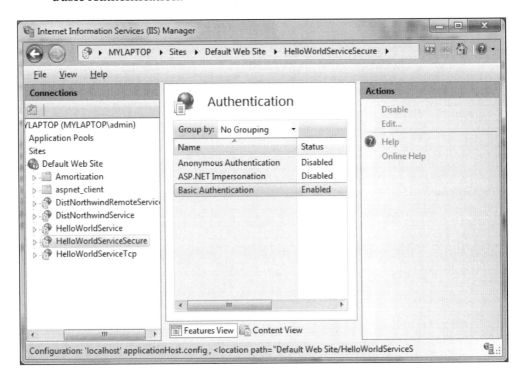

Anonymous Authentication must be disabled because when negotiating with the server, most browsers will try Anonymous Authentication first.

5. If your computer is within a domain, while the **Basic Authentication** node is still selected, click on the **Edit** button on the right-hand side panel and enter your domain name to both **Default domain** and **Realm** boxes:

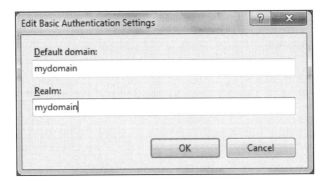

You should enter your domain name (normally your company name) here, not your computer name. For example, if your computer's full address is `pcNameA.companyNameB.com`, enter `companyNameB` here.

Now if you browse to the original service address, you will get an error **The authentication schemes configured on the host ('Basic') do not allow those configured on the binding 'BasicHttpBinding' ('Anonymous')**. This is because the `HelloWorldServiceSecure` service is still configured to communicate using Anonymous Authentication. Next, we will modify the service configuration file to use Basic Authentication instead.

Configuring the HTTPS protocol

Before we modify the service configuration file, we need to do more on the IIS site. We will enable the HTTPS protocol for our website so that the client can communicate with our service via the HTTPS protocol. This is especially important for Basic Authentication, since with Basic Authentication, the username and password are transmitted in Base64 encoded text, which can be easily decoded to clear text.

To configure HTTPS for our service, follow these steps:

1. Start IIS manager.
2. Select the root node on the left-side panel (it should be your computer name).
3. Double-click on **Server Certificates** in the middle panel:

4. On the right-hand side **Actions** panel, click on the **Create Self-Signed Certificate...** link:

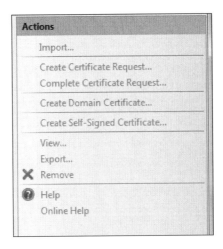

5. The **Create Self-Signed Certificate** dialog window should appear on your screen. Specify a name `MyTestCert` for the certificate and click on the **OK** button to close the dialog window.

6. Still in the IIS manager, select the website of the `HelloWorldServiceSecure` application. By default, this should be **Default Web Site**. Make sure you select the website, not the **HelloWorldServiceSecure** application, as binding settings apply to the whole website.

7. On the right-hand side **Actions** panel, click on the **Bindings...** link.

8. If https is not in the list of the binding types, click on the **Add** button; otherwise, select **https** from the list and click on **Edit**.

9. On the **Add Site Binding/Edit Site Binding** dialog window, specify the test certificate in the **SSL certificate** field:

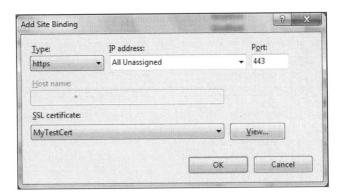

10. Click on the **OK** button to close the **Add Site Binding** dialog window and then click on the **Close** button to close the **Site Bindings** dialog window.

11. The bindings of your website should be similar to those shown in the following screenshot:

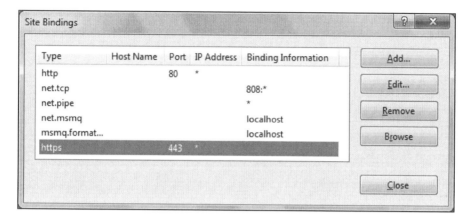

 In your production environment, you should create a signed certificate from a Certificate Authority like VeriSign. And in development time, if SSL brings too much overhead, you can host your service without SSL. It is recommended for security purposes to turn it on when the service is deployed to the production environment.

Configuring Basic Authentication on the service

Now IIS is configured to use Basic Authentication, but the service is still not. We need to configure the `HelloWorldService` service to be authenticated with Basic Authentication.

1. Open the `HelloWorld` solution.

2. Add a new solution folder `HostIISSecure` to the solution.

3. Add the `C:\SOAwithWCFandLINQ\Projects\HelloWorld\HostIISSecure\web.config` file to the new solution folder.

4. Add another solution folder `bin` under the `HostIISSecure` solution folder.

5. Add all files under the `C:\SOAwithWCFandLINQ\Projects\HelloWorld\HostIISSecure\bin` folder to this new solution folder.

6. Open properties of the `HelloWorldService` project, and add the following statements to the post-built event of the project. This will make sure the `HelloWorldServiceSecure` application will always have the latest service binary files as other hosting applications.

```
xcopy "$(AssemblyName).dll" "C:\SOAwithWCFandLINQ\Projects\
HelloWorld\HostIISSecure\bin" /Y
xcopy "$(AssemblyName).pdb" "C:\SOAwithWCFandLINQ\Projects\
HelloWorld\HostIISSecure\bin" /Y
```

7. Now open the `web.config` file and make the following changes to this file:

a. Change the service metadata attribute from `httpGetEnabled` to `httpsGetEnabled`.

b. Add the following `services` node just after the `behaviors` node. This will define an endpoint with our specific binding configuration:

```
<services>
  <service name="MyWCFServices.HelloWorldService">
    <endpoint address="" binding="basicHttpBinding"
      contract="MyWCFServices.IHelloWorldService"
      bindingConfiguration="secureHttpBinding">
      <identity>
        <dns value="localhost" />
      </identity>
    </endpoint>
    <endpoint address="mex" binding="mexHttpBinding"
              contract="IMetadataExchange" />
  </service>
</services>
```

c. Add the following `bindings` node just after the new node that we just added. This will define the binding with Basic Authentication:

```
<bindings>
  <basicHttpBinding>
    <binding name ="secureHttpBinding">
      <security mode="Transport">
        <transport clientCredentialType="Basic" />
      </security>
    </binding>
  </basicHttpBinding>
</bindings>
```

d. Now the `system.serviceModel` node should have four child nodes: `serviceHostingEnvironment` (existing node), `behaviors` (existing node), `services` (new node), and `bindings` (new node).

e. Save your `web.config` file.

In your `web.config` file, the `system.serviceModel` node should be as follows:

```xml
<system.serviceModel>

  <serviceHostingEnvironment >
    <serviceActivations>
      <add factory="System.ServiceModel.Activation.ServiceHostFactory"
        relativeAddress="./HelloWorldService.svc"
        service="MyWCFServices.HelloWorldService"/>
    </serviceActivations>
  </serviceHostingEnvironment>

  <behaviors>
    <serviceBehaviors>
      <behavior>
        <serviceMetadata httpsGetEnabled="true"/>
      </behavior>
    </serviceBehaviors>
  </behaviors>

  <services>
    <service name="MyWCFServices.HelloWorldService">
      <endpoint address="" binding="basicHttpBinding"
        contract="MyWCFServices.IHelloWorldService"
        bindingConfiguration="secureHttpBinding">
        <identity>
          <dns value="localhost" />
        </identity>
      </endpoint>
      <endpoint address="mex" binding="mexHttpBinding"
                contract="IMetadataExchange" />
    </service>
  </services>

  <bindings>
    <basicHttpBinding>
      <binding name ="secureHttpBinding">
        <security mode="Transport">
          <transport clientCredentialType="Basic" />
        </security>
      </binding>
    </basicHttpBinding>
  </bindings>

</system.serviceModel>
```

The service is now ready. You can go to `https://[your_pc_name]` `/HelloWorldServiceSecure/HelloWorldService.svc` and see the WSDL of the service.

You will be prompted to enter your credentials. You should then enter your Windows login credentials here.

 If you go to `https://localhost/HelloWorldServiceSecure` `/HelloWorldService.svc` (using localhost instead of your PC name in the URL), you will get a warning that **The security certificate presented by this website was issued for a different website's address**. You can ignore this warning and still see the WSDL of the service. However, in a following section, when you add the service reference, you must use your PC name, instead of localhost.

On the service WSDL page, you should see the following XML node:

```
<http:BasicAuthentication xmlns:http="http://schemas.microsoft.com/
ws/06/2004/policy/http"/>
```

This means the service is now secured by Basic Authentication.

Testing the service with Basic Authentication

To test the secured service, we need a test client. In this section, we will create a console application to test the secured service.

1. Add a console application project `HelloWorldClientSecure` to the solution.

2. Right-click on the new project and select **Add Service Reference...** from the context menu.

3. Enter `https://[your_pc_name]/HelloWorldServiceSecure/` `HelloWorldService.svc` as the address and `HelloWorldServiceRef` as the namespace. You will be prompted to enter your credentials. Enter your Windows login credentials here.

   If you get an error saying **An error (Details) occurred while attempting to find service** and the error details are **Metadata contains a reference that cannot be resolved**, you may need to give your IIS identity proper access rights to your `Windows\temp` directory.

You may be prompted to enter your credentials up to three times while Visual Studio is trying to discover or enumerate all the services for the desired name on your machine. In my environment it was trying to discover the service at three places—`HelloWorldService.svc/_vti_bin/ListData.svc/$metadata`, `HelloWorldService.svc/$metadata`, and `HelloWorldService.svc`.

If you are prompted more than three times for your credentials and you still cannot add the service reference, make sure you are using the correct URL for the service. You may need to replace localhost with the system name of your PC or you may need to include your domain name in the URL. This is because the host part of the URL must match the **Issued to** part of the self-signed certificate. You can open your certificate (from IIS manager) to see the exact party name that this certificate is issued to, and use this in your URL. In the following screenshot, the computer is not in a domain, so **Issued to** in this case is the same as the computer name. If it is within a domain, the **Issued to** field should look something like `MyLaptop.domain_name.com`. In this case, you should use `MyLaptop.domain_name.com` in the URL.

If your computer is within a domain, you also need to make sure you have set your default domain and realm in your bindings settings. You can refer to the previous section, Configuring the HTTPS protocol, for more details.

4. Now open the `Program.cs` file and add the following code to the `Main` method (remember to replace the user's credentials with your own one):

```
var client =
    new HelloWorldServiceRef.HelloWorldServiceClient();
client.ClientCredentials.UserName.UserName = "your_user_name";
client.ClientCredentials.UserName.Password = "your_password";
Console.WriteLine(client.GetMessage("Basic Authentication
caller"));
```

5. Set the `HelloWorldClientSecure` project as the startup project and run the program. You should get an output that looks similar to the one shown in the following screenshot:

Hosting a WCF service with Windows Authentication

In previous sections, we learned how to host a WCF service with, Basic Authentication. As you can see, with Basic Authentication, the client has to capture the user's credentials (the credentials are hardcoded, from a configuration file, or prompted for user to enter) and the credentials are transported in clear text, unless HTTPS is configured.

This might be an acceptable approach if the clients are outside of your domain, that is, from the Internet or extranet. However, for intranet clients, a better approach is to use Windows Authentication, so that you don't need to capture the user's credentials, instead, you can use the user's network credential token and pass it to the WCF service. In this section, we will configure our WCF service to use this authentication mode.

As we have the IIS application and the test client for Basic Authentication ready, we will just modify them to enable Windows Authentication. We do this as follows:

1. Go to **Control Panel | Programs and Features | Turn Windows features on or off** and check **Windows Authentication** under **Internet Information Services | World Wide Web Services | Security**. See the previous section in this chapter (*Enabling the Basic Authentication feature*) for a screenshot.

2. Go to **IIS manager | HelloWorldServiceSecure | Authentication**, disable **Basic Authentication**, and enable **Windows Authentication**. If **Windows Authentication** is not in the list, close IIS manager and then re-open it.

3. Start Visual Studio, open the `web.config` file located under the `HostIISSecure` folder, and change the attribute value of `clientCredentialType` in the `binding` node from `Basic` to `Windows`. Save the config file.

4. Expand the **Service References** folder in the **HelloWorldClientSecure** project, right-click on the **HelloWorldServiceRef** item, and select **Update Service Reference** from the context menu. The service reference will be updated without asking for additional credentials; this is because we are now using Windows Authentication, thus your current login token is passed to the service.

5. Open the client's config file `App.config` in the `HelloWorldClientSecure` project to verify that the attribute value of `clientCredentialType` in the `binding` node has been changed from `Basic` to `Windows`.

6. Open the `Program.cs` file in the `HelloWorldClientSecure` project and change the old code in the `Main` method as follows:

    ```
    var client =
        new HelloWorldServiceRef.HelloWorldServiceClient();
    client.ChannelFactory.Credentials.Windows.ClientCredential =
        System.Net.CredentialCache.DefaultNetworkCredentials;
    Console.WriteLine(client.GetMessage("Windows Authentication
    caller"));
    ```

7. Run the program again and you should get an output similar to the following screenshot:

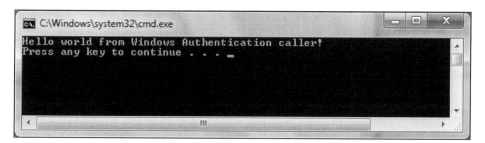

This output shows the service is now hosted with Windows Authentication and the client is passing the user's default network credential to the service. The current logged in user's Windows token, instead of the user's name/password, is now transmitted over the network.

 Besides setting the attribute value of `clientCredentialType` to `Windows` or `Basic` in the `binding` node of the service web configuration file, you can also set it to `InheritedFromHost`, which means the WCF service will inherit the security settings of the hosting IIS application. This option will be very helpful if you would like to specify multiple authentication schemes on a single endpoint.

WCF Security Guidance

Microsoft WCF Security Guidance is a Patterns and Practices project to improve web services security, especially for WCF services. It contains proven practices for building secure, distributed applications with WCF. With end-to-end application scenarios, it shows you how to design and implement authentication and authorization in WCF. You can learn how to improve the security of your WCF services through prescriptive guidance including guidelines, Q&A, practices at a glance, and systematic how-tos. It is a collaborative effort between Patterns and Practices, WCF team members, and industry experts. The guidance document can be downloaded from `http://wcfsecurityguide.codeplex.com/`.

Summary

In this chapter, we learned basic concepts of WCF security and hosted the `HelloWorld` service, using Basic Authentication and Windows Authentication. The .NET framework gives you a variety of configuration settings for WCF security. You should examine your WCF service needs and pick the most appropriate settings for your organization.

In the next chapter, we will explore basic concepts of WCF extension points and learn how to extend our `HelloWorld` service.

12

Extending WCF Services

As we have learned from previous chapters, WCF provides a unified programming model for building service-oriented applications. With WCF, you can build secure, reliable, transacted solutions that integrate well across different platforms and interoperate with existing investments. The WCF programming model is very comprehensive, yet it is also very flexible. You can extend this model to enhance the functionality or customize the framework for your specific needs. In the last chapter of this book, we will explore extension points of WCF services and learn how to extend a WCF service.

We will cover the following topics in this chapter:

- WCF runtime architecture
- Why extend a WCF service?
- Client-side extension points
- Service-side extension points
- Steps to extend a WCF service
- How to extend the HelloWorldService

WCF runtime architecture

The WCF runtime provides a set of classes responsible for sending and receiving messages. For example, formatting messages, applying security, transmitting and receiving messages by using various transport protocols, as well as dispatching received messages to the appropriate operations, all fall within the WCF runtime scope.

The following diagram shows WCF runtime (`http://msdn.microsoft.com/en-us/magazine/cc163302.aspx`):

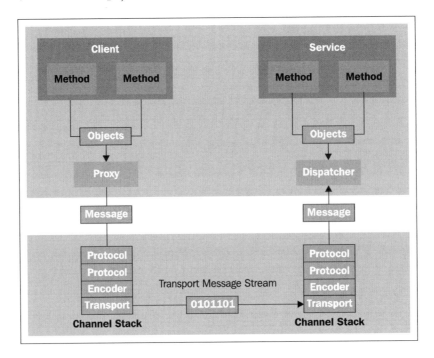

The sequence of a WCF service call might look as follows:

- A client application calls a WCF service through a WCF proxy
- The proxy translates the call to one or more WCF messages
- The messages are passed through channels and transported to the service
- On the service side, the messages are transported through channels
- Service dispatchers pick up the messages, making calls to WCF services and then returning the results back to the client

As you can see from this diagram, there are multiple layers and many entry points for a WCF service call. At almost every entry point, there is a possible extension interface that you, as a WCF developer, can extend. In fact, there are over 30 extension points in the WCF runtime. In this chapter, we will explore some common extension points and we will extend our `HelloWorldService` to log incoming/outgoing messages.

For a comprehensive list of WCF extension points, look at the MSDN documentation on WCF extensions. Additionally, you might want to check out the blog at `http://blogs. msdn.com/b/carlosfigueira/archive/2011/03/14/ wcf-extensibility.aspx` for WCF extension points. (This blog explains many of the WCF extension points up to .NET Framework 4.0, but they are all valid for .NET 4.5.)

Why extend WCF services?

There are many reasons why you might need to extend a WCF service, such as the following:

- Message validation
- Parameter validation
- Message logging
- Message transformations
- Custom serialization formats
- Custom de-serialization formats
- Output caching
- Object pooling
- Error handling
- Authorization
- Authentication

WCF extension points

The client and service runtimes expose various extensibility points that the developer can leverage. These extensibility points can be used to customize various WCF capabilities such as encoding messages, intercepting parameters, or selecting the operations to invoke on the service side.

Client-side extension points

Client-side extension is also called proxy extension. Some available client-side extensions are listed as follows:

- **Parameter inspection**: Performs custom validation, value modification, or special filtering for method parameters, before these method calls are translated to messages

- **Message formatting for serialization**: Customizes the serialization process by using a custom formatter object

- **Message inspection**: Implements cross-operation messaging features such as message logging, validation, or transformations functionality

- **Result processing**: Inspects the returned result, formats the message, and customizes the de-serialization process after the service invoke is finished, but shortly before the result is returned to the client

The following diagram shows three extension points on the client side (http://msdn.microsoft.com/en-us/magazine/cc163302.aspx):

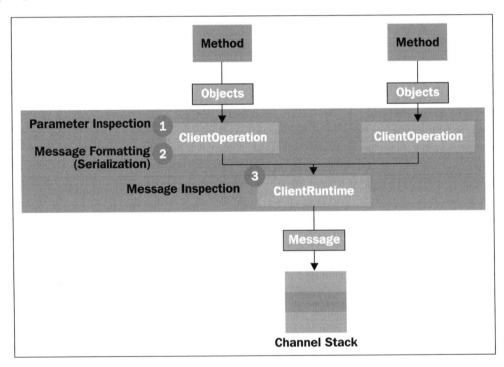

Service-side extension points

Service-side extension is also called dispatcher extension. A service-side extension can be used to perform message inspection, message formatting, and parameter inspection. For the message formatting extension, it can customize the de-serialization process for incoming messages and the serialization process for outgoing messages. In addition, there is an operation selector extension, which is to override the default operation selection behavior and an operation invoker extension to provide a custom operation invoker object.

The following diagram shows five extension points on the service side (http://msdn.microsoft.com/en-us/magazine/cc163302.aspx):

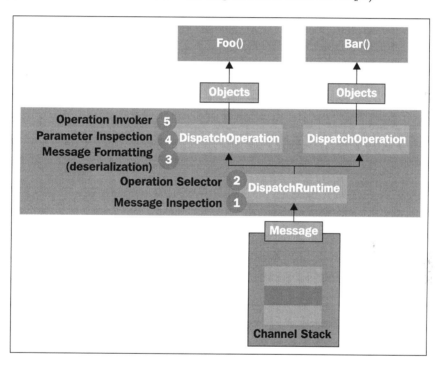

Extending a WCF service

As we have learned earlier, there are more than 30 extension points in the WCF runtime, but the most common situation is to customize the extension of a behavior. Discussion of all WCF extension points is beyond the context of this book and from this point on, we will focus only on the behavior extension.

To extend a behavior, `DispatchRuntime` and `DispatchOperation` need to be extended on the service side and `ClientRuntime` and `ClientOperation` need to be extended on the client side. This can be achieved by implementing corresponding interfaces such as `IParameterInspector`, `IDispatchMessageInspector`, and `IClientMessageFormatter`. These interfaces provide the necessary methods to allow parameters to be inspected, messages to be inspected, and to serialize and deserialize parameters to and from messages.

The following are standard procedures to extend a WCF behavior:

- Create an extension class, implementing the appropriate extension interface(s)
- Create a behavior class, implementing the appropriate behavior interface(s)
- Optionally create a behavior element class, if extensions will be applied through a configuration file
- Add behaviors to the runtime through code, attribute, or configuration

WCF extension classes

To extend a WCF service, you first need to create an extension class. As each extension point is modeled by an interface, you need to choose the proper interface to implement when creating an extension class. An extension class can implement a service (dispatcher) interface, a client (proxy) interface, or in some cases, both interfaces. If the extension class implements both the client and service interfaces, this same extension class can be used to extend a WCF service on both client and service sides.

All extension interfaces are defined in the `System.ServiceModel.Dispatcher` namespace. The following is a list of commonly-used extension interfaces:

- `IParameterInspector`: You can implement this interface to create a custom parameter inspector that can view and modify the contents of a call. The inspection can be done before or after the call in either client or service applications.
- `IDispatchMessageFormatter`/`IClientMessageFormatter`: You can implement this interface to create a custom formatter that serializes objects into messages and de-serializes messages into objects for a particular operation.
- `IDispatchMessageInspector`/`IClientMessageInspector`: You can implement this interface to inspect or modify inbound or outbound application messages either prior to or after an operation is invoked.

- `IDispatchOperationSelector`/`IClientOperationSelector`: You can implement this interface to customize the selection of the operation to invoke.

- `IOperationInvoker`: You can implement this interface to control the conversion from an untyped object and array of parameters to a strongly-typed method call on that object.

WCF behavior classes

In addition to an extension class, you also need to create a behavior class in order to extend a WCF service through behaviors.

There are four types of behaviors for a WCF service that you can extend:

- Service behavior
- Endpoint behavior
- Contract behavior
- Operation behavior

Each type allows you to apply extensions at different scopes. For example, `IServiceBehavior` can be applied at service, endpoint, contract, and operation level, but the `IOperationBehavior` can only be applied at operation level.

Each type of behavior is modeled by a different interface. All interfaces have the same methods, but each method has a different signature. You need to choose the proper interface to implement when creating a behavior class.

The behavior class can also implement the attribute interface, so it can be applied through attributes in the code.

All behavior interfaces are defined in the `System.ServiceModel.Description` namespace. The following is a list of commonly-used behavior interfaces with their scopes:

- `IServiceBehavior`: Service, endpoint, contract, and operation
- `IEndpointBehavior`: Endpoint, contract, and operation
- `IContractBehavior`: Contract and operation
- `IOperationBehavior`: Operation

WCF behavior element classes

If you want to add your extension class only through configuration, you need to create a behavior element class. A behavior extension element class represents a configuration element that contains subelements that specify behavior extensions, which enables the user to customize service or endpoint behaviors. You can override two methods in this extension class, CreateBehavior and BehaviorType, to let the WCF runtime get the behavior extension definition through the behaviorExtensions element in the configuration file.

> If your WCF service is self-hosted, you can create your extension behavior in your host code. In this case, you don't need to create a behavior element class.

With a behavior element class, you can register your extension class in the config file (or machine.config file). It is strongly recommended that you use fully qualified assembly names when registering your extension types. If the type is not uniquely defined, the CLR type loader searches for it in the following locations in the specified order:

- If the assembly of the type is known, the loader searches in the configuration file's redirect locations, GAC, the current assembly by using configuration information, and in the application base directory.

- If the assembly is unknown, the loader searches in the current assembly, mscorlib, and the location returned by the TypeResolve event handler. The CLR search order can be modified with hooks such as the Type Forwarding mechanism and the AppDomain.TypeResolve event.

> An attacker can exploit the CLR search order and execute unauthorized code. Using fully qualified (strong) names, uniquely identifies a type and further increases security of your service.

Applying the extensions

Once you have created the extension class, the behavior class, and optionally the behavior extension element class, you need to apply this extension to your WCF service.

The behaviors can be applied in three different ways:

- **Code**: The description of the service, endpoint, contract, and operation objects have a property with a collection of behaviors associated with that object. You can add your extension behaviors by using this reference.

- **Configuration**: For service and endpoint behaviors, you can add your extensions via the `system.serviceModel` or `behaviors` section in the service configuration file.

- **Attributes**: For non-endpoint behaviors, you can create an attribute class, which implements one of the behavior interfaces, and then apply the attribute to the appropriate service element.

Extending HelloWorldService

Now that we have learned the basic concepts and theories of WCF extension, let's do some practical work to further understand it. In this section, we will extend our `HelloWorldService` with a runtime behavior, inspecting and logging incoming and outgoing messages of the service.

Setting up the service

First, we will set up a copy of `HelloWorldService` with no extensions. We will extend this service in the following sections to inspect and log all incoming and outgoing messages.

To set up the service, follow these steps:

1. You can refer to *Chapter 2, Implementing a Basic HelloWorld WCF Service* and *Chapter 3, Hosting and Debugging the HelloWorld WCF Service* of this book to get the `HelloWorld` solution ready.

2. Create a new folder `HostIISExtended` under the `C:\SOAwithWCFandLINQ\Projects\HelloWorld` folder.

3. Copy all files from `HostIIS` to this new folder.

4. Start IIS manager, and add a new application `HelloWorldServiceExtended`, pointing to this new folder.

5. Test it with the following URL in a browser:

    `http://localhost/HelloWorldServiceExtended/HelloWorldService.svc`

You should see the WSDL description page of the `HelloWorldService` service. Click on the link to make sure you can get the WSDL of this new service.

Next let's add this folder to the HelloWorld solution in Visual Studio:

1. Start Visual Studio and open the HelloWorld solution.

2. Add a new solution folder HostIISExtended to the solution.

3. Add the C:\SOAwithWCFandLINQ\Projects\HelloWorld\ HostIISExtended\web.config file to the new solution folder.

4. Add another solution folder bin under the HostIISExtended solution folder.

5. Add all files under the C:\SOAwithWCFandLINQ\Projects\HelloWorld\ HostIISExtended\bin folder to this new solution folder.

6. Select the HelloWorldService project and go to the project's **Properties** page.

7. Add the following copy statements to the post-built events:

```
xcopy "$(AssemblyName).dll" "C:\SOAwithWCFandLINQ\Projects\
HelloWorld\HostIISExtended\bin" /Y
xcopy "$(AssemblyName).pdb" "C:\SOAwithWCFandLINQ\Projects\
HelloWorld\HostIISExtended\bin" /Y
```

This way it will make sure that the HelloWorldServiceExtended application will always have the latest HelloWorldService binary files.

Creating the extension project

To extend HelloWorldService, we need to create an extension class, a behavior class, and a behavior element class. We need to create an assembly for all of these classes, so that later we can apply this extension to the WCF service.

You can follow these steps to create a project for this extension assembly:

1. Open the HelloWorld solution.

2. Add a new class library project named HelloWorldExtension.

3. Delete the Class1.cs file from this new project.

4. Add the following three references to the project:

```
System.Configuration
System.ServiceModel
System.Web
```

5. Go to the project's **Properties** page.

6. Add the following copy statements to the post-built events:

```
xcopy "$(AssemblyName).dll" ..\..\..\HostIISExtended\Bin /Y
xcopy "$(AssemblyName).pdb" ..\..\..\HostIISExtended\Bin /Y
```

This way it will make sure that the HostIISExtended application will always have the latest extension binary files. As you will see in the following sections, the WCF runtime will search the bin directory of the host application to discover the extension class.

Creating an extension class

As we mentioned earlier in this chapter, to extend a WCF service we first need to create an extension class. Follow these steps to create this extension class:

1. Add a new class named MyMessageInspector to the HelloWorldExtension project.

2. Add the following five using statements to the new class:

   ```
   using System.ServiceModel;
   using System.ServiceModel.Dispatcher;
   using System.ServiceModel.Channels;
   using System.IO;
   using System.Web.Hosting;
   ```

3. Make this class implement the IDispatchMessageInspector interface.

4. Add the following method to trace a message:

   ```
   private Message TraceMessage(MessageBuffer buffer)
   {
       Message msg = buffer.CreateMessage();
       string appPath =
       HostingEnvironment.ApplicationPhysicalPath;
       string logPath = appPath + "\\log.txt";
       File.AppendAllText(logPath,
       DateTime.Now.ToString("G"));
       File.AppendAllText(logPath, "\r\n");
       File.AppendAllText(logPath, "HelloWorldService is
       invoked");
       File.AppendAllText(logPath, "\r\n");
       File.AppendAllText(logPath,
       string.Format("Message={0}", msg));
       File.AppendAllText(logPath, "\r\n");
       return buffer.CreateMessage();
   }
   ```

 Here we are logging to a file. You might want to log to the Windows event logs or a database in your own situation.

5. Give IIS identity of the HostIISExtended application write access to the HostIISExtended application folder (C:\SOAwithWCFandLINQ\Projects\ HelloWorld\HostIISExtended), as the extended WCF service will write to a file in this folder. You can find out the IIS identity of the application from the **IIS Manager | Application Pools |** application pool of the HostIISExtended application, **| Advanced Settings | Process Model | Identity**.

6. Now add the following two methods to call the method we just created, so that we can log each incoming and outgoing message:

```
public object AfterReceiveRequest(
    ref Message request, IClientChannel channel,
    InstanceContext instanceContext)
{
request =
    TraceMessage(request.CreateBufferedCopy(int.MaxValue));
    return null;
}

public void BeforeSendReply(
    ref Message reply,
    object correlationState)
{
    reply =
    TraceMessage(reply.CreateBufferedCopy(int.MaxValue));
}
```

In this extension class, we make it implement the IDispatchMessageInspector interface, so that we can extend the service (dispatcher) to inspect the messages. Then, we have added two inspector methods to inspect the outgoing and incoming messages. In this case, we just log the messages, but you can even modify the messages according to your own requirements.

Because the body of the request/reply message can only be processed once, here we have to pass a buffer of the original message to the TraceMessage method, create a new message from the buffer, and then return a new message to the original method, to ensure the original methods do not get affected. Also we make the AfterReceiveRequest method return null, because we don't need to correlate between the two methods (parameter correlationState in the BeforeSendReply method is the return result of the AfterReceiveRequest method).

The whole content of the `MyMessageInspector.cs` file is as follows:

```csharp
using System;
using System.Collections.Generic;
using System.Linq;
using System.Text;
using System.Threading.Tasks;

using System.ServiceModel;
using System.ServiceModel.Dispatcher;
using System.ServiceModel.Channels;
using System.IO;
using System.Web.Hosting;

namespace HelloWorldExtension
{
    class MyMessageInspector : IDispatchMessageInspector
    {
        private Message TraceMessage(MessageBuffer buffer)
        {
            Message msg = buffer.CreateMessage();
            string appPath = HostingEnvironment.
            ApplicationPhysicalPath;
            string logPath = appPath + "\\log.txt";
            File.AppendAllText(logPath, DateTime.Now.ToString("G"));
            File.AppendAllText(logPath, "\r\n");
            File.AppendAllText(logPath, "HelloWorldService is
            invoked");
            File.AppendAllText(logPath, "\r\n");
            File.AppendAllText(logPath, string.Format("Message={0}",
            msg));
            File.AppendAllText(logPath, "\r\n");
            return buffer.CreateMessage();
        }

        public object AfterReceiveRequest(
            ref Message request, IClientChannel channel,
            InstanceContext instanceContext)
        {
          request =
          TraceMessage(request.CreateBufferedCopy(int.MaxValue));
          return null;
        }
```

```
public void BeforeSendReply(
    ref Message reply,
    object correlationState)
{

    reply =
    TraceMessage(reply.CreateBufferedCopy(int.MaxValue));

}

}

}
```

Creating a behavior class

Next we need to create a behavior class. In this behavior class, we will apply the extension class to the WCF runtime.

Follow these steps to create the behavior class:

1. Add a new class named `MyMessageInspectorBehavior` to the `HelloWorldExtension` project.

2. Add the following five `using` statements to the new class:

   ```
   using System.ServiceModel;
   using System.ServiceModel.Description;
   using System.ServiceModel.Channels;
   using System.ServiceModel.Dispatcher;
   using System.Collections.ObjectModel;
   ```

3. Make this class inherit `Attribute` and implement the `IServiceBehavior` interface.

4. Add the following method to apply the behavior:

   ```
   void IServiceBehavior.ApplyDispatchBehavior(
       ServiceDescription serviceDescription,
       ServiceHostBase serviceHostBase)
   {

       foreach (ChannelDispatcher cDispatcher
       in serviceHostBase.ChannelDispatchers)
       foreach (EndpointDispatcher eDispatcher
       in cDispatcher.Endpoints)
       eDispatcher.DispatchRuntime.MessageInspectors.Add(
       new MyMessageInspector());

   }
   ```

5. We also need to implement the following two methods, though in this example we don't do anything within them:

```
void IServiceBehavior.AddBindingParameters(
    ServiceDescription serviceDescription,
    ServiceHostBase serviceHostBase,
    Collection<ServiceEndpoint> endpoints,
    BindingParameterCollection bindingParameters)
{
    //do nothing
}
void IServiceBehavior.Validate(
    ServiceDescription serviceDescription,
    ServiceHostBase serviceHostBase)
{
    //do nothing
}
```

In this class, we make it implement the `IServiceBehavior` interface, so that we can apply our extension behavior to the WCF runtime. We also make it inherit the `Attribute` class, so that this extension behavior can be applied by using attributes in code (though we are not going to take the code approach in this chapter).

The full content of the `MyMessageInspectorBehavior.cs` file will be as follows:

```
using System;
using System.Collections.Generic;
using System.Linq;
using System.Text;
using System.Threading.Tasks;

using System.ServiceModel;
using System.ServiceModel.Description;
using System.ServiceModel.Channels;
using System.ServiceModel.Dispatcher;
using System.Collections.ObjectModel;

namespace HelloWorldExtension
{
    class MyMessageInspectorBehavior : Attribute, IServiceBehavior
    {
        void IServiceBehavior.AddBindingParameters(
            ServiceDescription serviceDescription,
```

```
        ServiceHostBase serviceHostBase,
        Collection<ServiceEndpoint> endpoints,
        BindingParameterCollection bindingParameters)
    {
        //do nothing
    }

    void IServiceBehavior.ApplyDispatchBehavior(
        ServiceDescription serviceDescription,
        ServiceHostBase serviceHostBase)
    {
        foreach (ChannelDispatcher cDispatcher
            in serviceHostBase.ChannelDispatchers)
            foreach (EndpointDispatcher eDispatcher
                in cDispatcher.Endpoints)
            eDispatcher.DispatchRuntime.MessageInspectors.Add(
                new MyMessageInspector());
    }

    void IServiceBehavior.Validate(
        ServiceDescription serviceDescription,
        ServiceHostBase serviceHostBase)
    {
        //do nothing
    }
    }
}
```

Creating a behavior element class

To apply the extension though configuration, we need to create a behavior element class. This class will tell the WCF runtime how to discover and apply the extension class to the WCF runtime.

The following steps create this behavior element class:

1. Add a new class named MyMessageInspectorElement to the HelloWorldExtension project.

2. Add the following using statement to the new class:

    ```
    using System.ServiceModel.Configuration;
    ```

3. Make this class inherit BehaviorExtensionElement.

4. Add the following code to define the behavior:

```
public override Type BehaviorType
{
    get { return typeof(MyMessageInspectorBehavior); }
}
protected override object CreateBehavior()
{
    return new MyMessageInspectorBehavior();
}
```

In this element class, we just override one property and one method of the `BehaviorExtensionElement` class. The `BehaviorType` property will tell the WCF runtime what type our extension behavior is, and the `CreateBehavior` method will tell the WCF runtime how to create the extension behavior class.

The full content of the `MyMessageInspectorElement.cs` file will be as follows:

```
using System;
using System.Collections.Generic;
using System.Linq;
using System.Text;
using System.Threading.Tasks;

using System.ServiceModel.Configuration;

namespace HelloWorldExtension
{
    class MyMessageInspectorElement : BehaviorExtensionElement
    {
        public override Type BehaviorType
        {
            get { return typeof(MyMessageInspectorBehavior); }
        }
        protected override object CreateBehavior()
        {
            return new MyMessageInspectorBehavior();
        }
    }
}
```

Applying the extension to HelloWorldService

The last step is to apply our newly created extension class to `HelloWorldService`. Because we have created a behavior extension element class, we can apply this extension only through configuration.

1. Start Visual Studio.

2. Open the `HelloWorld` solution.

3. Open the `Web.config` file under the `HostIISExtended` folder.

4. Add the following `extensions` node to be a child node of the `system.serviceModel` node:

   ```
   <extensions>
     <behaviorExtensions>
       <add name="myMessageInspectorBehavior"
            type="HelloWorldExtension.MyMessageInspectorElement,
         HelloWorldExtension, Version=1.0.0.0,
         Culture=neutral, PublicKeyToken=null"/>
     </behaviorExtensions>
   </extensions>
   ```

   Here when specifying the extension element, we are fully qualifying it with the element name, name space, version, and culture. As we have said earlier in this chapter, this will make our extension more secure than just specifying its name. Here we don't specify a public token, but to make it even more secure, you can assign a public key token to the element.

5. Add the following node as a child node of the `behaviors` node:

   ```
   <myMessageInspectorBehavior/>
   ```

   So the whole `behaviors` node should resemble the following:

   ```
   <behaviors>
     <serviceBehaviors>
       <behavior>
         <serviceMetadata httpGetEnabled="true"/>
         <myMessageInspectorBehavior/>
       </behavior>
     </serviceBehaviors>
   </behaviors>
   ```

   This will apply the behavior extension that we have added in the preceding step to our `HelloWorldService` in this IIS application. This means whenever this service is invoked, this extension will be applied. We will test this with a test program in the next section.

The following is the content of the `system.serviceModel` node:

```
<system.serviceModel>
  <serviceHostingEnvironment >
    <serviceActivations>
      <add factory="System.ServiceModel.
      Activation.ServiceHostFactory"
        relativeAddress="./HelloWorldService.svc"
        service="MyWCFServices.HelloWorldService"/>
    </serviceActivations>
  </serviceHostingEnvironment>

  <behaviors>
    <serviceBehaviors>
      <behavior>
        <serviceMetadata httpGetEnabled="true"/>
        <myMessageInspectorBehavior/>
      </behavior>
    </serviceBehaviors>
  </behaviors>

  <extensions>
    <behaviorExtensions>
      <add name="myMessageInspectorBehavior"
        type="HelloWorldExtension.
        MyMessageInspectorElement,
          HelloWorldExtension, Version=1.0.0.0,
          Culture=neutral, PublicKeyToken=null"/>
    </behaviorExtensions>
  </extensions>

</system.serviceModel>
```

Testing the extended HelloWorldService

Now that we have the service extension applied to the service, we can test it with a program. In this section, we will re-use our `HelloWorldClient` to test the service. We will verify that the extension has been applied to the service successfully through the `web.config` file.

But before testing it with the `HelloWorldClient` application, you can test it via a web browser. Just go to `http://localhost/HelloWorldServiceExtended/HelloWorldService.svc` and you should see the WSDL description page of the extended `HelloWorldService` service.

Click on the link to make sure you can get the WSDL of this extended service.

If you didn't get the WSDL description page of the extended service and instead get an error page saying **Internet Explorer cannot display the webpage**, it is because your IIS identity doesn't have write access to the `HostIISExtended` IIS application folder (`C:\SOAwithWCFandLINQ\Projects\HelloWorld\HostIISExtended`). You can refer back to the previous section *Creating an extension class* for more details about this.

Once you successfully get the WSDL of the extended service, you can follow these steps to test the service with the `HelloWorldClient` application:

1. In Visual Studio, open the `app.config` file from the `HelloWorldClient` project.

2. In the config file, change the endpoint to the following address:

   `http://localhost/HelloWorldServiceExtended/HelloWorldService.svc`

3. Now rebuild the solution, set `HelloWorldClient` as the startup project, and run the program. You should see the same result as in *Chapter 2, Implementing a Basic Helloworld WCF Service*.

4. Open Windows Explorer and go to the `C:\SOAwithWCFandLINQ\Projects\HelloWorld\HostIISExtended` folder.

   Here you will find a `log.txt` file. Open it and you will see some logs as shown in the following screenshot:

5. To debug the extension, you can first set a breakpoint within the `TraceMessage` method in the `MyMessageInspector.cs` class and then step in to the extension from the client program or attach to the `w3wp.exe` process and then run the client program to hit the breakpoint.

This test proves that our `TraceMessage` service extension method has been invoked by the service for all incoming and outgoing messages. As you can see in this example, we didn't change any code in the service, we are using the same client program as before, yet the extension has been applied by changing a few lines within the configuration file. You can use the same mechanisms to plug in your extensions in your environment to any existing services at any time.

Summary

In this chapter, we learned the basic concepts of the WCF extension and extended service behavior of the `HelloWorld` service. In this sample extension, we just logged all incoming and outgoing messages, but in your environment, you can do much more than just logging messages. There are many extension points and you should examine your WCF service needs and pick the most appropriate extension points according to your application requirements.

This is the last chapter of the book. Through this book, we learned how to create, host, and debug a WCF service. We also learned WCF exception handling and applied best practice to our WCF service development. As Entities Framework is now the standard data access ORM, we explored LINQ, LINQ to Entities, and replaced our data access layer with LINQ to Entities. We also learned WCF transaction management by using LINQ to Entities and configured the security for our WCF service. Then in this last chapter, we extended our WCF service to log all incoming and outgoing messages. At this point, you should be very comfortable in creating and configuring your own WCF service, customizing its transaction and security settings, and extending it if it is needed. I hope you can apply your WCF knowledge to your real work and enjoy it.

Index

Microsoft Message Queuing
      (MSMQ) 24, 325
Microsoft Service Factory website
   URL 81
Min operator 164
MsmqIntegrationBinding 18
multiple database support
   testing, of WCF service 296

N

netMsmqBinding 324
NetMsmqBinding 18
netNamedPipeBinding 324
NetNamedPipeBinding 18
netPeerTCPBinding 324
NetPeerTcpBinding 18
netTCPBinding 324
NetTcpBinding 18
non-debugging mode
   client applications, running in 77
   WCF service, running in 77
non-HTTP WCF activation
   enabling, for hosting machine 69
Northwind database
   about 118
   modeling 246, 247
   preparing, for WCF service 122, 123
   product record, updating 129, 130
   querying 124, 125
   WCF service, connecting to 123, 124
NTLM Authentication 326

O

object initializer, LINQ 147
Object-Relational Mapping. See ORM
ODBC 168
Open Database Connectivity. See ODBC
operation contract
   about 19
   example 19
OperationContract attribute 37
Oracle Pro*C 168
ORM 168

P

Plain Old CLR Objects. See POCO
POCO 104, 180
Pro*C 168
ProductBDO class 248
ProductDAO.cs file 118, 119, 130
ProductLogic.cs file 120
ProductService class 127
Products table
   modeling, with version column 237
Program.cs file 147, 185
project
   LINQ to Entities item, adding to 175-180
proxy extension. See client-side extensions
proxy file
   generating 48, 49

Q

Query Analyzer 162
query expression, LINQ 160-163

R

RealNorthwindDAL project 118
RealNorthwindService.cs file 95
RealNorthwindService project 81, 124
RealNorthwind solution
   creating, service library template
      used 83, 84
receiveTimeout attribute 18
records
   deleting, from database 184
   inserting, into database 184
   querying 182, 183
   updating 183
reference
   adding, to BDO project 249
relational database management systems
      (RDBMS) 168
Remove method 184
runtime architecture, WCF 342

S

SaveChanges() method 212, 243
Secure Sockets Layer (SSL) 324

Thank you for buying
WCF 4.5 Multi-Layer Services Development
with Entity Framework

About Packt Publishing

Packt, pronounced 'packed', published its first book "Mastering phpMyAdmin for Effective MySQL Management" in April 2004 and subsequently continued to specialize in publishing highly focused books on specific technologies and solutions.

Our books and publications share the experiences of your fellow IT professionals in adapting and customizing today's systems, applications, and frameworks. Our solution based books give you the knowledge and power to customize the software and technologies you're using to get the job done. Packt books are more specific and less general than the IT books you have seen in the past. Our unique business model allows us to bring you more focused information, giving you more of what you need to know, and less of what you don't.

Packt is a modern, yet unique publishing company, which focuses on producing quality, cutting-edge books for communities of developers, administrators, and newbies alike. For more information, please visit our website: www.packtpub.com.

About Packt Enterprise

In 2010, Packt launched two new brands, Packt Enterprise and Packt Open Source, in order to continue its focus on specialization. This book is part of the Packt Enterprise brand, home to books published on enterprise software – software created by major vendors, including (but not limited to) IBM, Microsoft and Oracle, often for use in other corporations. Its titles will offer information relevant to a range of users of this software, including administrators, developers, architects, and end users.

Writing for Packt

We welcome all inquiries from people who are interested in authoring. Book proposals should be sent to author@packtpub.com. If your book idea is still at an early stage and you would like to discuss it first before writing a formal book proposal, contact us; one of our commissioning editors will get in touch with you.

We're not just looking for published authors; if you have strong technical skills but no writing experience, our experienced editors can help you develop a writing career, or simply get some additional reward for your expertise.

WCF 4.0 Multi-tier Services Development with LINQ to Entities

ISBN: 978-1-849681-14-8   Paperback: 348 pages

Build SOA applications on the Microsoft platform with this hands-on guide updated for VS2010

1. Master WCF and LINQ to Entities concepts by completing practical examples and applying them to your real-world assignments

2. The first and only book to combine WCF and LINQ to Entities in a multi-tier real-world WCF service

3. Ideal for beginners who want to build scalable, powerful, easy-to-maintain WCF services

SOA Patterns with BizTalk Server 2009

ISBN: 978-1-847195-00-5   Paperback: 400 pages

Implement SOA strategies for BizTalk Server solutions

1. Discusses core principles of SOA and shows them applied to BizTalk solutions

2. The most thorough examination of BizTalk and WCF integration in any available book

3. Leading insight into the new WCF SQL Server Adapter, UDDI Services version 3, and ESB Guidance 2.0

Please check **www.PacktPub.com** for information on our titles

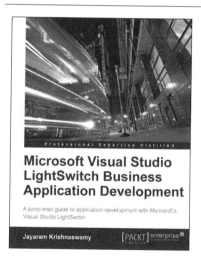

WCF Multi-tier Services Development with LINQ

ISBN: 978-1-847196-62-0   Paperback: 384 pages

Build SOA applications on the Microsoft platform in this hands-on guide

1. Master WCF and LINQ concepts by completing practical examples and apply them to your real-world assignments

2. First book to combine WCF and LINQ in a multi-tier real-world WCF service

3. Rich with example code, clear explanations, interesting examples, and practical advice â€" a truly hands-on book for C++ and C# developers

Microsoft Visual Studio LightSwitch Business Application Development

ISBN: 978-1-849682-86-2   Paperback: 384 pages

A jump-start guide to application development with Microsoft's Visual Studio LightSwitch

1. A hands-on guide, packed with screenshots and step-by-step instructions and relevant background information—making it easy to build your own application with this book and ebook

2. Create entities and screens both from scratch and using built-in templates

3. Query using built-in designer and by coding (both VB and C#)

Please check **www.PacktPub.com** for information on our titles